THE COMPLETE BRING YOUR WORTH COLLECTION

THE BITE-SIZED ENTREPRENEUR,
BRING YOUR WORTH &
BUILD FROM NOW

Damon Brown
www.DamonBrown.net
www.BringYourWorth.tv
JoinDamon.me

COACHING & SPEAKING REQUESTS:
DAMON@DAMONBROWN.NET

"In The Bite-Sized Entrepreneur, *Damon Brown lays waste to both the misconceptions and pesky little lies we tell ourselves about why we can't make our side hustles a reality. A thoughtful, provocative read, Brown will help you understand why you have more time than you think to follow your passions—and offers smart, actionable advice to help you implement the right strategies so you can make your side hustle successful within the boundaries of the life you live today."*
–Kayt Sukel, *author of* The Art of Risk *and* This Is Your Brain On Sex

"In The Ultimate Bite-Sized Entrepreneur, *Damon Brown proves that you don't need to don a hoodie, move to Silicon Valley and sacrifice all your sleep (and sanity) to make it in the world of self-employment. Through his road-tested wisdom and interviews with successful innovators who have built businesses on their own terms, Damon provides practical, tactical advice to grow your business one small, delicious, perfectly bite-sized step at a time."*
--Jenny Blake, *author of Pivot: The Only Move That Matters Is Your Next One*

"You can create the life you imagined and still be an entrepreneur. Damon's new book will give you the easy way to implement strategies and do just that. Entrepreneurship is the best gig ever only *if you do it the way Damon lays out. Otherwise, you'll be working for the worst boss you ever had."*

--Cameron Herold, author of Double Double: How to Double Your Revenue and Profit in 3 Years or Less

"For every would-be entrepreneur who's wondered if it's possible to "crush it" without crushing yourself, this book is for you! In this concise read, Inc. columnist Damon Brown lays out a road map for launching a satisfying and successful business without overturning the life you currently have."

–Meagan Francis, founder, the Life, Listened podcast network

"Sure, it starts with passion, but what do you know about living the life of an entrepreneur? The Bite-Sized Entrepreneur *gives smart, succinct advice about how to follow your business dreams, including why to treat Tuesday like Monday; the difference between busyness and productivity; and three effective ways of saying 'no.' Highly recommended for would-be entrepreneurs and freelancers."*

--Kelly K. James, *author of* Six-Figure Freelancing, Second Edition: The Writer's Guide to Make More Money

"A practical and actionable guide to accomplishing your goals that can help anyone master the mindset needed to become a self-made success."

–Scott Steinberg, *author of* Make Change Work for You: 10 Ways to Future-Proof Yourself, Fearlessly Innovate, and Succeed Despite Uncertainty

PUBLISHED BY:
Bring Your Worth

The Complete Bring Your Worth Collection
1st Edition
Copyright 2023 by Damon Brown
Edited by Jeanette Hurt
Cover designed by The Bec Effect
Cover photo by Alex Goetz

To Uncle George for laying the blueprint.

I'm not in charge of you, and I'm not manipulating you. I'm simply establishing the conditions for you to get to where you said you wanted to go.

Seth Godin

TABLE OF CONTENTS

(FROM THE BALANCED BITE-SIZED ENTREPRENEUR)

SELECTED BOOKS BY THE AUTHOR

CAREER REMIX:

GET THE GIG YOU WANT WITH THE SKILLS YOU'VE GOT

THE PASSIVE WRITER:

5 STEPS TO EARNING MONEY IN YOUR SLEEP

(W/ JEANETTE HURT)

OUR VIRTUAL SHADOW:

WHY WE ARE OBSESSED WITH DOCUMENTING OUR LIVES

ONLINE

Book I:
The Ultimate Bite-Sized Entrepreneur

76 Ways to Boost Time, Productivity & Focus on Your Big Idea

"What is the work that you can't not do?"

-Scott Dinsmore,
How to find work you love

FOREWORD

I wrote THE BITE-SIZED ENTREPRENEUR book to understand how things manifested so quickly. Three years before writing it, I was a San Franciscan tech journalist seriously dating a wonderful woman. Less than a thousand days later, I was a married San Diegan in a house with a white picket fence (Seriously!), taking care of my 1-year-old son and reeling from the sale of my first startup, Cuddlr. How did I transform so quickly? Like Aurelius' *Meditations* or David Thoreau's *Walden*, this book was an elaborate note to self.

What remains humbling is that you have experienced the same question: How can I fulfill my calling while keeping my life intact? I'm honored to be on this journey with you, and this special edition captures the best of THE BITE-SIZED ENTREPRENEUR trilogy along with exclusive discussions directly influenced by meeting people like you at during my talks all around the world.

Whenever I am in need, I love to pull my favorite philosophical book off the shelf, pick a random page, and take in the wisdom. It always seems to be what I need to hear at the time. My intention, and my hope, is for this ultimate collection to play the same role in your life.

-Damon Brown, November 2017

ON STARTING
(THE BITE-SIZED
ENTREPRENEUR)

To Alec,
who inspired me to do my first TED Talk &
build my first successful startup before he could
even speak.
Thank you.

"Most of us have two lives. The life we live, and the unlived life within us. Between the two stands Resistance"

-Steven Pressfield, The War of Art

A Word on Passion

Passion is the compass that points you in the right direction above the fog of the moment and the uncertainty of the future. Passion is also the instinct that pushes you to destroy everything else to get that brass ring.

Passion will leave you stranded if you do not put in the time. Passion will also give you the heart of steel needed to thrive when the less dedicated will falter.

Passion is our vice and our victory. Use it wisely.

INTRODUCING YOU, THE BITE-SIZED ENTREPRENEUR

I never intended to be an entrepreneur. I just had an idea.

At the time, I was a freelance tech journalist living in San Francisco. A friend of mine was struggling to remember a quote. I asked, innocently, "Isn't there an app for that?" There wasn't, and I found myself becoming an entrepreneur for the same reason most creators do: I realized something I needed did not exist and, if I didn't create it, it might never exist.

The odd part wasn't the journey to creating what would become the app So Quotable: it was who was actually making the journey. I wasn't a young, hooded Harvard dropout like Facebook's Zuckerberg, nor was I a brash, brilliant college dropout like Apple's Jobs, nor a rich, hip L. A. kid like Snapchat's Spiegel.

I was a journalist and author, an African American man in his mid-30s who, aside from negotiating rates with magazines, had no business experience.

In fact, at the time, I was about to propose to my now-wife. By the time So Quotable ramped up to launch three years later, I had bought my first home, married that long-time girlfriend, and we had our first kid. In the midst of the launch, a colleague helping out on the tech side bailed, and I found myself learning Apple's iPhone programming language with one hand while rocking my newborn in my other, spare arm.

I wasn't sure if the app – or even I – would make it to the finish line, but I also had not felt so alive in a long time. I'd wake up in the middle of the night with new ideas and realize elegant solutions to my app challenges during dinnertime. It was like I had two babies instead of just one. It was the passion to make my mark: I wasn't staying up late and getting up ridiculously early to watch my favorite show or to have "me" time. It was a nobler cause.

I was also doing things my way. Instead of staying in Silicon Valley, ditching my girlfriend, and dressing like a college student, I moved out of Silicon Valley, settled down behind my proverbial white picket fence, and created the type of entrepreneurial life that *I* envisioned.

And, to my surprise, it worked. So Quotable launched in time for my first TED talk and gained a great cult following. The success connected me with two others to launched Cuddlr, a social plutonic app for connecting for hugs. Cuddlr hit #1 on the Apple App store twice, got us on the cover of *The Wall Street Journal*, and was acquired less than a year after it arrived. I handled the Cuddlr launch through daily 4 a.m. Skype calls with my international colleagues, with occasional breaks to coax my new toddler back to sleep.

The truth is that the success didn't happen with the media coverage, the TED talk, or even the Cuddlr acquisition, but from doing and completing the work. As they say in Silicon Valley, real creators ship – and the product shipped! As soon as I met someone, told them about So Quotable, and said "You can download it off the Apple App Store now," I won.

You absolutely have the ability to follow your passion, fulfill a public or personal need, and make a legacy for yourself within the structure of your 9-to-5, your family life, or your daily grind. Never before have we been more capable to pursue our passions within the time we have. Like kids jumping Double Dutch rope, we have more room for our dreams than we think – it's just a matter of good strategy and timing. And perhaps that side hustle we create will become the foundation for the rest of our careers.

Bite-sized entrepreneurs incorporate brilliant startup techniques into their daily lives, giving themselves the focus and drive to pursue new passions while still being true to where they are in their personal and professional lives. *The belief that you have to sacrifice your livelihood to leave your entrepreneurial mark is a lie.* It isn't about losing the life you have, but adding value to create the life you want.

There are many things a bite-sized entrepreneur is not. She is not a dilettante, dabbling in various pursuits to combat boredom or gain prestige; a bite-sized entrepreneur doesn't give up when things get difficult. She is not a shallow businessperson, keeping the dedication superficial; a bite-sized entrepreneur dedicates every available ounce of free time to understanding her passion. She is not an obligated creator, getting her ego too invested into the idea to change; a bite-sized entrepreneur gives her passion space to transform organically into the business it was meant to be. Finally, she is not a patient person, assuming that one day she'll have all the time in the world to pursue her true passion; a bite-sized entrepreneur ain't waiting until retirement.

I'd love to be your guide on your entrepreneurial journey. Like my *Inc. Magazine* online column which inspired this book, I am giving you simple, digestible, and actionable insights that can be interwoven into your current life structure. You can flip through the 21 strategies in any order, though you may notice a natural flow if you read it straight from top to bottom. All of these ideas are explored with people who have successfully executed what you currently feel: A calling to create something bigger than yourself within the parameters of your current life. Everyone's journey is different, which is the point: Realizing your business aspirations is not, and should not, be a one-size-fits-all process.

Let's make an impact on our own terms. Today.

-Damon Brown, August 2016

"Rule of thumb: The more important a call or action to our soul's evolution, the more Resistance we will feel towards pursuing it."

-Steven Pressfield, The War of Art

1
THE PASSION TRAP
Passion favors sweaty palms

Are you waiting for inspiration? Passion? A muse? I wouldn't count on it. When it comes to business, particularly entrepreneurship, you're better off leaning on just doing the work.

Artist and entrepreneur Jessica Abel describes the process well:

Passion for a practice or a subject comes from your investment of time and energy. Whatever your passion turns out to be is a combination of what you're into, your circumstances, and what happens to fall across your path, added to what you decide to spend your time on and what you're willing to take risks to do more of, with a just a tiny dash of natural talent.

The term "practice" has a double meaning. We have you practicing something every day, like playing the piano. We also have you doing the practice, as in growing the mental and emotional discipline to stay committed to a goal. It's not a coincidence that the same word is used in daily rituals and commitments, like meditation.

The truth is that passion will not get you out of bed every morning. Like love, it can be fickle and moody and fairweather. Passion makes you more susceptible to burnout and extreme thinking.

Doing the work, though? It sustains you, because it never changes, and it gives levity when things are great and when things suck.

All you have to do is show up every day.

2
LIES WE TELL
Be gentle with others, give yourself tough love

We all share common challenges when it comes to the tough road of entrepreneurship, but we also give common comforts to ourselves to push into another day.

In short, we lie to ourselves.

You don't know if the rockstar client will come through, a successful fundraise will happen or even if a larger competitor will snuff you out. There has to be a suspension of disbelief-- otherwise, you wouldn't attempt to run your own business in the first place. Passion sometimes needs a little help trumping common sense.

There's absolutely nothing wrong with having faith in the future, but it is crucial that we recognize the times when we're placating ourselves for self-management. Here are the biggest comforts I say to myself. Perhaps you can relate.

I'll start this project/this business when I have more bandwidth

There is always tomorrow--until there is not. Like becoming a parent, there will never be an ideal time to launch your business. You will always need more resources than you have, more time than you got, and more energy than you can muster. If Steve Jobs, Elon Musk, and other visionaries waited until everything was perfect, then we wouldn't be talking about Jobs, Musk and their contemporaries right now.

As wine seller turned successful entrepreneur Gary Vaynerchuk said in an impassioned message: "I worked weekends and holidays every day starting at fourteen years old to make [my business] happen. I think back to all the time I put in of real, hard work before I saw any of the benefits." Don't wait for a red carpet.

I'll save my business/my finances if I can just net this one client

One client often isn't enough to save your business. Worse, if you put all your focus on netting one client, all things tend to fall to the wayside (even if you do get the client).

For instance, if your company gets any acquisition or investment interest, it is easy to start focusing on the potential payoff rather than the day-to-day work and the long-term strategy. And if it falls through, your company will take a while to get back on course-- assuming it ever will.

I'll stay up all night/skip today's meals because that's how you crush it
Entrepreneurs will have you believe that skipping that night of sleep or "crushing it" all day without eating is the key to success--there is even a startup or two dedicated to the idea. Sacrifices need to be made (I definitely walk the walk on that one), but there is no real correlation between depriving your body of needs and creating the next unicorn startup. In fact, you are more likely to burn out. Pushing yourself beyond your limits should be viewed as a contextually necessary evil, not as a default.

Consider this: If you do successfully reach that

fundraising/monetization/users goal, then you'll have another goal after that and a business that will demand even more from you. I know many an entrepreneur who flamed out before reaching even the first milestone, defeating the whole purpose of moving forward. We often work harder than we should because we want to feel like we're crushing it--and that feel is more important than the actual impact. There is a difference between killing it and killing yourself.

I'll get work done on the plane/vacation/ break

There is always more work to do: Another email to send, another pitch to perfect, and another glitch to correct. A major challenge is allowing ourselves to get away. The second part of the challenge? Letting others allow us to get away.

We assume we'll get work done on the flight in or during our travels, so we start pushing work into that so-called free time and start making promises that we may not be able to keep. It usually has one of two outcomes: You actually begin to relax after you realize how exhausted you are, but carry the guilt of making promises you won't keep, or you stress yourself out juggling the demands of travel and the needs of work, not really resting and, likely, not doing your best work because you are tired. Sometimes when you try to do two things, you actually fail at both.

I'll work with this PITA client one last time

Stop lying to yourself. Money, sympathy, or even status quo can compel us to repeat a client who is a pain in the ass (PITA). When we get another opportunity to work with the client, we tend to forget about the issues that stressed us out in the first place--like parents deciding to have another kid. It's not until you're knee-deep in the same situation that you say, "Ah, that's why I swore I'd never work with them again."

Assume that you'll get another, better client (or clients) to replace them. Our fear is often driven by the feast or famine cycle: Keep every client you have, as you don't know when you'll get another one! In reality, we can't actually get new, quality clients if we're spending all our time inefficiently catering to our ill-fitting ones.

I need to quit my job/end my relationships so I can truly dedicate myself to my big idea

Kids will come, money will go, and jobs are necessary, but time is the one asset you can't get back. Waiting for a big chunk of time is usually a waste of time. You fall into the extreme thinking trap: You need to go big or not go at all. There are certain times when you have to leap, but that's usually after you've already recognized an opportunity and have done the homework... and that work takes time.

Keep in mind that Twitter, Yammer, and other billion dollar companies began as side projects founders did while focusing on their day job. Imagine if they waited until they could "go big". Plant the seed today.

3
EFFECTIVE PROCRASTINATION
What you aren't procrastinating on is more important

Procrastination is a bad, four-letter word, something to be avoided at all costs. For entrepreneurs, it is a sin somewhere between working for free and being a poor networker. I recently heard a quote, though, that changed my outlook on procrastination:

"The work you do while you procrastinate is the work you should do for the rest of your life." - Jessica Hische

Procrastination is usually viewed as the absence of work (and, therefore, the loss of profit and productivity), but what if it was a compass to your true calling? Perhaps the things you do that make time fly by faster can be integrated into your actual work.

In retrospect, the procrastination idea has already changed my career. I was perfectly happy researching and writing books, but writing my first major book, *Porn & Pong: How*

Grand Theft Auto, Tomb Raider and Other Sexy Games Changed Our Culture, on the history of sexuality and video games, put me on my first book tour. It was amazing! I spent five years working in solitude, and now I was finally able to discuss my theories and share my inside stories with the world. In fact, I began to enjoy the in-person intimacy more than the actual writing. I could have ignored that impulse and gone back to writing, but instead I shifted my focus to public speaking and soon got onto the TED stage doing more of what I love.

I would delay getting back to my writing so I could connect with people. Now I craft dynamic speeches in addition to writing books, turning my procrastination vice into my strength - and integrating my previous career into it in the process.

Here's how you can turn your procrastination into a powerful tool:

Listen
What activity are you doing now to prevent you from going back to the work you claim to enjoy? Mindless activities, or what you do

without feeling stressed, could represent you going on instinct rather than forced action. In other words, figure out what you do in your life that feels natural.

Distill

What are the basic traits of your procrastination? Write down what you actually get from the activity. My love of long conversations boils down to connecting with others, getting different viewpoints, and arguing new ideas. Think about your own favorite procrastination and distill it down to two or three things you get out of it - without judgment.

Pivot

How can you integrate your natural inclinations into your practice? For instance, if you love sitting in a coffee shop talking for hours, then perhaps you need more face time with your clients. It doesn't mean you have to change your entire business, but that you are pivoting to include more of what you actually love.

How can you integrate your favorite procrastination into your business life?

4
IDEA DEBT
Too many ideas mean none get done

I recently did an idea purge. I love committing my thoughts down onto index cards since they are simple, portable, and easy to organize. I started decluttering over recent months and I realized my pile of cards has gotten out of hand. The most amazing discovery: A new idea I thought I came up with was written on a piece of paper from a year before! Talk about going in circles.

If I could have smacked myself in my own head, I would have.

Author Kazu Kibuishi has a great term for this psychological weight: **Idea debt**.

I try not to look at what I'm going to do as this amazing great grand thing. I'm not just fulfilling some old promise that I made a long time ago. Now I'm actually solving problems in the moment, and that's so much more exciting than trying to fill years of what I like to call my "idea debt." That's when you have this dream of this awesome thing for years. You think, "Oh, I'm going to do this epic adventure. It's going to be so great." The truth is, no matter what you do, it will never be as great as it is in your mind, and so you're really setting yourself up for failure.

Kibuishi is talking about perfectionism: Waiting for the perfect time to start the perfect idea. Entrepreneurs (and, in a tip to my background, journalists) can't have this perfectionist approach because we A) have to bow to bigger deadlines, and B) we would never survive as entrepreneurs. Point me to a founder who believes her product is perfect to ship and I'll show you someone who won't be a founder for long. There are always more ways to improve a product or service. Getting to market is the only reason why we should stop.

If perfectionism isn't the big problem for entrepreneurs, then what is the issue? Idealism. Underlying Kibuishi's description is the idealization, the grand structure, the bells and whistles of our great scheme. And the idealization, structure and bells and whistles of another great scheme. Oh, and the other one we have, too. As entrepreneurs, we often have too many things planned out that weigh on our daily lives. At least for me, the "cool ideas" I have are far outweighing the time, energy and, frankly, quality control I'm able to muster.

So, ideas are getting killed. Slaughtered. Put out to pasture. Index cards have been chucked, unfinished manuscripts have been tossed, and untouched research has been recycled.

I ask three questions with every jotted note:

Why haven't I executed on it yet?
Again, I found ideas from a decade ago. From my passionate productivity to my sacrifice of sleep, I've managed to pursue and complete many goals. Chances are, there is a legitimate reason why this idea is on an old scrap of paper versus being a properly executed plan.

Why am I holding on to it?
Often, the idea of something is way more powerful than the will to create it. And if it is that powerful of an idea, then it will come back stronger after you dump it.

Why am I defending it?

By keeping that idea lingering you have to, by nature, defend it against criticism from others and even from yourself - otherwise, the idea would have been forgotten long ago. Unfortunately, we are so encouraged to defend our ideas and our beliefs, it's easy to neglect that we've outgrown them. And those ideas take space from potential new projects.

As I've purged my unfinished, incomplete ideas, I've realized how much ego I have tied up into what *could* be.

What idea should you be letting go?

5
BUSYNESS
Be productive, not busy

Projects, people, and passions can keep us on the move, but there is a distinct difference between busyness and productivity. Productivity feels like you do not want to stop. Busyness feels like you cannot stop.

Chronic busyness is rampant today, even though we know that it isn't good for us. Why do we keep ourselves excessively busy? There are three big rewards we get out of it:

Fulfills the ego

Like sociologist Brene Brown's take on comparative suffering, our busyness has become an acute measurement of our entrepreneurial worth: "You stayed up all night? I've been up for 72 hours straight working on my business." What we tend not to brag about is efficiency, as the wiser person may have paused, strategized, and executed the same goal in a shorter period of time. It is definitely the age of the hustle, but I'd love to see us upgrade to the thoughtful hustle: How can we maximize our time? Busyness for the sake of busyness isn't it.

Fulfills the guilt
Feeling guilty when we actually do take a break is common, particularly during crucial periods. Even notable entrepreneur Elon Musk famously said he is afraid of vacations. However, it is during the pivotal points in your business where you actually need to pace yourself to stave burnout. You can minimize your guilt by having a structure in place that actually allows your business to continue uninterrupted while you are away.

Fulfills the silence
Being still often scares us, as it can make us feel anxiously bored and even to think about the things we've been avoiding with busyness. There is so much to be discovered when we allow ourselves to stop and quiet down. In fact, we may suddenly be given an elegant answer to the challenge we've been so busy trying to conquer.

6
A GOOD BURNOUT
Always maximize your time on the sidelines

If there is one thing we don't talk about in entrepreneurship, it is burnout. Company failure, spousal abuse and self-destroying habits are often accepted, but you're not allowed to admit you are exhausted. I know people who were so burnt out that they just disappeared without a trace. No judgment from me: I walked the precarious line myself, juggling raising my baby, bootstrapping a top Apple app, and maintaining my writing career.

No one is Superman or Wonder Woman. It's a shame that we don't talk about burnout more because, like the proverbial dark night of the soul, there are some amazing, priceless gems we can gain only in the space between ending and doing. Keep these strategies in mind, particularly if you can actually make time to process your burnout.

Stop
Burnout means you don't have the energy or focus to continue on. It means excessive late

nights, drawn-out meetings, and extra drama have to go away, simply because you physically, mentally, and emotionally can't carry the weight. Good! They shouldn't have been there in the first place.

In my reflective time after my startup was acquired, I've done judicious editing in my life: removing excess, ending relationships, and pausing action. Decisions are now based on gut, even if that means missing opportunities. Urgency is as addictive as envy, and just as deadly, since it is the comparison to the person you think you deserve to be as opposed to the comparison to the competitor you think you see. A forced pause makes you reconsider where you put your energy, since your stamina is now limited.

Restrategize
What are you actually working toward? The day-to-day grind leaves little to no room for actual strategy, as you've got real, tangible business problems at your doorstep. The problem is that you don't restrategize until you or a loved one gets sick, your career takes a left turn or... you suffer burnout. Burning out

shouldn't be looked at as a failure, but as an internal switch going off to tell you the parts of your life that have been neglected need to be attended to. It might feel like the timing couldn't be worse, but it is always the right time for your body, mind, and soul.

The only way forward is to make career decisions more conducive to the life you need. As Warren Buffett famously said, the most valuable thing entrepreneurs can say is "No." What stuff are you carrying that you shouldn't have been carrying in the first place?

Prioritize

Like when I was guiding the growth of my startup, my time is limited to what must be done *now*. However, unlike an overflowing email box or an app update demanding my attention, the things that are demanding my time are my sons, my intuitive leaps toward new ideas, and my own personal balance. I'm still running on a compressed time schedule, except it isn't filled with work, but with self-care. In a sense, I'm still taking in the last startup roller coaster ride -- at least emotionally. And I'm already gaining more clarity on my higher purpose as an entrepreneur.

Whether your hamster wheel is a startup or a corporate gig, we all struggle to prioritize. Instead, we triage based on the values we had before we got on the ride -- prioritizing based on an outdated model that doesn't take into account anything we've learned before. Been doing the same thing for five years without a break? Then you are organizing and prioritizing your work, and your career, based on whatever you learned a half decade ago. It is difficult to take everything in while you're trying to put out the next fire, but it's not impossible.

Burnt out? Embrace it as much as you can. The next journey will begin soon enough.

7
CLUTTER
New opportunities can't come in without space

My office is filled with lots of mindfulness and strategic tools, but the most useful one is a brand-new shredder. It cost $50 with coupons. Powerful enough to eat through papers, folders, and credit cards for 30 minutes straight, the little monster turned my save-for-a-rainy-day piles into buckets of confetti. The debris filled two garbage cans roughly my height and width.

What are you still carrying that you don't need? The cathartic act of destruction, of removal, and of closure gives us space for our next act. It forces us to make peace with the past. It also gives us pause to honor what we've done.

The physical clutter
In one pile, for instance, I found my business card from a few years ago. It said JOURNALIST in big letters, proudly referred to publications that don't exist anymore, and

highlighted projects and books that, at the time, represented the peak of my career. Speaking at TED was still a dream. Being a startup founder wasn't even on the radar. This random scrap piece of paper represented an acknowledgement of my growth, something that we entrepreneurs are want to do. It also made me realize that I was just as likely to find my 2016 business card one day and quietly acknowledge, again, how much my career had evolved–an inspiring, high-level thought while I do the day-to-day entrepreneurial march.

The virtual clutter
It can be just as inspiring to do a virtual purge. In fact, the real challenge in the future won't be us drowning in papers, but being overwhelmed by stuffed email accounts, bursting app screens, and bloated cloud drives. As I argued in *Our Virtual Shadow: Why We Are Obsessed with Documenting Our Lives Online*, "The way we are using technology, our idea is that we document everything now and sort it out later." Well, the sooner you make "later" happen, the more mental and emotional space you'll give for future growth.

It's overwhelming, but here is where you can start:

- **Buy a shredder or another efficiency-focused product.** It's worth getting services and products that will create room for your future business. The virtual side is equally important. For example, a computer efficiency program can delete orphaned data and compress your useful files so you can work faster.

- **Take an afternoon to assess.** Imagine you are working in a new office on a new computer. We have unparalleled focus, clarity, and relief when we're working with a clean slate. Decluttering and deleting isn't on the same level, but spending three hours organizing can bring us much closer to that nirvana. Time is our most valuable asset, but the return on investment here is high.

- **Prevent indecisiveness by hiding your stuff.** If you are on the fence about tossing any physical or digital goods, try putting them away, like in a dark part of the closet or in a file deep within your computer memory. Check in a few months later. If you haven't accessed them, then you probably don't need them. The hiding technique is popular among clothing decluttering experts.

Sorting, removing, and tossing our entrepreneurial baggage may the ultimate way to assess our past–giving us clarity for which previous pitfalls to avoid and where we should be focusing on next.

When is the last time you cleared the decks?

"During the process of rising, we sometimes find ourselves homesick for a place that no longer exists. We want to go back to that moment, before we walked into the arena, but there's nowhere to go back to."

-Brene Brown, Rising Strong

8

GROWTH SPURT

Take extra care during any transitions

I am in a growth spurt, just like my toddler. My favorite entrepreneurial clothes, which fit perfectly yesterday, are ridiculously small today. Ideas are moving faster than my attention span can handle. I need more rest, yet I'm overstimulated by all the possibilities now. I've outgrown my past and am stretching hard to build my future. "Comfortable" is a word I haven't used in a very, very long time.

You could argue that entrepreneurs are always in a growth spurt, but that's not really true. You cannot always be expanding, changing and breaking your foundation, and as much as our ego wants us to believe we're always pushing boundaries, it isn't possible to be in a continual state of growth. In fact, not pausing to evaluate can actually hurt our progress. No, a growth spurt is when you are expanding your customer base to a new demographic, you are pivoting your company to a new arena or you are moving your business to another level. It is scary, frustrating and exhilarating.

I see it every day when I am with my toddler, just as I see it every day when I look at myself in the mirror. Here's how I take care of both of us:

Feed yourself well

You don't know what you're doing anymore, so everything takes more time and energy than planned. Let's face it: There is a certain amount of autopilot that happens when we have a good rhythm going. Now, that rhythm is gone.

Like a growing child, your appetite is absolutely insatiable. In the past six months since selling my startup, I have read more books, been more thoughtful and asked more questions than any other time in recent memory. Why? I'm spending every moment figuring out how the hell to structure this next phase. My brain needs to be fed.

Give space

Similar to my son, you need an unusual amount of space to grow. Unlike him, however, you already have responsibilities, obligations and patterns that can keep you from growing into better opportunities. For you, me and other adults, we gain space by saying No. A lot. (Actually, that's not too different from a toddler, either.)

It wasn't until well after I transformed from journalist to entrepreneur that I realized how much I needed to remove from my life: From restructuring my relationships to chucking out outdated ideas. To flip Shonda Rhimes' TED Talk celebrating her year of saying yes, creating a Year of No is one of the best things you can do for your business.

Follow desire

What risks did you want to take now that you were too afraid or unable to take before? The beautiful part about instability is that one smart, calculated risk could be as disruptive as two or three calculated risk - no matter how many changes you make, you know you will never be the previous person again. The past is gone and cannot be rewound. The previous rules don't apply anymore.

Passion is your only clear compass.

9

FAVORS THE PREPARED

Make a contingency plan for success

How do you prepare for failure? It makes sense to have a Plan B, like a nest egg you can crack if it all goes south, or a set vocation that you know is in demand, or perhaps an alternative business you can launch. Only the most risk-tolerent - and, perhaps, reckless - of us go into an endeavor without any type of security. In fact, it may be more motivation for you.

Now, how do you prepare for success? I've found that most of us have made peace with failing, but actually don't have a plan for when we succeed.

In 2014, I co-founded the social meetup app Cuddlr with a couple other people - super small operation with barely a budget. I spearheaded the launch strategy and mapped out our plan from pre-launch to about six months out. My co-founders expected a cult following, I expected a more mainstream opportunity. What we got was a smash hit, getting an incredible amount of press and running to the top of the Apple App store within its first week. We're lucky we had a framework plan for post-launch, but it was difficult to ride the rocket ship even with that. Imagine if we had no plan for success! We probably wouldn't have been acquired.

The challenge for my co-founders and me, as well as many entrepreneurs, was that our focus was on evangelizing our service. But what if people love our service? It becomes preaching to the choir. There has to be a strategy if you actually win. It's akin to a presidential candidate being focused on the debates, but not having a set plan for when she actually gets into office. It's a recipe for disaster - even though you got what you wanted.

Here is some food for thought.

Plan it all the way through
What if you get that gold-star client or make that financial goal this year? Consider the next goal you have in mind. For instance, what kind of maintenance will be required to keep that hard-to-get client? Or how, exactly, will you be using that additional profit from a financial

milestone?

Line up your mentors

A fresh success often means dealing with new issues that require a brand new strategy. Do you have a brain trust ready? The key isn't to have people who know what you know, but know what you'll need to know once you succeed. Again, planning for success means you assume you'll need a higher level of insight.

Look at different types of success

Entrepreneurs like myself often have many opportunities happening all at different stages, which means you may reach your goal with two medium-sized clients versus the big whale you've been trying to score. Does that affect the outcome? Run through a few ways success could happen for you. You may be surprised at how a slightly different outcome will affect your post-success strategy.

10
GOING PUBLIC
Recognition does not equal success

I'll never forget when my journalism law professor, the late Richard Schwarzlose, recommended I get E. B. White's *The New Journalism*. I was halfway through Northwestern's prestigious Magazine Publishing graduate program and realized that I didn't want to publish magazines. I wanted to write. "Go find *The New Journalism*" he said with a pat. "And you'll see what's possible." Published in 1973, *The New Journalism* had excerpts from edgy non-fiction writers who incorporated fiction techniques to unparalled effect. Tom Wolfe, Joan Didion, and Gay Talese were among them and are still considered literary giants today. I slept with the book under my pillow.

The most outrageous contributor was Hunter S. Thompson, the scoundrel who got in deep with The Hell's Angels, revealed southern racism at the Kentucky Derby, and truly exposed the dark side of Las Vegas. He consistently reported while being drunk and high and anti-social. He also was a master of words. To the untrained eye, it would be easy to assume that the former somehow enabled the latter. That would be a lie.

When Hunter S. Thompson died of an apparent suicide in 2005, one of his most shared quotes was from an old 1974 *Playboy Magazine* interview:

"One day you just don't appear at the El Adobe bar anymore: You shut the door, paint the windows black, rent an electric typewriter and become the monster you always were – the writer."

In other words, behind Thompson's drunken binges and crazy partying was sober work. It is always work. It will always be work. Work is behind everything.

Today, it isn't necessarily cocaine sniffs and tequila chasers. It is tweeting about the next novel you are going to do when you haven't written the last five books you've talked about. It is launching a kickstarter campaign for something you know you don't have the passion to follow through on. It is networking at conferences, at parties, and at coffeeshops about your brilliant idea that you could have – should have – started literally years ago. It is the flash before the fire, the dessert before the main course.

It is cheating.

We worry about selling out for security or big bucks, but the most dangerous selling out is you removing the work and soaking in the fun and the accolades that are supposed to be a reward for that very work. There is mounting scientific proof that saying you are going to do something and getting props for it taps the same part of your brain that recognizes reward for actually *doing* it. In other words, you could lose the motivation to achieve your goal simply because you've already gotten part of the reward: Recognition.

The results are sad. It is the drunk journalist who doesn't know what questions to ask, it is the potential writer posting endlessly about the new book he should be drafting, and it is the wannabe entrepreneur publicizing an app that they haven't even started developing. What they fail to understand is that the real spoils aren't recognition, awards, or money, but growth, insight, and impact – and that only comes with work.

There is no hack to that.

11
DIRTY WORK
Get your hands dirty as much as possible

My best entrepreneurial moments happened when I was tasked something I had no business doing. In creating my first app, So Quotable, I spent the first few years getting lots of support from a tech-savvy friend. One random day before it was going to launch, this person disappeared without a trace – and with the code. I was pissed. So, while taking care of my newborn baby, I learned to program for Apple devices, designed the user interface, and released the app within four months. It came out in time for my first TED Talk.

As my co-founders and I launched my second app, Cuddlr, circumstances shifted my role from a silent media and cultural strategist to the public face of the app. By the time we were acquired a year later, I was doing the majority of the interviews.

I'm proud of how I rose to those occasions, but I share this because I am 100 percent, absolutely positive that I wouldn't have done any of this unless it was necessary. Who in their right mind would get up before dawn to program with one hand while rocking their infant in the other? No one, that's who.

When I talked to my best friend, author A. Raymond Johnson, about the So Quotable experience, I compared it to being a lounge singer that suddenly became a singer-songwriter. I always had a vision, but now I could see the concept, map it out, and release it my damn self. I was a one-man band. I was free. My experience with Cuddlr essentially doubled down on that feeling, as I led our tiny company through intense media blitzes, demanding customers, and an eventual acquisition. They were journeys that few entrepreneurs are able to experience from inside the arena.

You may not be able to afford a capable programmer, a strong PR team, or a great logo artist. It may be late nights of you proverbially mopping the floor, taking out the trash, and doing the dishes by hand. But when you eventually are able to hire others to help, you'll have an unmistakably keen vision for how to run your business efficiently and wisely.

It is an insight the suckers who simply hired out the dirty work will never, ever have.

12

SKIP MONDAY

Strategize early to better execute later

It usually happens around Sunday afternoon: The vague, uncomfortable reminder that tomorrow is Monday. You get revved up to start the week at your A-game, but the pressure can often crush any real or perceived progress. It can be a rough cycle.

Instead, consider shifting your usual Monday work to Tuesday. Whether your business is based on the traditional work week or loosely framed around consultant hours, it is a simple strategy that can save you both time and anxiety.

No one is paying attention on Monday

When do brands announce things they don't want to get attention? Friday afternoon. And despite the norm, I'd argue that Monday morning would be a close second, as everyone is antsy to get out what they've been working on or thinking about since late last week. The same can be said for important internal and external meetings, major sales launches and anything else that requires serious attention. It's like we all have a gag order for two and a half days and, suddenly, we have the opportunity to talk. Things quiet down by Tuesday morning - making the second day of the week perfect to make your announcement or to have a conversation.

No one is ready for Monday
Office Space clichés aside, we have to do a mental shift after two days off. Even if, like me, you work over the weekend, there's a difference between quietly getting things done and manning the workday phone, email and social media. Respect that you, and most every one else, are still in second gear. Treat Monday as you would Friday: Laying the groundwork for the upcoming days, but leaving the serious thought and actions to later.

No one is listening on Monday
When it comes to connecting with others, Monday is a pretty rough day. Monday is considered one of the weakest days to post on social media (Wednesday, arguably, is the best) as well as one of the worst days to cold call (Friday takes the award here). Save your heavy

discussions and your "asks" for another day. Tuesday is an excellent candidate.

No one is satisfied with his or her progress on Monday

As a 5-day culture, we create this immense pressure to be as productive as possible every week. It may motivate you sometimes, but any less than stellar work or unfinished business comes back to bite us in the behind on Monday. It's like the Ghost of Friday's Past begins haunting on Sunday night - and by Monday morning, you are feeling the weight to make up even more for last week's lackluster productivity (even if it isn't actually lackluster). The expectation of bigger, better results can be an internal struggle or, worse, projected onto other people, including employees and colleagues, which means that even if you don't feel that way on Monday, there are others that are struggling. Why not sidestep the melodrama? Make a simple, limited list of what must get done on Monday, create a dialog with others enforcing the focused approach and save the heavy lifting for a less psychologically day: Tuesday.

13

TOO BUSY

Being too busy shows poor business vision

Based on our most common conversations, busyness today is an epidemic--even more so than it was for previous generations with less technology available. In fact, it can be a point of pride.

The truth is that we are not too busy; we just have too many choices to make clear priorities. One of the worst things you can say to someone in business is that you "are too busy."

Unfortunately, other people may be smart enough to understand your real message, even if you don't realize it yourself.

You don't care.
It's OK, as you can't care about everything--the very nature of something being a priority is that other things are less cared about. The first step, though, is to know yourself well enough to understand that you don't really care. The next step is to find a gentle way to say no. Start here.

You are inefficient.

Perhaps the most damning view is that you simply can't handle your business time efficiently. This perception goes double for fellow entrepreneurs: Many of us launched successful startups while juggling other personal and professional commitments. We're the last people you want to tell "I'm too busy." Instead, explain that you're working hard to give excellent attention to your current projects and, if possible, you will make room for other projects in the future.

You aren't serious about your business.

How many times do successful businesspeople turn down work? Quite often, actually, but it is because of their clarity of focus, not their busy schedule. It is a novice move to burn bridges or close doors prematurely, as your busy season today may turn into a slow churn tomorrow.

14

A GENTLE "NO"

Saying "no" is more important than saying "yes"

Rejection is a part of business, particularly entrepreneurship, but the biggest, most important rejections have to come from you. You can't accept every offer. You can't pursue every idea. You can't please every customer.

Unfortunately, between our "winner takes all" mentality and our fear of turning away work, we rarely develop the skills necessary to say No. In fact, saying No is easy. Stopping an action without destroying a potential future relationship is hard.

Here are three strong, kind and honest ways to say no--and actually learn about potential collaborators in the process:

"**When we work together, I want to make sure you have my full attention.**"
One of my biggest pet peeves is when a business partner commits to working together, but obviously has too much on his plate. The

problem is that I do my best to make sure that I'm not overextended so he gets the attention and details deserved - and I assume others do the same.

"I need to respect those to whom I've already committed."

It reminds me of the adage "If someone gossips to you about other people, you can bet they are gossiping about you to other people." The same could be said for other business dealings: People who are unwilling to say No to you, even though they know they can't give you quality time, are the same people who will willingly sacrifice their commitment to you to work with someone else to whom they can't say No.

A potential collaborator may not like that you are prioritizing others' previous needs over their current needs, but they should respect it. If they don't respect your commitment to others, then that often reflects their own principles - and it may be a warning sign to keep in the back of your mind.

"We should make sure the timing is good."

Your business should naturally evolve,

whether it means changing your product scope or identifying a new customer base. It means yesterday's great projects are today's misfires and last year's potential partnerships are now pretty lukewarm. There are amazing collaborators, clients and mentors I would love to work with right now, but as I focus in on my core business, I've had to gently let them know that our time to work together isn't here... yet. It leaves the door open for later opportunities and also confirms that you respect other people's time and are keen not to waste it.

"There's no problem with being where you are right now. We can be where we are and at the same time leave wide open the possibility of being able to expand far beyond where we are now in the course of our lifetime."

-Pema Chodron, Comfortable With
Uncertainty

15

EMBRACE LIMITATION

Limited resources foster creativity and genius

I wrote about a dozen books over seven years, so it isn't unusual for others to talk to me about their ambitions to write. Overall I found that the biggest reason people haven't written a book yet is not a lack of literacy, nor the inability to understand publishing (indeed, you can Google self-publishing resources and have a book out by next week). The excuse was always something intangible, that things just hadn't come together yet.

"I haven't found the time.", "I need money to do it right.", "I am not living in the right place to really promote it."

Often, these are lies we tell ourselves. As we discussed in LIES WE TELL, "You will always need more resources than you have, more time than you got and more energy than you can muster. If Jobs, Musk and other visionaries waited until everything was perfect, then we wouldn't be talking about Jobs, Musk and their contemporaries right now."

Those books as well as major consulting gigs and even my last acquired startup were all done under some kind of resource poverty: Time, money or location. Call me crazy, but those actually made the opportunities not only better, but increased the chances of those opportunities actually showing up.

Personal scarcity

Isn't it amazing how we manage to get our projects done just in the nick of time, no matter how long the deadline? We always pace ourselves, expanding and contracting our productivity, based on the time available. Our biggest constraints are often personal: Relationship needs like our families, physical needs like our rest, or emotional needs like our hobbies. After having my first kid, my workweek was slashed from 60 hours to about 15 hours - and I launched two startups, did two TED talks and blossomed my career while being his primary caretaker. It's not about time, but efficiency.

Financial scarcity

We may dream about being billionaires, but complete financial freedom can actually be a detriment to productivity. Artists and entrepreneurs often thrive when they have fewer resources simply because they must be more creative and innovative. Waiting until your money is better is often a mistake.

Location scarcity

It's not about Silicon Valley. I have meet fascinating entrepreneurs in nontraditional areas like Cincinnati, Detroit, and Miami aiming to put their city on the map or bring it back to past glory. I also know entrepreneurs who are sitting on their laurels until they can move to a major city, which is akin to an author waiting until they meet an agent to type any words. The question is, where can you make the most impact?

16

MARTYRDOM

Sacrificing your well being won't help your business

Passion usually gets us into our entrepreneurial profession, as there would be little other reason for us to take such giant risks. It's a double-edged sword, though, as passion can make us push ourselves too hard. It also can have us make short-term decisions that don't make any sense for our well-being or, ironically, for our actual long-term business.

We should expect to make adjustments within specific periods - people call it "crunch time". For instance, I spent more than a year getting up in the wee hours of the night to launch my startups and my speaking career, but I put a set time limit on that insane schedule, which helped me stay balanced throughout.

Unfortunately, it is way too easy to begin sacrificing important things and making crisis mode your default. Here are the big three parts of your life that are not worth putting at the sacrificial altar.

Sleep

I'm guilty as charged on this one, which is why I can speak from experience. Media mogul Arianna Huffington has written a best-selling book on the importance of sleep. Jeff Bezos, who is easily controlling half of your online commerce, gets eight hours a night. Science has proven that it is more productive to get more sleep and work less than it is to do the opposite (and why a nap should be on your daily agenda).

Food

A "nutritious" shake may save 15 minutes time, but it doesn't give your mind and body the break it needs to process problems nor to rest between intense work blocks. Not eating at all is truly a recipe for disaster, and the older we get, the less our bodies will tolerate the stress.

Relationships

What's funny is that we never really sacrifice our relationships, but just burn out our social currency. You become the friend that only calls when she needs something (and, as an entrepreneur, you will definitely eventually need something). Not cultivating and managing your relationships ends up hurting your business growth - doing the opposite of what you may claim you're not cultivating and managing your relationships for.

17
SCARY VACATIONS
Never stopping isn't a sign of strength, but of fear

Legendary entrepreneur Elon Musk recently shared a private issue with the press: He is afraid of taking a break. He was quoted as saying:

The first time I took a week off, the Orbital Sciences rocket exploded and Richard Branson's rocket exploded. In that same week, the second time I took a week off, my rocket exploded. The lesson here is don't take a week off.

It may be a brilliantly logical man showing his superstitious side, but his phobia of vacation echoes what many of us believe: You can't afford to stop. Evidence now shows that you can't afford not to stop, but there are many reasons why you believe you can't have or don't deserve a break.

You don't have the structure in place
Have you enabled your business enough so you can actually be unavailable for a few days?

Very few of us have. It goes beyond vacation, though: Personally, unexpected health issues and family emergencies have put my own work at a standstill. Enabling co-workers, subordinates, or even our brain trusts is key to feeling better about taking a break. It also requires putting your ego aside and realizing that denying yourself time to recharge doesn't equate "crushing it" as an entrepreneur.

You fear competitors will quickly leave you in the dust
Often in our minds, competitors are No-Doz snorting freaks of nature that never rest. They are just waiting for us to pause so they can take the lead. Even the noblest professions have a ruthless edge, but stopping actually can give our minds the chance to create the strategy we need to win.

The greatest entrepreneur of our generation, Steve Jobs, took infamously long walk breaks. Stopping also prevents us from tinkering too much on our products. Finally, we are less likely to go to extreme thinking and ruin what we've spent so much time building.

You are afraid of facing what you've left behind

Startups can easily demand all of our time, to the point that many of us have given up on having any type of healthy social or family life. But what happens when your business closes or you have a successful exit and you have nothing else to focus on but your life outside of work? It's a scary thought, especially if there is a trail of broken promises and strained relationships laying in your ambitious wake. Unfortunately, avoiding personal conflict just prolongs, if not exacerbates the issues that aren't being addressed. Facing those demons is akin to the popular proverb about planting trees: "The best time to do it would be 20 years ago. The second best time to do it would be today."

When is the last time you actually stopped?

18

THE SMARTEST PERSON
Your network really is your net worth

We create startups with the idealistic intention of building a community around it, yet often don't take the time to create a community within our own personal entrepreneurship. This dawned on me when I was in Silicon Valley and, organically, my friends and I had created our own brain trust.

A hodgepodge of techies, entrepreneurs and artists, we'd gather together every week to drink, connect, and recap. It became a magnet, as regulars would inevitably have a friend in town or another colleague interested in coming through and they, too, would stop by whenever possible. The diversity in people pushed our conversations beyond any discussions we could have had in a less public forum.

I left the Bay Area a while ago, but I'm still connected to the valuable people I met. Now we've spun off into interesting ventures, like tackling Silicon Valley diversity and leading the discussion on tech's human impact. More than that, they became the trusted colleagues and mentors for my startup adventures.

In short, they are my brain trust: A diverse, collective sounding board for my next entrepreneurial moves. And every entrepreneur should have one.

Do you have people to listen to your ideas and help you take things to the next level? Here's how you can cultivate them.

Rise to the occasion

As the saying goes, if you're the smartest person in the room, then you need to go find a better room. Your collective should push you to be more strategic, more ambitious and more successful, rather than stroke your ego based on past actions.

Being around smart, accomplished people will push you to higher heights. Attending my first TED Conference was both thrilling and intimidating, but the experience turned me into a regular attendee and, a few years later, a TED speaker myself. Connecting with the American Society of Journalists and Authors made me realize how much further I could go with my writing, inspiring me to become an active member and eventually join its Board of Directors. You should connect with people who help you recognize and encourage you to be your highest self.

Make the time

Our lives can be a blur of late nights/early mornings, airport hopping and crunch times. Cultivating a reliable set of colleagues and mentors should be built into your schedule, just as you would make time for strategic planning or for budget allocation.

Consider the return on investment. I recently offered to take a wise colleague out for an expensive meal. What I got was advice that helped me wrap up my startup gracefully. The priceless insight not only required me setting aside time for the dinner, but also energy building and cultivating the relationship to the point where I could have a long dinner with them. Relationships take time.

Talk to folks in other disciplines

Artists can often be bad businesspeople not

because they are awful at math, but because they don't mingle with MBAs and accountants who could give them advice. It is easy to stay in the comfort zone and, as we get older, it gets harder to leave it.

Connecting with different professionals becomes even more important after we get established. Early in our career, we are eager for leads, feedback and direction. As our work stabilizes, though, we think we already have the contacts we need and assume the work will continue to flow. It's not until we need the insight of an advertising specialist, or a media journalist, or another highly-focused professional outside of our field that we realize how narrow our circle has become. You don't want to be facing a difficult business decision and have no one to give you an informed opinion on it.

How are you building a reliable entrepreneurial community for yourself?

19
BE BORED
Not doing encourages daring ideas

We talk today about powering through pain, fatigue, and exhaustion to reach our entrepreneurial goals, but sometimes stopping is exactly what we need to do to understand what we should be doing next. And stopping, sometimes, requires being bored.

Best-selling The Personal MBA author Josh Kaufman explained it well on entrepreneur Tara Gentile's *Profit Power Pursuit* podcast:

I'm actually thinking about taking the Internet out of my office entirely. The more you can make it harder for yourself to focus on anything else, that's valuable. I think there's a lot to be said for "strategic boredom". Just removing all the other things that could be potential distractions... just get rid of them temporarily. And if you can make what you want to do the most interesting thing that you have in your environment, then a lot more gets done that way.

Kaufman calls it "strategic boredom". Whatever you are doing, whether it is a strategy session, a pitch deck or a new manuscript, has to be the most interesting thing happening in your world at that moment. Your social media timeline, mindless busy work and other potential distractions have no place here. Personally, I've found my own work elevated when I minimize the amount of focal points I have - which sometimes means physically unplugging the Internet.

When is the last time you allowed yourself to be bored? If you can't imagine it, then you likely fear it. Here are three reasons why it scares us.

We waste time being afraid of wasting time
Boredom is considered a bad thing today, as we associate it with unproductivity. We always want to feel like we are busy by being on social media, going on business trips, or doing all-nighters for the business. However, our most insightful strategies and ideas happen when we are walking somewhere, taking a moment to think or actually resting for a moment.

In fact, a recent study cited by the Harvard Business Review found that we are more productive when we take time to look at nature. Having been raised in the city, I associated nature with boredom well into adulthood, as perhaps you did, too. As the study shows, though, nature is really a catalyst for us to pause and access the moment. It gives our brains a chance to process and strategize-- and avoid potentially time-wasting moves in the future.

We worry that inaction will make things fall apart

The entrepreneurial world seems to operate on two gears: Stop or Run. You are either running towards profitability or paddling to stay afloat. It is extreme thinking, and it is what keeps us willingly sacrificing our health and our relationships to reach another business milestone.

Crunch time is real, but insane hours, emotional stress, and ridiculous malnutrition are meant for significant stretches, not as the default. Is every moment crucial? Probably not, or your definition of crucial isn't really valid.

The truth is that our ego wants to believe that we are sacrificing everything at this moment because it is what is required of us to succeed. Working without pause also helps us avoid boredom, and that very silence that would make us face the truth about the decisions we've made and the ones we keep on making.

We fear we aren't good enough, so we tinker when we shouldn't
The fear of boredom also means that we will mess with things when we really should let them flow naturally. Picture the nervous artist fussing over a painting that is already done or a businessperson aggressively addressing a harmless contractual point at the last minute. We have the ability to destroy all our hard work simply because we can't just sit still and shut up.

Mounting scientific evidence says that creatives--the risk takers and the entrepreneurs--are more likely to overthink their ideas and strategies to the point of neurosis. The deck is already stacked against us. Don't be your own worst enemy.

20
AFTER THE WIN
We are most vulnerable after a success

If we love anything, then it is talking about the struggle to succeed. It is about being focused, about showing up every day and about potentially betting the farm to win.

But what happens after we win? Well, a lot happens.

Entrepreneur Toni Ko felt lost after she sold her cosmetics company to L'oreal for a reported $500 million. Co-founder Marc Lore felt disappointment when his company was acquired by Amazon for $550 million. I went through my own challenges after my popular app, Cuddlr, was acquired.

The toughest part, though, is allowing ourselves to struggle again in our next pursuit. That's why we are more likely to fail after we win big. And it often isn't the positive, swing for the fences failure, but the soul crushing kind. *The Ego is the Enemy* author Ryan Holiday shared exactly why with entrepreneur Tim Ferriss:

Ego is dangerous when you're aspiring to something, no question, but when you are successful and you've built this thing and then you're trying to do your next thing, when you're convinced that everything you touch turns to gold, that's where ego is the most destructive.

It breaks down into a couple reasons. First, your ego, like all of our egos, is insatiable and is hungry for more praise. It is the equivalent of the lab rat being given a sugar cube: It is fine beforehand but, once the sweet treat is introduced, it will get agitated and angry if it doesn't get it again.

We have to train ourselves not to take our success as the default. Instead, the practice of our work should be the default.

Second, you have taken your mastery for granted. Do you remember the first time you started your profession? I started crafting stories when I was a toddler, so I seriously cannot remember when I began narrating to an audience. The longer you've been doing something, the less you remember the pain, struggle and hard work it initially required. It is why you should diversify your social circles and create side hustles to make sure you are not mentally complacent.

The best cure? Always be a beginner at something.

21

WE NEED YOU

No one can duplicate your unique genius

I spent a remarkable amount of time studying astrology, and I blame Kelby, my first "girlfriend". Cresting and ending as a high school summer over-the-phone-only romance, our relationship was mostly talking about how different we were and how, astrologically, we weren't supposed to work. Around that time, I saw Linda Goodman's *Star Signs* on my grandmother's shelf. I read it several times that summer, from top to bottom, and began reading other books about astrology, which led me to Carl Jung, the Myers-Briggs Test, and more sociology.

Many years later, I'm a broke post-grad student living as a freelance writer in Chicago. I get some stuff published, but I can barely make my apartment rent which was decided based on a job opportunity that vanished. As I reached my wits' end, a friend of a friend connected me with a major online portal. It was looking for editorial content and wondered what I could write about. I highlighted technology, video games, sexuality and – screw it – astrology. It immediately hired me as an astrologist, pulling in a salary that I would even consider decent today. And I had some of the most fun ever as a freelancer. I had no idea.

Stuart Butterfield and his partners just made a mint selling the photo website they founded, Flickr, and decided to reinvest some of it into creating a video game company. They wanted to specifically focus on the online experience. Unfortunately, they invested millions into the PC realm right when mobile was rising. Realizing their folly, the founders had a hard conversation with investors and decided to shut down the company. The investors were in deep, too, at least $17 million. The founders had a meeting laying off virtually the entire team, during which Butterfield burst into tears. The founders went back to the drawing board.

While they were working on the game, though, they created an elaborate internal chat system that allowed them to quickly communicate and share files with each other. With nothing to lose, they began sharing the chat system with friends at Microsoft and other companies. The team was surprised at the response and realized that their little side project, not their robust video game, was the real hit. They named it Slack. By Summer 2016, Slack was the defacto corporate chat choice and was worth $4 billion. It was only four years old. Butterfield had no idea.

Let's talk about you. The crazy idea in your head may be the very next thing the world needs. There is no use in waiting for a sign (unless you absolutely need to, which, in that case, consider this your sign.) You can't rely on timing, as it may take you weeks, months, or even years to do your thing, and you have no idea what the world will look like at that moment. You can't rely on others, as no one else shares the exact vision you have, so no one else can tell you whether to go forward or not. And you can't rely on the past, as doing more of what was done yesterday is a waste of all of our time, particularly yours.

What you can do is listen to that nagging voice that is telling you that you have a higher purpose. What you can do is begin moving towards that higher purpose. What you can do is start walking. Today.

Steven Presssfield sums it up well in his classic book *The War of Art*:

"Creative work is not a selfish act or a bit for attention on the part of the actor. It's a gift to the world and every being in it. Don't cheat us of your contribution."

What are you being called to contribute right now?

ON PRODUCTIVITY
THE PRODUCTIVE
BITE-SIZED ENTREPRENEUR

To Abhi,
whose smile reminds me of the beauty of life itself.
Thank you.

"In fact, there is no inherent problem in our desire to escalate our goals, as long as we enjoy the struggle along the way."

- Mihaly Csikszentmihalyi, Flow

How Not to Be Productive

When I wrote the first THE BITE-SIZED ENTREPRENEUR, my intention was to arm you with everything you needed to find and trust your passion, and use that direction to create your ultimate side hustle.

You and other wonderful readers sent me great feedback about your own personal journeys in entrepreneurship, along with your questions. Lots of questions. I quickly realized that you were hungry for more.

I liken it to going to one of those upscale, gourmet Vegas buffets: You can sample just about anything and everything that a restaurant has to offer, but once you've tried it all, you know what food you really love. Once you know what you prefer, your next move should be going straight to a restaurant that specializes in that dish.

THE PRODUCTIVE BITE-SIZED ENTREPRENEUR is specialty served on a platter. If the first book laid the foundation to ignite your passion, this follow-up is here to help you sustain it. After all, once you make room in your life and grow into your successful side hustle, then your main focus has to be on maintaining and strengthening your business. Your business is always a reflection of yourself. This book will make you a more productive version of yourself.

If you are looking for productivity hacks, then this is probably the wrong book for you. It's actually my fault, not just because I wrote this book you have in your hands, but because I have an aversion to the popular word "hack". Part of it is my background, as, in journalism, a hack is someone who is a lazy writer. Part of it is the second life of my career, as a tech entrepreneur, where a hack is a quick, smart shortcut to a problem.

Here's the issue: There is no shortcut to productivity. There is no hack.

In being around extremely productive people and observing my own most productive periods, I've found that strong productivity is less about banal, universal shortcuts and more about preparing your mindset. In culinary culture, preparers do a mis en place, an organization of their tools, raw foods, and other items, just in the right place so that, when order after order comes in at the heat of the night, they don't need to think about what's next. Smart productivity is the same way. It is instinctive from preparation and habit.

I learned this first hand, as my most productive time wasn't 15 years of working 60 hours a week as a freelance journalist and author, but the three years of working 15 hours a week as a journalist, author, entrepreneur, and speaker after my two sons were born. As I said in THE BITE-SIZED ENTREPRENEUR, "I found myself learning Apple's iPhone programming language with one hand while rocking my newborn in my other, spare arm." The very limitation of time accelerated my productivity, but I also had to be mentally ready to step up my game.

To be the most productive, you have to make room for inspiration, set the plate for action, and give patience for recovery. Keep in mind that inspiration doesn't mean waiting until you feel like doing something, but putting in the proper R & D (research and development) so you are likely to find the creative spark and the strategic genius. Setting the plate is keeping obstacles clear of your momentum. Recovery is respecting your own balance, celebrating your progress, and assessing your next move.

Being productive every single day is a fruitless goal. To maximize productivity, you have to accept that you will not be able to give 100% every single moment of your life. Constantly working means you aren't taking time to integrate lessons learned during action, just as much as staying idle means you aren't testing theories in your head.

Productivity is a cycle, not a sprint.

I call the productivity process "pursuing, doing, and renewing". It is an infinite iterative flow where we research our interests, implement our theories, and assess our growth. It is not unlike Eric Ries' landmark Lean Startup method, in which you ship the "minimal viable product", or MVP, to get feedback from others as much as possible. In the case of productivity, we're getting feedback from ourselves.

THE PRODUCTIVE ENTREPRENEUR is broken down into three sections loosely based on the process: Pursuing, Doing, and Renewing. Like other THE BITE-SIZED ENTREPRENEUR books, you can read the strategies in any order, but your productivity will be much stronger if you go through it from top to bottom. If you are new to entrepreneurial pursuits, it also may be worthwhile reading the original THE BITE-SIZED ENTREPRENEUR to get a solid foundation for the basics.

It would be indulgent to spend more time laying the groundwork for a book on productivity, so let's get started. Enjoy!

-Damon Brown, September 2016

I: PURSUING

"At the beginning of any new idea, the possibilities can seem infinite, and that wide-open landscape of opportunity can become a prison of anxiety and self-doubt."

-Peter Sims, Little Bets

1

CREATE LIMITATIONS

You automatically take as much time as you are given

It began with getting up at 5 a.m. That was the plan. Our baby would wake up at 6, and, since I was the primary caretaker at home, I'd be able to get a sufficient amount of business done before then. I quickly learned that meant I didn't shower unless he took a nap, so I started getting up at 4:30 a.m. Then I realized I couldn't make morning tea or coffee unless I got up at 4:15 a.m., and that I had to refuse my steadily increasing workload unless I woke up at 4:00 a.m.

The scales kept adjusting until I found a new wakeup time: 3:15 a.m. It was an hour after the bar's last call, making it officially morning. Three o' clock still carries the smell and the silence of the night, though, and it gave me the isolation and darkness that fueled my creativity. I traded my extreme late nights of younger years for very productive mornings. I had space.

My son became my end-of-day clock, and when he rang around 6 a.m., I had usually already talked to my New York contacts, written an article, and tackled a new business strategy for my first app, So Quotable. The time shift became invaluable when I launched my app Cuddlr, not only because my main co-founder was in the U.K., but later when I needed significant time to steer its significant userbase and eventual acquisition.

Around the time of my change, I caught a popular article that said we used to sleep in two shifts as recently as a couple centuries ago.

[Virginia Tech History professor Roger Ekirch] found that we didn't always sleep in one eight hour chunk. We used to sleep in two shorter periods, over a longer range of night. This range was about 12 hours long, and began with a sleep of three to four hours, wakefulness of two to three hours, then sleep again until morning.

That was all I needed to hear. "Maybe this temporary thing will work...forever!" I told myself one morning before sunrise.

After several months, however, I realized that this should not – or rather, could not – be my default. My moods began swinging. My body began to ache.

I told myself to hang in there, that I'd keep at it for a year. As the 12th month arrived on the horizon, I hit the equivalent of a runner's wall, and I limped to the finish line.

Clearly, it was time for a change. I decided to look at my priorities. I started saying no to gigs, accepted that parts of my to-do list wouldn't get done, and gave myself at least one alarm-free morning every week. The aches went away, my mind cleared up, and everything became more focused. The year following this experiment was even more productive, as I zeroed in on only the projects about which I was most passionate – simply because I didn't have the time to do anything else.

My years of working at odd hours and [insert chuckle here] "waiting to be inspired" to create were replaced by a stable, disciplined regiment. In an instant, my 60-hour-work week was sliced down to 15 hours a week. I viewed myself as a marathon runner doing a daily, three-hour leg.

My first year as a parent became one of the most productive years of my life.

Have you ever found yourself more productive when you have less time? It reminds me of an old programming adage: Programmers always manage to get things done with just the amount of computer memory they are given. It's the same reason why we always seem to spend through the money we have, or feel like we complete things just before the deadline is about to strike. We automatically take as much space as we are given.

When we are aware of how much little time we have, though, we begin compressing. As Brain Pickings' Maria Popova shared in a recent article, our relative view of time slows down when we feel threatened. In this case, the threat could be not getting the last sentence down in an idea or not sending out that client email before you run out of time. You realize how many minutes you spend checking social media, fixing a snack, or gazing out of the window. Those moments of disengagement can become the quiet time killers that keep you from being more efficient.

I learned this rather recently. In my compressed work year, I did my first TED talk, gave a keynote speech at American University, programmed and designed my first app, made TV appearances on Al Jazeera America and other outlets, and joined multiple startup advisory boards – all while being my first son's primary caretaker while still maintaining an active writing career. Not only was I driven by passion for both my family and my work, but also by my acute awareness that time was limited. My proverbial alarm clock was going to wake up around 6 a. m., which, from 3 a. m., gave me about 180 minutes each day to get my passion projects accomplished.

Here are some thoughts on how to maximize your time:

Monotasking

As I discuss in my book *Our Virtual Shadow: Why We Are Obsessed with Documenting Our*

Lives Online, scientific studies now prove multitasking doesn't really exist. What we view as multitasking is just picking up one task, dropping it quickly for another task, and then repeating the same process over and over again until they are both done. Instead, concentrate on getting one thing done well. The completion will boost your energy-and focus-for the next item on your list.

Return on investment

Forget the money ROI – what is your time ROI? We lose the most time by wasting it on items that shouldn't be high on our priority list. For all the great opportunities I fulfilled during my compressed year, I said "No" to even more opportunities than I accepted. I still do.

Slice and dice

In her book *Six-Figure Freelancing*, Kelly K. James talks about breaking the day up into 15-minute segments. This former lawyer gets things done by essentially giving herself a time limit for her work.

Time, not money, is an entrepreneur's most precious resource. A life change taught me this lesson, but you shouldn't wait for that to happen.

2
DEVELOP YOUR CORE
Do many things with one purpose

Have you noticed that the most productive people usually aren't exhausted? I mean, they get tired, but you rarely see them ready to pass out in a random corner or forced to take a mandatory vacation based on doctors' orders. On the other hand, those who seem the most stressed and burnt out seem to get things done within a hair of failure. If the wind blew the wrong way, you'd expect them just to topple over right where they once stood.

You can point to personality, disposition, or stamina, but I believe it comes down to one special difference: Focus. The most productive people are focused, usually on one priority. The least productive people are focused on many things, usually on many priorities, which, of course, means that nothing really is a priority. It is multitasking versus monotasking and diffused energy versus concentrated energy. Have you ever taken a magnifying glass and made a pinpoint with the rays of the sun until smoke started to rise? Productive people bring that level of concentration to their goals.

It gets confusing, though, when the most popular productive people seem to be spread so damn thin. For every creative like Jiro Ono, the singular-focused master chef featured in the film *Jiro Dreams of Sushi*, there are lots more like Richard Branson, the multimedia mogul who has built music, movies, airlines, and even spaceships under his Virgin brand. Oprah Winfrey, Jeff Bezos, and others always seem to have a new venture, yet never seem to be as stretched as much as the average Joe multitasking through his relatively simple life.

The truth is that Jiro and Richard and Oprah and Jeff are the same. Their expressions are obviously different, but they all have one simple, clear intention to their career. That's why it is absolutely crucial that you say "No" as often as possible. Can you imagine how many times Jiro said "No" to expanding beyond his small, exclusive restaurant (watch the movie to get a better idea), or the few number of times Oprah actually says "Yes" to a new project idea?

The beautiful part is that each of these successful individuals instinctually knows what next step for their business should likely be and what would be a misfire – simply because they have taken the time to know themselves and, therefore, found their purpose. Why do you do want to do what you do? If you want to be the most productive, then you have to know your end game.

And, in a Zen-like paradox, the better you know yourself, the less options you have to grow, as everything won't be for you, but the more narrow that focus, the more productive you will be in the areas that you *do* care about.

One of my favorite analogies is from Martha Stewart's *The Martha Rules*. My mentor Andrea King Collier told me about the following excerpt years ago. It ended up changing the course of my career:

We once [listed] all of our media platforms and traced how the little pansy flower had been covered in each one: Our magazine featured cupcakes decorated with sugared pansies; on television, I demonstrated how to apply pressed pansies onto paper, creating lovely stationary; on my daily radio show, I explained to listeners that the word pansy *stands for thought and remembrance; the syndicated newspaper column described how to press and dry pansies...*

And she keeps going! For the media mogul, productivity didn't mean reinventing the wheel to feed her many, many platforms, but taking one core idea and adapting it to each audience. My "pansy" is intimacy and technology, which turned me into a tech culture journalist, a speaker on human connection, and, most recently, the founder of a tech app that facilitated person-to-person intimacy. I'm happy with how my career has gone so far, but it also meant saying "No" to opportunities that would have derailed my journey or diluted my focus.

At the beginning of any new opportunity, the possibilities can seem infinite, and that seemingly exciting wide-open landscape of opportunity can turn into a prison of anxiety and self-doubt. Forget losing productivity; If you get too overwhelmed, you might end up losing yourself.

Learning, developing, and protecting your core is key to being the most productive entrepreneur possible. You should be able to say it in one short sentence, like an elevator pitch cut in half.

Do you know your core?

3

DEATH BY NETWORKING
You can only talk about an idea so much

I just did something I hadn't done in a while: I went to a networking event. The more time passes, the more I get out of connecting within organic environments and, occasionally, bonding at a small conference. Besides, with now two young kids and a busy business, I don't have much time.

During the cocktail hour, I chatted with an older gentleman, a serial entrepreneur. He asked me if I knew the scene, as he didn't know anyone. I was puzzled, then relieved as I admitted that I hadn't been to a networking event in a while.

We then both realized that we had been too busy *doing* rather than *talking*.

Networking is absolutely important: It grows your brain trust, exposes you to new ideas and gives you a break from the day-to-day grind. But going regularly specifically to networking events has an effect of diminished returns, especially if you are going to them within the same circles. Are you starting to recognize the same people at networking events? Then it's probably time to stop.

One of the great things about parenthood and other external responsibilities is that it forces you not to waste time. Back in Silicon Valley, I would spend hours every week at networking events - as did most people I knew. Mind you, I didn't do the TED Talks, startups, and bigger books until after I left the Silicon Valley networking scene, started a family, and took my time more seriously. I don't think that's a coincidence.

Before I go to an event, networking or otherwise, I ask myself one question:

Is there something more productive I could be doing with this time?

No wonder I, a travel and connecting fanatic, have only gone to only two conferences this year. With all that "extra" time, I wrote a book. I implore you to ask yourself the same question.

4
WRITE IT DOWN
Ideas go on paper, not on keyboard

Paper is definitely down in popularity, as we are more likely to open up a note application or send a quick email to ourselves than to physically write down something. Even classic journals like Moleskine are going digital.

It's all the more reason to check out NPR's recent interview of two University of California, Los Angeles researchers comparing students' handwritten note taking versus typed out notes. The results were stunning:

"When people type their notes, they have this tendency to try to take verbatim notes and write down as much of the lecture as they can," Mueller tells NPR's Rachel Martin. "The students who were taking longhand notes in our studies were forced to be more selective -- because you can't write as fast as you can type. And that extra processing of the material that they were doing benefited them."

The scientists found that laptop and written note-takers were equal when it came to facts and figures, but laptop note takers did "significantly worse" when it came to internalizing concepts.

The prevailing theory is this: When you write something by hand, your brain actually has to process the information because it is often not possible to write down every thing being said. Typing, on the other hand, lends itself to speed. You are more likely to try to capture every word rather than jot down the intent.

It is not practical, if impossible to write down everything by hand, but there are some key situations where writing would be more effective than typing:

- Capturing a lecture or presentation
- Preparing for your own lecture or presentation
- Documenting an initial business meeting to set expectations
- Creating a framework for your new business idea

I did a TED Talk on the power of writing our big ideas on little pieces of paper. It doesn't have to be on a little piece of paper, though. It can be on whatever you wish. It is the manual act of writing itself that is valuable.

Today we default to texting something into our smartphone or whipping out the laptop, but we often forget the power of handwriting. Here is why you should consider writing your next thoughts down instead of typing them out.

Filter your thoughts

We go through a filtering process when we write things down. If you're like me, you can type much faster than you can write--and the additional time and energy required to move your pen means you are more thoughtful in what you capture on the page. It's not limited to words, either: Doing a quick sketch or diagram can sometimes be the key to focusing your thoughts and expressing hard-to-articulate ideas.

Remember what you were thinking

I write everything down on an index card whenever I have a big idea or need to work something out, as cards are compact, portable and efficient. Some of my index card ideas are rubbish, but the ones that are the most valuable eventually get put in a recipe box. (Thankfully, post-TED Talk, they are no longer all over my office.) Now I can access brainstorms or thoughts I had months, even years ago--and they are often strong ideas I would have long forgotten. It's like having a Google for my brain.

Articulate the abstract

Consider it an elevator pitch to yourself. While ideas are broad and encompassing, words are limiting and linear. Use this to your advantage: Find the right language to express your next product or venture. Writing out your thoughts takes them out of your head and forces you to capture them in a cohesive manner without potential distractions or aids like PowerPoint, spellcheck or the World Wide Web. Your scribbles can be both raw in concept and structured in words--a powerful combination.

When is the last time you tried writing down your thoughts, rather than typing things out, to get through an impasse or to work out a strategy?

5
EMPTY YOUR SCHEDULE
Scheduling a blank day boosts productivity

One of the safest things you can do personally is overcommit yourself. It is also perhaps the worst thing you can do to your business. The security of proving how busy you are and using busyness as a gauge for success will ultimately drop the quality of your interactions, your service and your health. Fighting to be the busiest entrepreneur in the room is an arms race you don't want to win.

My personal cure for overscheduling is to simply schedule a blank day. It doesn't even have to be an entire day. On a regular basis, I will set aside four to 12 hours dedicated to bettering my mind. My phone goes to voicemail, my email is paused, and meetings are pushed to a later date.

These aren't vacation days, but days of self-driven thought, productivity and realignment. Imagine what you could do with a scheduled day of betterment?
• Modify your business plan

- Catch up on must-read materials
- Call previous clients to reconnect

An "unscheduled" day is integral to my business, but it can feel awkward when you first try it. Here's how you can make your own blank day.

Schedule

Yes, you need to schedule your blank day, particularly if you have other people looking at your calendar. Block off the time. Setting it up like a regular meeting trains you to take the blank time seriously. For me, seeing it on my calendar makes me anticipate that day and gives me something to look forward to.

Commit

It is tempting to schedule one or two regular work activities, but even a brief retreat back into your daily grind can take you out of the zone. Instead, commit to the time away just as you would if you were on a Wi-Fi free plane, or sitting in a place with poor cell phone reception, or spending quality time with a loved one. In other words, your office is officially closed for the day.

Maximize

Once you realize your day is open, the possibilities will begin to emerge. Remember, it's not a day of rest, but a day of gathering your mental resources without outside commitments. For me, my blank days are when I finish books, go for thoughtful walks and catch up with dormant clients. They are days to restrategize, retool and recommit. It is me sharpening my axe so I can be a more effective warrior.

6

WHEN TO LET IT GO

Knowing when to stop working is just as important

Except for death and parenting, few things inspire as many quotations and axioms as entrepreneurship. They usually encourage us to keep going: "Fight another day," "It is darkest before the dawn," "Failure just eliminates another bad option," and so on.

Other people need encouragement to keep going. Entrepreneurs, though, need encouragement to *stop*. We're too motivated as it is. Anyone who enters the odds-adverse entrepreneurial world has to be, on some level, an optimist. If anything, we push when we should be still and we goad when we should be receptive. In fact, as discussed in the original THE BITE-SIZED ENTREPRENEUR, our restlessness can destroy something that is already on its way to success.

In my experience, there are three great reasons not to make any more moves on an opportunity:

The launch date/commitment time is already here

Legend has it that Alex Haley's publisher had to send a representative to the author's house to literally pull the *Roots* manuscript out of his hands. As this famed African saga was inspired by Haley's family tree, the author could have kept adding more and more details. But it was too late.

You have a commitment to excellence, but you have a bigger commitment to serve your audience. A great product or service is useless if it never ships.

You did everything you could

Sometimes, there are flaws, challenges, or gaps in what we are presenting, but there is absolutely nothing we can do about it. I experience this regularly in the journalism world, where external factors like page layout, the publication date, and budgetary constraints can severely affect the end result. It is a lesson in doing the best you can… and letting go.

It is in someone else's hands

The roughest part of entrepreneurship, at least for me, isn't the ideation/creation phase, nor the so-called crunch time before launching a product, but the gap where you wait for someone else's response. It could be the audience after a launch, or a partner after you made a big decision, or even a vendor once an important request was submitted. You know the result is important, but there is nothing more for you to do.

Everyone has a method of calming his or her inner control freak. My regular process is talking out loud through the various scenarios and having a plan A, B, and C in place. For me, having my next chess moves planned calms things down. And, once feedback is given, I'll know exactly what move I should start executing.

7
WALK IT OUT
Get on your feet to recharge your productivity

It has been a turbulent summer of sorts for many of us, with the political unrest, stock market volatility and crazy, dangerous weather. I've been dealing with my own unique stress, reflecting on my anniversary escaping Hurricane Katrina, selling my popular app Cuddlr, and transitioning out of a 3 a.m. daily work routine.

So, one day recently, I just got up from my computer, left the house and started walking. Probably about four miles that day.

I've always loved walking, particularly when I lived in the heart of San Francisco, where it would be a rare day when I didn't walk to tech functions throughout the evening (the city is seven by seven miles, so walking everywhere isn't an unrealistic accomplishment). I then moved to Southern California in which most cities, unlike New York, Chicago and D.C., aren't conducive to walking everywhere. I also started a family, and those hours spent walking-or hours spent doing anything-seemed as impractical as they seemed wasteful. But now I'm taking the time to walk, whether it be in the morning or in the night, as I'm realizing it is how I clear my mind and how I process my day. It has been like a meditation, though many of us who do walk regularly may not even realize the positive impact it has on our mental balance.

Walking for clarity isn't a revolutionary idea. According to *The Last Great Walk* author Wayne Curtis, the health benefits of regular walking came into view about a century ago-particularly when it came to keeping ourselves young.

What is new is that entrepreneurs are actually starting to value it. Consultant Nilofer Merchant has a short, excellent TED talk on why business people should take walking seriously. As we spend more time on tech and less time taking care of ourselves, I tend to agree.

Here's how you can incorporate walking into your daily entrepreneurial life.

Do walking meetings

Walking can be an excellent time to take conference calls, especially those that have you mostly on mute. If you are fortunate enough to work near your colleagues, take them with you on a brief jaunt. It may help you work out knotty ideas or even ease the tension of a particularly sensitive conversation-Steve Jobs famously had his most important discussions on his feet.

Get smart

It is also a great opportunity to listen to business books or, on the free side, to podcasts. I now listen to Startup, Will Lucas' Of10, and other favorite entrepreneurial podcasts almost exclusively during my walks. It not only makes the time more valuable, but it assuages any guilt that I'm out of the office.

Keep it brief

A walk doesn't have to be an extreme, epic journey-it could be walking to a farther coffee shop for your morning drink or spending an extra 10 minutes taking the long way to lunch. You can look at the additional time as a brief reprieve from the constant device buzz

Track your walks

If you're into measurable results, consider utilizing a wearable, whether it be a FitBit or Apple Watch, or an old-school pedometer. The ability to see how many steps or miles you've walked can help encourage you to keep going and, perhaps, walk even further the next time you go out.

8

STOP MEASURING TIME

Never mistake time for commitment

Time is often how we measure our commitment to an idea. Someone who put in 20 years developing something successful is looked at as persistent, visionary, and patient. On the other hand, calling someone an "overnight success" is usually a backhanded complement, as it shows a person who potentially got lucky or stumbled upon a brilliant idea. The quick ride to success is looked at with both admiration and envy. They didn't earn their stripes.

The one important thing time does not measure is commitment. Side hustlers, folks that take time outside of their main gig to take their passion seriously, can easily be more committed than full-timers. Can you imagine taking time away from your rest, your leisure, and your life outside of your full-time job to make your dream a reality? Perhaps you can. Perhaps you are doing that right now.

Time spent does not indicate passion nor focus,

hence it not equating commitment. Social scientists are now poking holes in the 10,000 hours theory made popular in Malcolm Gladwell's influential *Outliers*. Gladwell argued that mastery of a particular skill happens when someone puts in 10,000 hours of study and practice, citing Bill Gates, The Beatles, and other modern icons. The rub, though, is that we don't know how *focused* people were during those 10,000 hours. Picture Salvador Dali spending countless days doing still life and never progressing into the abstract, disturbing art for which he is known. He was fully present during those proverbial 10,000 hours, and that gave him the vision to create beyond the literal bread and baskets that he painted early in his career. Again, time does not equate *quality time*.

Instead, as Dali went abstract, The Beatles went psychedelic, and Gates went visionary, you should measure your productivity by your evolution. Your growth could be a radical, public departure. Your growth could be a subtle shift inside. It doesn't matter.

As spiritual writer Pema Chodron puts it, "In

order to go deeper, there has to be a wholehearted commitment. You begin the warrior's journey when you choose one path and stick to it. Then you let it put you through your changes."

Focus on transformation based on what you are doing, not on the time you spend doing it.

II: DOING

"The professional does not wait for inspiration; he acts in anticipation of it."

-Steven Pressfield, Turning Pro

9

DO LESS WITH MORE IMPACT

Being productive every day is a fool's errand

If busyness is our number one obsession today, then constant productivity is a close second. I'm part of the problem: I not only analyze how some of the most interesting leaders stay focused, but I am obsessed with being productive myself. I had my Masters by my very early 20's and wrote 18 books in the past decade. I've got my own issues.

So perhaps you'll listen when I say this: *You are not meant to be productive all the time.* We seem to think that there is some magic formula that turns our mushy, balanced-oriented human brains into tough, binary computers. There is not.

The best way to be productive is to let yourself be less productive.

Take it one goal at a time

It's no coincidence that some of the most recognized entrepreneurs ruthlessly focus on one thing at a time. Focusing on multiple things doesn't make us get more done, but simply makes us less productive in several areas.

Focus in intervals

I call them palate cleansers, after the refresher you eat or drink between meal courses. The idea is to focus on something for a short, intense period of time, then to give yourself a break.

Break early, break often

Walking, quiet time, blank days, Internet unplugging, and other disconnections do marvelous things to your productivity because your brain will continue to problem solve while you take in the quiet.

If you really want to get amazing things done, then trade in busyness for productivity. And that happens best in intense cycles, not in breathless marathons.

10

THE NECESSARY THING

Sometimes you can only do one thing well

When I was burning the candle in the middle (well beyond burning it at both ends) and considering giving up, one of my mentors, Rosemary Taylor, gave me a simple directive.

"Chop wood, carry water."

In other words, sometimes the best thing you can do is do the routine, the necessary thing, that needs to be done at the moment, and concentrate on absolutely nothing else. Focus on the first thing, the necessary thing, and then go to the next thing on the list.

That's it. And that is enough for today.

11

ALTERNATE TASKS

Palate cleansers can refresh your focus and productivity

As an entrepreneur, I tend to run hot and cold. I'm burning the midnight oil for weeks, then I have several days where my intensity and, seemingly, my passion seems to dissipate. Unfortunately, that means wasting excess energy when all the work is done and potentially not being as thorough as possible when the energy is low. I know the extreme decision-making trap firsthand.

One practice that helps immensely is palate cleansing. You are taking something to wash away the previous experience to make way for the next one. Mint, bread, and even plain old water are popular palate cleansers, but what if you applied it to your daily actions? Here's food for thought.

Focus on something else

In food, a palate cleanser is usually a light drink or snack that makes your senses focus on something else. It serves as a bridge between two courses. The courses themselves are usually strong or intense. The palate cleanser serves as a break between two extreme experiences, helping you digest the former and get prepared for the latter.

The irony is delicious, here: The more focus you want, the more you need to step away.

Make time to rebuild your focus
I love deep diving into work, but intensity, by its very nature, is in limited quantity. In fact, researchers estimate that you can only hold your complete attention onto something for a couple of hours. (It's the reason why public speakers follow the adage, "Say what you're going to tell them, tell them what you're going to tell them, and then tell them what you just told them.")

It is the reason why it doesn't make much sense to do a 20-hour day with little or no breaks: Your productivity will drop, sooner rather than later, and you may actually be wasting time rather than maximizing it. The 25-minute Pomodoro Technique is the epitome of short focus, but even a 15-minute break every hour or two would be much more efficient than creating a marathon day.

Give room for thought

Why do palate cleansers make you more productive? While you may have checked out, your brain is still focused on the previous project and creating smarter strategies for you to use when you start again. As I recently talked about, resting may be our most powerful entrepreneurial tool. People in traditional lines of work usually can't build their own schedule from scratch! It is a perk that may have gotten us into entrepreneurship, but something we tend to forget after we become entrepreneurs.

A short, daily meditation is my palate cleanser, as is going for a walk and, whenever possible, taking a brief nap. Yours may be checking social media, doing a quick exercise or reaching out to a colleague for a quick chat. We all should find ways to take our ostrich-like heads out of the sand.

12
OVEREXTENDING YOURSELF
Burning out doesn't have to happen

It is remarkably easy to do too much, particularly when you love what you do. Does work not feel like work? You may be fortunate enough to be in that situation, but that also means you are less likely to know when you are tilting towards burnout, physically in need of rest, or pushing yourself too hard. Entrepreneurs may have more passion around their career than most, so we are more susceptible to losing ourselves in the excitement of work.

Self-care is a part of taking care of our business, because if we break down, then our business will break down, too. Here are some solid ways to help stave off overextension.

Wait to commit
We feel pressure to say "Yes" to opportunities right away because we're afraid of missing the boat or, worse, our measured response will scare away the person who's offering the opportunity itself. I've found that some

opportunities are fleeting, but the number is nowhere near the number of opportunities that we think are fleeting. In other words, when it comes to determining the rarity of an opportunity, we tend to sit on the paranoid side. Unfortunately, that means we are more likely to say "Yes" to things even when we don't have the resources to take them on. And... suddenly we're overextended.

Instead, try taking a moment to consider letting go of the opportunity being offered. It could be five minutes, it could be an entire evening. Give yourself as much space as can be allotted. You may be surprised at the new considerations that suddenly pop up, ideas that would not have otherwise crossed your mind until, perhaps, it was too late.

Check your gut

Some opportunities can feel particularly rare because they are actually a little too ideal. Fortunately, our gut can give us the warning that we should look deeper. For myself, I may get a feeling that someone is holding back information or that the deal may end up in a different place than intended. It is often right, but the most important part to understand is that your gut isn't specific - it just realizes when something feels off with a situation. And it very well may be telling you that a new opportunity will be too much of a strain on your resources.

Ask a colleague

Sometimes the one to help you stay in check is a trusted confidant. If you have your brain trust in order, then you already have people around you who know your goals, your intentions and your weaknesses. An objective party can warn you when you are veering off your path or potentially falling prey to one of your blind spots.

Look back a year from now

One of the best ways to prevent overextending yourself is to envision how you'd like to spend your time, energy, and focus a year from now. What will you be doing? How will you be doing it? What seeds do you need to plant to get there?

There are few reality checks bigger than realizing the work you are doing now won't get you to where you want to be. No one intends to be unproductive towards his or her dreams. It's just that, when we overextend ourselves, we are too overcommitted and scattered to prioritize the things that will move us closer to our goal over the busy work we're already doing. Think about where you want to go and plan on saying "No" to plans that don't move you forward. "No" should be your default, and seemingly nonessential opportunities should have to be important enough to convince you otherwise.

13
MASTERING TIME
How you can maximize your schedule

Time management master Laura Vanderkam has written several books, including the best-seller *168 Hours*, on how even the most in-demand leaders maintain incredible productivity. She and I agree that the most precious resource you have isn't money, but time.

I got a chance to connect with Vanderkam when she spoke at the recent American Society of Journalists and Authors conference. She shared three master tips to strong time management.

Write down how you spend your time
Create a time journal, not unlike people concerned with their eating habits create a food journal. How can you maximize your time if you aren't sure how you're really spending it?

Vanderkam admitted that she thought she worked 60 hours a week but, after keeping a time journal for several months, realized it was closer to 40 hours a week. By keeping a journal, you can squeeze out the inefficiencies and better understand why you may not feel as productive as you think you should be.

Do a (time) portfolio review

Do a portfolio review of how you spend your time, just like you would for stock performance. In this case, however, you are looking at the allocation of your time assets. Are you spending 10 percent of your time sending and tracking invoicing? Then we're talking five to six weeks out of every year.

Vanderkam found that virtual assistants, interns and smart software can help immensely - and the financial outlay pales compared to the time you save. How else could you be growing your business with the proverbial 10 percent of your year you'd get back?

Done is better than perfect

The ultimate time suck is perfection. Spending too much time perfecting a product or service not only can hurt your business, but it can create opportunity cost for the other great, new things you could be working on.

Vanderkam highly recommends this: "Let it go. Done is better than perfect." Think about the last time you spent an inordinate amount of time for an incremental improvement on a completed project. Now imagine all the other things you could have been doing with that time. At a certain point, spending more time on something will provide significantly diminished returns. Being honest about when you reach that point is perhaps the toughest, most important skill in great time management.

14

PUT THE COFFEE DOWN

Drinking coffee at the wrong time will hurt your day

Unlike many entrepreneurs, I didn't drink coffee through school, nor in young adulthood, and it didn't keep me going during business all nighters and crunch times (adrenaline did that). No, I didn't fall in love with coffee until well into my grown-up life when I began appreciating its bitter, robust flavor.

Thankfully, it was just before taking on a 3 a.m. schedule, but the energy boost has always been a perk, not a reason.

Culturally we usually have coffee first thing in the morning, but I realized that it was much more powerful and effective when I had it later in the day--like 11 a.m. The days went smoother and I focused better. Now science is backing it up, though there are many reasons to hold off on that first cup of java.

Your body doesn't need coffee early
Your body begins pumping cortisol when you

147

wake up in the morning, kind of like a smelling salt to help you rise and shine. The boost happens between 8 a.m. – 9 a.m., followed by other boosts midday and in late afternoon. Drinking coffee first thing in the morning is like adding lighter fluid to an already-growing fire: You quickly burn extra bright, and you burn out just as fast.

However, drinking a cup between 9:30 a.m. to 11:30 a.m. provides an energy bridge between your early cortisol rises. Around 11 a.m. is my sweet spot. It is also important to put the science in context: 8 a.m. was once the perfect time for me to have coffee, but that was when I was waking up at 3:15 a.m., so 8 a.m. was my midday cup.

Coffee can mask your true entrepreneurial feelings
For a caffeine-sensitive person like myself, coffee can make one feel like everything is coming together: You're being super productive, ideas are coming easily, and business is going in the right direction! All the above may or may not be true, but I want to feel that way because of the passion for my

148

business or the rewards of a hard-earned strategy, not because a bean is making me feel brilliant.

As a stimulant, coffee can make us excited about awful ideas, abrasive about our opinions and unable to settle down (or perhaps that's just me!). It can bring out the opposite skills we need to be the best entrepreneur we can be. The potential issue is compounded when we drink it when our bodies are already revving up for the day. Overdoing the coffee first thing in the morning can have us starting the day making bad decisions.

It breaks up your day
The 3 p.m. drag is real, particularly after a heavy lunch, but late morning is often when we really begin to slow down from the rush. The average work day starts with a 6 a.m. jolt of the alarm, the body shock of shower water, the dash for the train or car, the social stimulation of people or traffic and the productivity burst with the intent of catching up or getting things done early in the day. In other words, you're running a sprint until lunch is on the horizon. No wonder we slow

down at lunch and need a nap around 2ish.

The 11 a.m. coffee creates a natural break in the day--the transition from sunrise to sunset. On more mellow days, I'll replace my late morning coffee with a strong tea or fruit-infused water. When I do coffee, though, I take it a step further and make it a physical transition by making my coffee by hand with a French press. It takes about five minutes, grinding the beans, pouring in the hot water and pushing down the stopper. For me, it is like a meditation on what I already got done today and what I will get done later. It is a thoughtful pause.

15

KNOW YOUR PRIME TIME
Everyone peaks at different moments

When I was young, my golden hours were from 1 o'clock until dawn. It was something about the silence of the night, the gap between bedtime and rise, that turned me alive. I'd have all kinds of ideas. My writing would flow. An optimistic glaze would cover my world. It wasn't until I couldn't stay up all night (hello, family) that I realized how much my creativity was fueled by certain rituals - and, in this case, certain schedules.

I recently heard the term "golden hours" from People Matters founder Jodi Wehling. I take it as more than just your most productive time of the day. No, it's when you are at your peak in creativity, vision and inspiration - even without a cup of coffee. Here Wehling describes them:

Pay attention over the next week and identify when your best work hours are.

Then guard them with your life. Block the time and

mark it as "busy". Resist the temptation to book this time for a meeting.

This is your time. It is worth twice as much as other times in terms of what you can get accomplished.

As a leader, it is terribly easy to let outside forces dictate your schedule. If you get more successful, then defending your own needs becomes harder, not easier.

There are two great, actionable ways to make your golden hours work:

Say no

Nope. Uhn-uh. Can't right now. I recently talked about three smart, strategic ways to say no and save your relationships. Denying people access to you 24/7 is the only way you can preserve your productivity.

Create a blank day

Block off an entire day and make no meetings, phone calls or messaging available. Not only will it give you the space to think, which we rarely create, but it also will give a glimpse into when your golden hours actually are.

Undisturbed, I'm productive mid morning, mid afternoon and late evenings, which is much different than when I started my career or even during my early morning rituals a couple years ago. Having a blank day will show you your natural productivity patterns *at this moment*.

Save your energy
Bracket your golden hours with less intensive activities. For instance, if I have meetings or interviews, I place them before or after my most productive moments. It is a great way to preserve your outside work needs and protect your golden hours.

When are your golden hours?

16
THE HARDEST 1%
The last step is by far the most dangerous

I launched my first app, So Quotable, after many years of development, with the app's programmer abandoning the project at the last minute, and four months of learning Apple programming language in the wee hours while taking care of my first son. It was brutal. It launched as a workable, functional product just in time for my first TED talk. I showed it with a mixture of pride and shame, as I could quite see the bubble gum and duct tape that kept it together. I knew it inside and out, so I knew all of its flaws.

Shortly after launch, I showed it with trepidation to a professional, successful programmer who knew my journey. He paused wordlessly for a moment, then gave this big smile.

"I'm impressed!"

"Ha! It's pretty damn rough. What are you impressed by?"

"You shipped."

He knew, I knew, and now you know a secret: You will never want to ship. What you create will never be good enough for the public. If you are doing your job right, then you can name at least five things you would change about the thing you are about to give the world. If you aren't insecure about your next big reveal, then you are either lazy or lying.

Artists don't create. Artists ship. Wrote something that you never show to another soul? You just made a diary entry, not a novel. Make a brilliant product that is stuck in almost done? You just created an amazing demo, not something people can actually use. At this point, your influence will be nil. To paraphrase motivational speaker Steve Harvey, you'll be safe, but you'll never soar.

Off the top of my head, I know several talented people who thrive in the 99% zone: brilliant artists, founders, and creatives – nay, *aspiring* artists, founders, and creatives – who charge like a wrecking ball towards their goals. And then, just as the final piece comes into place, they stop. I bring this up not from a place of judgment, but just to show you how deadly that final 1% can be for anyone creative. The dream of what could be is a strong, seductive opiate compared to the cold reality of your realized idea, filled with bumps and bruises and compromises and constraints, exposed to the elements of criticism and judgment.

It's never starting an idea that shows you are serious about your commitment. It is finishing an idea.

III: RENEWING

"With affluence and power come escalating expectations, and as our level of wealth and comforts keeps increasing, the sense of well-being we hoped to achieve keeps receding into the distance."

- Mihaly Csikszentmihalyi, Flow

17
OPTING OUT
Always know why you are doing what you are doing

Why are you at work today? I don't mean your paycheck work, but your so-called passionate work. For us, work could mean pushing out another product, going to a networking event, or updating your website. Why are you doing it right now? Why are you compelled to produce, to move... to show up?

The question is not as banal as it seems. Mainstream musicians come out with a new album every 18 months, often not because they are inspired like clockwork, but because they (and/or their publishers) are afraid the public will forget their name. Authors churn out books to keep themselves known, too, and even if they currently have a best-seller, they will want to have another one coming as the current one takes its' inevitable fall off the charts. Entrepreneurs fight for success, get that success, and then immediately chase after the next success as they don't want to be viewed as a one-hit wonder.

I can relate to two out of three of these things (hint: I don't play any instruments).

What all three of these examples, and countless other similar scenarios, have in common is fear. We are afraid of losing our place in the world. If we stop, then we will be replaced with a newer, smarter model. We must feed the beast.

It may be the most widely used performance hack. It is also the most short sighted.

It's like performing with a gun to your head: Sure, it gets you motivated to be productive, but at a certain point your body, mind, or soul will give out and you will have to stop, no matter the consequences. That's called burnout. It's called being productive the wrong way.

Instead, you have to listen to, understand by, and give respect to your natural cycle. You will not be productive all the time. You are not meant to be productive all the time. In fact, you are best when you are not productive all the time, as less productive periods give you the opportunity to think, to strategize, and to optimize your energy for the next sprint.

If you want to understand why we often don't respect our own productive cycles, then you have to look at how we view others. As creatives – and entrepreneurs, no matter the ilk, are creatives, too – we face a tremendous amount of pressure to perform. You came up with a brilliant melody? Come up with another one. Can we get another game-changing novel? When are you going to get another startup idea that will shift business forever? We are all guilty of having these expectations, explicitly or implicitly, on the creatives we admire the most. It is why we get desperate, angry, or dismissive at the Salingers of the world: People who produce based on some personal schedule, not on some worldly expectation.

Vulture's Rembert Browne articulated the psychosis well in an article about Andre 3000, Frank Ocean, and other mainstream performers who produce seemingly on their own time:

High quality multi-talents with both infrequent

outputs and low profiles make us uncomfortable. We love them, but we're jealous of them, and, possibly, deep down we hate them, because they're doing what we all want to do: Opt out. The way they've decided to live reminds us of how wrong we're all doing it. When people go against the grain of the system, it's a reminder that we're the robots — and the weirdos are the actual humans.

The lessons here are many. First, productivity comes in two forms: Productivity for the public approval and productivity for your passion. It's possible to discover transformative ideas and map out brilliant strategies *without anyone else knowing and with no public proof.* It's OK.
Second, if you produce all the time, then it is easy to lose your voice for the sound of the crowd. The outside voices could be your customers, your family, or your backers. Remember, the people have invested in *your* voice, not the other way around.

No one is going to tell you when it is time to put the tools away and sit down for a second. Only you know when that moment is. And you absolutely always know when that moment is. You just need to be brave enough to listen.

18
LOOKING FOR A CRISIS
Avoid making up things to feel productive

If you are like me, then you get excitement from making difficult situations manageable and impossible scenarios work. Business, and startups specifically, strive on people disrupting monolithic systems and solving long-term problems.

The issue is that the very same bug that gets under our skin to fix things can also make us addicted to the rush of chaos. VC Mark Suster calls it "urgency addiction" and defines it well better than I can:

People with the "urgency addition" thrive on the pressure. We rise to the occasion as it stirs our creative juices. There is something about the adrenaline rush of being under time pressure that excites us and teases out our creativity. We get away with having the urgency addiction because we perform well under pressure. Not everybody does.

The problem, Suster says, is that there a lot of

things that are urgent, but few that are important. As he mentions, productivity guru Stephen Covey discussed the idea many years ago in the seminal book *First Things First.*

I have sympathy for Suster and his type of urgency addiction, but I believe it goes a bit deeper than that.

There are two types of urgency addition: personality and environmental.

Suster's great post breaks down what it's like for someone who has a personality leaning towards urgency. As he says, everything is a crisis, and rushing to get things done makes him feel accomplished. More worrisome, he gets a great adrenaline rush from when he finishes things, saving himself from ruin just in the nick of time.

My urgency addiction, however, is different. Throw me on a proverbial desert island and I will be as calm as the breeze. Put me around other people, though, and it can be terribly easy to absorb their attitude - particularly if they are in crisis mode. I'd call this an environmental urgency addiction.

A good personal example for me would be my young family. If you have kids, then you know that minor things to adults are big, imposing things to little ones, which means meltdowns, tears and frustrations. Transpose that energy into a startup (yes, there is a direct parallel between the two experiences) and you can see how a chaotic environment can put me into urgency mode over things that are relatively minor. You are orbiting the giant hairball, as the late Gordon MacKenzie put it, and trying not to get caught in it.

Whether you are a personal or environmental urgency junkie, there are a few survival tactics to keep your head together.
• Remind yourself that it isn't a crisis
• Ask yourself if it will matter 5 minutes, 5 months or 5 years from now
• Forgive yourself for going there

In *The War of Art*, Steven Pressfield found that creatives were more susceptible to "creating soap opera in our lives". However, unlike the amateur, "The working artist will not tolerate trouble in her life because she knows trouble prevents her from doing her work." We need the excitement and the adventure, but it is much easier to make personal drama than it is for us to sit down, shut up, and put that passion into our art.

Think about all the things that feel like a crisis in your life right now, and then how many are real, absolute crisis that have no chance of being resolved on their own. If you channeled that excess anxiety over imagined crisis into your work, then how productive would you be today?

19
LESS, BETTER EMAIL
Do less emails, more actions

Inbox Zero is a great, wonderful goal, where you have no emails sitting in your mailbox. It is also fairly unrealistic for an entrepreneur. How often do you have every deal, relationship and invoice wrapped up like so many loose threads tied into a neat bow? I actually achieved it once recently, and keeping it is a daily battle.

Clearing our inbox may be a Sisyphean affair, but we're ignoring another part of the problem: The length of the messages we get. The longer the email, the longer it often takes to get to the actual action item. And as much as fellow communication specialists decry the shortening of our language in texts, emojis, and, well, Slack, we still manage to write emails the length of newspaper articles.

Can't we just get to the point? Evidently not.

Fast Company's Liz Funk recently ran a good (and short!) piece on the rules to briefer stronger emails. It's worth reading in whole, but I particularly like her best rule:

"2. Never send an email that's more than five sentences long"

That's right. How much more effective would your messaging be if you got straight to the point? It's not a matter of being curt or brisk, but circumventing all the unnecessary fluff that goes into your email discussions.

Sticking to five sentences means you can't acquiesce when it comes to an "ask", nor can you hide in "maybes" when you actually mean "no". Instead, you are forced to be clear, succinct and respectful of everyone's time - including your own.

All of Funk's top three rules are worth considering, too:
  1. Take the number of words you think your email should be, cut that number in half, and that's what your word count should be.
  2. Never send an email that's more than five sentences long.
  3. Put the most important information first.

I'd add a few more rules myself:

4. Consider email part of a bigger conversation, not the whole conversation, so it isn't necessary to put every single detail in one note.
5. Assume the reader does not have much time to pore over your email.
6. If an email is becoming abnormally lengthy, then perhaps email is not the right medium.

Most of all, I appreciate Funk's the simple summary of why you should care:

For solopreneurs, freelancers, and sales professionals who make their living pitching, having a perfectly crafted, short email introduction can drastically increase your success rate. For those making an ask via email, a message that is brief and adds value is more likely to receive a response. For everyone else, sending shorter emails doesn't always take less time, but it does stack the odds in your favor for whatever you aim to accomplish.

Isn't that enough to take the five-sentence challenge? I know it is for me.

20

CREATE "ME" TIME

Even ambitious entrepreneurs can create space for themselves

Entrepreneurship isn't conducive to balanced health, balanced relationships or, really, balanced anything. The rub is that the very vacation, break, or me-time you are postponing could give you the insight you need to move your business forward. We expect to be geniuses at business, but don't give ourselves time to recharge our brains.

I get it: My daily life has been raising my young family, writing and public speaking, and, most recently, leading my startup to acquisition. Here are three ways I keep myself together.

Meditate
Perhaps you, like I once did, think of monk-filled temples or planning to learn it during a trip to the mountains. I view it now as just taking a moment to be fully present in your life: No multitasking, no planning, and no distractions. I rarely get silence, so I will carve

out a time daily to sit cross-legged, close my eyes, and breathe in and out. I just do it for a few minutes a day, usually every day. And, as my Buddhist friend A. Raymond Johnson once shared with me, even riding a bike or washing the dishes can be turned into a meditative activity. It is about stopping, fully taking in your life and enjoying it.

Do one selfish thing
It is crucial to do something daily that has absolutely nothing to do with anyone or anything else. It means it won't grow your business, help your family, or improve your money. If you can carve out time to juggle your business, your personal relationships and other commitments, you can make 10 minutes to do something fun just for you. For me, as a music fan, it might mean taking a random moment in the day to listen to John Coltrane uninterrupted. It is surprisingly refreshing.

Have downtime
As entrepreneurs, we often try to kill two birds with one stone by incorporating our research or work into our downtime: Reading a business book or watching a TED Talk on our

business area. I argue that this isn't really downtime, but light work. To mean, downtime means doing something not related to your work at all: It may mean watching a viral video to see what the talk is about, going on a walk in your neighborhood, or spending a few minutes catching up with an old friend.

21
THE WHISKEY METHOD
Look back to go forward

Forgetting the past will not make you more productive. It is a common misconception. Smart planning, excellent ideas, and impressive vision will not help you if you don't possess two traits: Confidence and gratitude. Both reside in your history.

The past reminds you of what you have overcome, which gives you confidence to move forward, and it shows you what you have accomplished, which gives you gratitude for the current moment.

Confidence can be relatively easy to find, but gratitude is a rather slippery one. The most productive people have their own wise method of finding it: *The 4-Hour Work Week* author Tim Ferriss writes briefly in a gratitude journal every morning and night, while media mogul Oprah Winfrey meditates often.

I regularly meditate and occasionally journal, too, but my most effective process is reminding myself where I was a year, five years, or even ten years ago.

I call it the Whiskey Method.

A few years back, the popular scotch whiskey Johnny Walker had a wonderful ad campaign. They would take a popular icon or even an upstart entrepreneur and show their timeline to their modern success. As a made-up example, "1966 Backup Guitarist, 1967 Debut Album, 1969 Rock Legend" would be for Jimi Hendrix. It would end with a simple motto: "Keep walking".

The problem is that we tend to lionize people, particularly ourselves, *after* they've made it. We often don't define what "making it" means, nor do we celebrate the many, many victories it takes to even get there. We don't respect the journey. And, as writers more thoughtful than I have said, you can't expect to be given more if you don't appreciate what you already have. Why would your so-called muse deliver more creativity and insight when you didn't give her props for helping you in the past? The Whiskey Method is that gratitude.

Here is mine:
- 2005 Published First Book
- 2010 Published First Best-seller
- 2013 Started First Startup
- 2014 Did First TED Talk
- 2015 Sold Second Startup

It is both inspiring and humbling to me that I just began writing books about a decade ago, and you are now reading my 18th one. It is even more beautiful that I started my entrepreneurial journey only three years ago, yet have had enough adventures to share with others. I immediately feel like forgiving myself for the mistakes I've made this month, this week, or even this day.

The frustrations, setback, and challenges in my day-to-day grind begin to fall away, as I realize not that much time has passed. I am still a student. And now, as I realize how quickly I've transformed as a person, I start to respect the progress I make today – and that means I'll be more productive than I would have been otherwise.

22

SILENCE IS GOLDEN
Periodically shut up to make progress

It's always more comfortable to take action. It is the negotiator who can't handle the uncomfortable lull in the conversation, the artist who keeps fiddling with her finished work or the child who has to do what he was just told not to do. The absence of something is always more frightening than having undesired results from our actions.

If we embraced silence as part of the natural ebb and flow of our lives, then we would be stronger, smarter, and savvier when it is actually time to take action. Meditation, yoga and other practices can help get your mind into a clearer space.
You can also just stop talking.

A recent Duke University study found that quiet actually improves memory and awareness, per *Nautilus Magazine*:

Kirste found that two hours of silence per day prompted cell development in the hippocampus, the brain region related to the formation of memory, involving the senses. This was deeply puzzling: The total absence of input was having a more pronounced effect than any sort of input tested.

Here's how Kirste made sense of the results. She knew that "environmental enrichment," like the introduction of toys or fellow mice, encouraged the development of neurons because they challenged the brains of mice. Perhaps the total absence of sound may have been so artificial, she reasoned--so alarming, even--that it prompted a higher level of sensitivity or alertness in the mice.

Like taking a short nap or planning a blank day, creating quiet time is a conscious act towards productivity disguised as a leisure activity. We schedule power meetings, brainstorms, hackathons, and vacations. Why aren't we scheduling silence? It is worth blocking off a daily hour of quiet - not inactivity, but silence - and seeing how it changes your productivity.

23

BULLETPROOF

The more you know yourself, the more space you have to be productive

Pressure to be productive can actually stress us out to the point where we are no longer potent, and it usually comes from two places: internal and external. The internal pressure reminds you that there is a particular, often idealized goal you planned to reach and you will absolutely not reach it if you do not hit a certain level of productivity. The external pressure tells you that other people will judge you or, worse, stop you from reaching the goal if you aren't being productive fast enough.

The internal pressure can be relieved by setting realistic milestones, creating limitations to encourage focus, and maintaining your self-care. The external pressure is much more nefarious. It is the competitor that you know now, or perhaps the unknown competitor in the near future that can snuff you out at any time. It is the loved one that, whether he said anything or not, you know is just waiting for you to fail so he can be proven right. It is the loyal customers who you think will be disappointed if you do not deliver as quickly as you would like. It is the invisible "they". And, to use a popular sports saying, "They cannot be stopped, only contained."

Containing the external pressure can be done in one simple way: Understand what you are not. By knowing what you are not, you have little to worry about with other people derailing or duplicating your success. A good example is the ride-sharing services Lyft and Uber. On paper, they sound like similar companies, both employing everyday drivers to turn their own vehicles into ad hoc taxis. The identities couldn't be more different, though: Uber pushes the remote, cool personal limo feel, as it originally only utilized black cars, while Lyft represents the fun, collegiate experience, with its cars initially having big pink moustaches stuck on their bumpers. Talk about branding! I know many creatives that hate the word "branding", but that's what you are doing when you say you only work with small organizations, or your boutique caters to the working class, or your startup was created for hungry millennials, and so on. It is what separates *you* from *them*. And separating yourself is a hell of a lot easier when it comes from your own identity, as you don't have to work so hard to be authentic. I heard Uber co-founder Travis Kalanick speak at TED and there is no way you could see him and believe he created Lyft. The Uber brand is a representation of him, through and through. You nor I could recreate Uber, even with a billion dollars. Uber belongs only to Travis. People can compete, but they cannot replicate.

Identifying what you are not, and therefore quieting the external pressure, is important for two reasons. First, putting the focus on proving something to the outside world is a ridiculous task: If you are doing anything worthwhile, then there will be critics, and those critics will never be silenced. It is a waste of precious time. Second, worrying about the external pressure will take you out of your own natural productive cycle. Get in the wrong headspace and you could be shipping products to please the public when your work actually needed more time to gestate, or taking on more duties to hush critics when you should be better managing your tasks at hand. Again, you have an instinct for when you should be pursuing, when you should be doing, and when you should be renewing. Not having a rock-solid identity could have you dramatically trying to force productivity based on the fickle public.

Master marketer Seth Godin explains it further:

"At some point, you need to decide who you are. You need to understand the scale of what you built. You need to decide what the brand is when people hire you and when they engage with you... [and] we can't jump to the next thing instantly nor can we complain that picking one scale keeps us from doing the other thing. We have to embrace it. The fact is that it helps us that we have a sinecure, that we have a niche, that we have a thing that we do, 'cuz then, when other people want to be in our space just for kicks, they can't! They are not us at our scale with our contribution to make."

The more you clarify what you are not, the more bulletproof you become. Then you can take your time, follow your own productivity cycle, and push away worries about being replaced – because you can't be.

24

SHADOWBOXING

Fact: Most of your fears will not come to pass

Entrepreneurship is all about anticipation. You have to know what the market wants before you deliver or, when it comes to the financial end, what the markets will bear before you price your product. You have to guess what your competition is going to do when you launch your service. You have to be ready for when your idea goes viral because, as argued in THE BITE-SIZED ENTREPRENEUR, you have to prepare for success as much as you do for failure. And why, again, are we more prone to anxiety and sleepless nights? Honestly, it could be a chicken and egg paradox, as entrepreneurial personalities tend to be focused on the future anyway.

The question is, what do you do with all that nervousness about tomorrow?

Nothing.

Recognize it, sit with it, accept it, and let it leave.

The spiritual writer Pema Chodron has a great analogy for us. It is unedited and shown at length for full effect:

There's a Zen story in which a man is enjoying himself on a river at dusk. He sees another boat coming down the river toward him. At first it seems so nice to him that someone else is also enjoying the river on a nice summer evening. Then he realized that the boat is coming right toward him, faster and faster. He begins to yell, "Hey, hey, watch out! For Pete's sake, turn aside!" But the boat just comes right at him, faster and faster. By this time he's standing up in his boat, screaming and shaking his fist, and then the boat smashes right into him. He sees that it's an empty boat.

I laughed out loud when I first read this story more than a decade ago. I laughed again when I stumbled upon the story again this past week, the same week where I swung my fist angrily at many empty boats. Some situations, I believe, I actually made worse because of my reactions. In fact, they weren't even actual situations *until* I reacted! As a comedian once said, I could kick my own ass.

Before beating myself up about it, though, I paused and realized that this is all part of our process. We are always surrounded by empty boats careening at reckless speeds into our emotional, mental, and professional lives, and, frankly, for many of us, those three lives are all the same. It becomes about reacting to things that are real, not to things that make us feel a certain way. It is separating our facts from our fears. It is about accepting our anxiousness for the future and understanding that it has absolutely nothing to do with what will happen in next minute. Because we don't know that.

Be thankful for your empty boats, as they carry one of the most valuable insights: your personal fear. My boat is different than your boat. The boat represents your issues, your scars, your past. It is entirely possible to live your life swinging at shadows, taking actions based on some vague anxiety about the future. Many people spend years fighting for security – no matter what the price. When you step into entrepreneurship, though, you have to understand why you are driven and what motivates you. It is the key to success, as someone who doesn't know why they are getting up in the morning, sacrificing their time, and risking their livelihood for something will not be an entrepreneur for very long. Others may have the luxury of clinging to routine, repetition, and stability to keep their fears at bay. We do not have that option.

As a result, the moments where we can see, feel, and identify our fears are truly gifts to our future selves.

"Fear is often an indicator that you're going in the right direction," *Unmistakable* author Srinivas Rao puts it. "It repeatedly indicates your next new level."

Do you know what you are afraid of now? Congratulations. Now you know your pain point, the area where you need to grow, and that knowledge will get you a step closer to mastering yourself. It is an insight people who never take the entrepreneurial journey will rarely understand.

ON BALANCING
THE BALANCED
BITE-SIZED ENTREPRENEUR

To Parul,
my partner on this wild, wonderful journey.
Thank you.

WHY THIS BOOK SHOULDN'T EXIST

This book almost didn't happen. The first Bite-Sized Entrepreneur book came quickly, as did The Productive Bite-Sized Entrepreneur. I had just sold my startup, Cuddlr, after an 11-month run as co-founder, and spent a year writing about my experiences for Inc. Magazine, specifically leading a high-profile startup while being a fully-present, hands-on stay-at-home dad of a baby. There was a lot to say! Fresh from Silicon Valley, the belief was that you could not succeed as an entrepreneur and maintain a romantic partnership, nevertheless a family. I wanted to show people that it was possible.

And then, suddenly, I was done.

The first book rocketed up to the top of the Amazon Entrepreneurship books, with the second one following behind, and I began juggling media interviews and requests along with the writing, the consulting and the entrepreneurial advising – you know, how I actually made a living. And I'm still a stay-at-home dad with a new toddler and, now, another son.

I had to make a choice: Focus on the goal of completing the trilogy or admit that the goal didn't fit my new world. So, I'm going to kill myself to write THE BALANCED BITE-SIZED ENTREPRENEUR?

"How absurd", I told my closest confidantes, "for me to burn myself out writing a book about creating balance."

So, I stopped.

In retrospect, it wasn't a stop, but rather a thoughtful pause. Much has happened in the year since the last Bite-Sized Entrepreneur, but most of it was internal. I learned how to be fully present for two kids, pay more attention to my body (the first books talked about me waking up at 3:15 am to lead my company – and the aftermath), and become grateful for the bit of wisdom I was able to share already in the best-selling books.

More importantly, I began listening to you. I lean towards strategy, so I had all the books planned out, from general launch dates to major discussion points. What I didn't realize until my pause is that you, not me, would tell me what you need. *You tell me how I can best serve you.*

I traveled the world speaking about the Bite-Sized Entrepreneur methods, from Durham, NC, to Bogota, Colombia, to my previous hometown of San Diego. What's amazing was that I'd get the same two questions:

"Do I have enough to start?" and "Do I have enough to keep going?"

I always respond to the first question quickly, drawing in the topics of starting small, ideally as a side hustle, and organizing your life based on priorities, to maximize productivity. It's the first two books! Maintaining, though, was what you really needed. Sure, you can get started and have your prioritizes in order, but if your mind isn't in some sense of balance, then all the resources, time, or passion in the world won't bring you to your definition of success.

Therefore, THE BALANCED BITE-SIZED ENTREPRENEUR goes deeper. How do you manage within chaos? How do you know what to focus on? How do you know when to quit? There are no easy answers, nor should there be. If you haven't already, read through the first two books, particularly The Bite-Sized Entrepreneur, to build a strong foundation for the concepts addressed here. You should know why persistence always trumps patience and why "No" is the absolute best word for your growth.

And, after reading this book, you'll have a better sense of how to maintain that beautiful structure and mindset you established based on the first two in the trilogy. This third book wouldn't have been possible without me spending a year growing enough to write it. I hope it was worth the wait for you. It was for me.

-Damon Brown, October 2017

I: LET GO

"All spiritual traditions emphasize the need to keep you attention in the present time. As long as you remain present, everything you need is present with you."

-Caroline Myss, Sacred Contracts

1

THE 3-MINUTE RULE

A few focused minutes will change your entire day

Our attention spans are arguably getting shorter, but our need for depth is getting heavier. It does not feel like enough to commit a little or to make small edits. Today, we have romanticized the broad stroke, the sweeping changes, and the dramatic declaration. Perhaps it isn't that our attention spans are shorter, but rather that a remarkable amount of things are clamoring for our attention, and that, to paraphrase both futurist Jared Lanier and iconic entrepreneur Seth Godin, is too much for our lizard brains to handle.

In other words, we feel like we have to make dramatic shifts to make any type of long-lasting impact on our lives.

The good news is that we can push slowly and confidently to our goals. We can take little steps, so small that they're almost unperceivable in our daily lives, and significantly change our insight, our strength, and our overall viewpoint.

Here's what you can do in three minutes a day.

Meditation

It started when I moved to New Orleans. I felt like I need to get quiet, not on the outside (NoLa is never a quiet place!), but on the inside. So I sat in my little bed, crossed my legs, and just closed my eyes. I repeated the same thing nearly every day since 2004.

The catch is that my practice is three minutes. I'll occasionally do five minutes on rough days, when I feel like I can't sit still, or on great days, when I actually crave the silence it provides. Just recently, I tried doing twice a day: Midmorning, after I get our youngest son down for his first nap, and mid-evening, after I get our youngest down for his sleep.

The key is that it is so tiny that it has stayed with me, from being a young man escaping Hurricane Katrina to a full-time journalist living in downtown San Francisco to a new entrepreneur (and dad) in San Diego to, now, as a veteran stay-at-home dad and consultant in Toledo, Ohio. I can *always* spare three minutes to sit. You can, too.

Goal setting

Poker champion Phil Hellmuth wrote his six major life goals on a piece of paper and put it on his bathroom mirror (he hit five out of six within a few years, including winning the World Series of Poker). Entrepreneur Elon Musk put his goal for the electric car on a random Tumblr blog and, ten years later, Tesla was the leader in the vehicle space.

I write down my goals on index cards, sometimes once a quarter, sometimes once a year, often with a deadline. It takes three minutes. In 2014, I did a TED talk about the power of index cards, which was nine minutes longer than the time I take to write down my ideas. Chances are you already know what you want. Write it down. It won't take long.

A few things happen when you put it down on paper. First, you are forced to articulate your vision, which makes it more concrete than something floating in your mind. Second, you've got a compass to guide all your decisions. Got a new opportunity? If it doesn't fit into your ultimate goals, then it can (and should) be a quick "No". Third, as the late motivational speaker Jim Rohn said, you can actually keep track of your growth. What were your goals a year ago? If you don't know, then you can't see – and celebrate – how much you've grown.

Again, three minutes of your time.

Enjoy your environment

Consider the world your playground. For me, it hit me when we had our first kid, and those daily miles-long walks I took to clear my mind were unrealistic. Instead, my exercise and motion had to come from pacing carrying my son, walking while I was on the phone, or, later, pushing his stroller up and down San Diego hills.

What I began to do is savor opportunities to move more. I'd travel through airports and take the stairs rather than the escalator. Later, when I'd have the time during layovers, I'd skip the people mover and even the trains to briskly walk to the next terminal. These bite-sized improvements led to me being in some of the best shape of my life, despite the natural chaos of running an ambitious home career with two young kids.

For you, it could be parking a little further from the grocery store, skipping the elevator in two story buildings, or other small changes.

Consistent action, not dramatic action, fuels growth.

2
PUT YOUR MASK ON FIRST
Assume tomorrow won't provide your rest

There's a reason we are comfortable sacrificing it all to make our businesses a reality: We assume we'll get a break tomorrow. To paraphrase Orphan Annie, tomorrow is always a day away--but meanwhile we could end up being useless to the very people we say we are sacrificing everything for.

Consultant Alan Weiss calls this the Oxygen Mask Principle. If you're in an emergency situation on an airplane, you are told to put your oxygen mask on first before assisting a less competent companion. He breaks it down in his podcast, The Way I See It:

You can't help the client or your family, you can't do pro bono work, you can't help others in the profession, you can't help anyone unless you yourself are comfortable. You need a healthy selfishness.

Weiss wrote *Value-Based Fees*, one of my favorite business books, and it is refreshing to hear such a driven businessman discuss the need for balance. As I talked about in *The Productive Bite-Sized Entrepreneur*, being busy does not equal productivity--and continuous exhaustion will not only make your work sloppy but ultimately wreck both you and your business.

Ironically, prioritizing your self-care is the best way to take care of others. How are you taking care of yourself today?

3
YOU NEED LONGER DEADLINES
Unnecessary pressure often creates disappointing results

It is Monday morning and I've already had a failure this week. I have a product I worked hard to finish and roll out today, but the pieces didn't come together on time. It was sometime mid-Sunday, shortly after lunch that I realized I'd have to suck it up and let it go.

What is fascinating is that there was no reason for my new product to launch today. No one, aside from a couple confidants, knew it was going to launch. In fact, my work would probably go on fine without it. Coincidentally, just a few weeks ago, someone in my brain trust suggested I try to let go of "false deadlines".

A false deadline is a hard stop you give yourself for some non-consequential reason. It could be to placate your ego, it could be you want to get a project off your plate, it could be you're just sick of looking at it on the to-do list. The fact is that it actually doesn't matter: You have no external pressure to perform. It is all internal.

Can you relate? Here's how I calm myself down when I see myself setting up (and failing) a false deadline.

Where did this deadline come from?

If you pause for a second, then you may find the origin of your deadline isn't even relevant anymore. I've worked on projects where the aggressive timeline was based on another department's needs - yet when the other group pushed its timeline out, we didn't change ours! The result was us rushing around for quite literally nothing.

When did this deadline become a priority?

I'm a big advocate for not waiting until tomorrow to create the life you want, but it is just as important to know today what moves are *ideal* and what moves are *necessary*. An ideal goal can sneak into the necessary goal category and, suddenly, the amount of pressure you give yourself to reach this ambitious end is significantly higher. I help others be productive and I still struggle with this phenomenon.

What will happen if you don't meet this goal?

This last point is critical, as you have to be able to identify what you fear will happen if you don't meet this false deadline. You can't process the anxiety around meeting the deadline if you don't know what, exactly, you are feeling.

For me, I'm proud of what I've created, so missing today's deadline means I have to wait longer to share it. Disappointing? Definitely. Career threatening? Far from it. And oftentimes, when I have missed a false deadline, opportunities to make the product greater have popped up after the fact - making the temporary pain all the more worthwhile. It's just a matter of remember this *while* it is happening.

4

CHECK THE WEATHER FIRST

Even the best effort is a waste when the timing is wrong

Life is probably significantly different for you now than it was five years, one year, or maybe even one month ago. The sentiment is strong for me, especially in the wake of a cross-country move, but there are other reasons why I've been thinking about change lately. Being back in the Midwest, where I had my teenage years, means trading a decade of neutral West Coast seasons for the gorgeous, crisp turning of the leaves. Winter actually feels intimidating now, but not because I'm afraid of the cold (my biggest TED Talk was in wintery Whistler, British Columbia, Canada). Rather, the prospect of shorter days and frigid nights makes me feel closer to nature, as if, post-California, I am suddenly exposed after being sheltered away from the rest of the world.

It feels invigorating to follow the flow of the seasons and actually, consciously, let things naturally whither away. There are ideas that later became principles and passions that became dogma. The pursuit of a big, hairy, ambitious goal became the focus rather than remembering why I created the goal in the first place. For many reasons, big goals that I set for myself as recently as a year ago now seem almost silly. Contrary to common belief, it is not easier to give up. It is actually easier to keep fighting, as at least you feel like you're making progress.

When you pause, though, you can see how ridiculous it feels planting a tomato seed during an ice storm or crossing a raging river when it isn't anywhere near frozen. It's just that, before the quiet moment, you aren't paying attention to the natural flow of your world. You're just trying to reach your goal.

The near-misses, almost-wases, and should-have-beens have been plentiful lately and, frankly, feel more robust than they've been in my life in a long while. So do the coincidences and absolutes, as if fate stepped in and said 'Nah, you're going that way. I'll make sure of that!' It pleases my ego to say that I am one determined individual, which is why life has to react so forcefully when I should be going in a different direction. And, as the world slows down and I slowly get over myself, I am becoming amazed at how, to paraphrase Steve Jobs, seemingly random dots of events begin to make a pattern.

But you can only see the evidence when you're looking back. Going forward requires trusting that fall will follow summer. And it always does.

5
FAILURE IS SUCCESS
Holding your nose during a failure misses the point

Failure is a prerequisite for getting what you want, and often it puts us in the direction to get what we actually need. It gave Apple's Steve Jobs a mission, Shark Tank's Daymond John a vision, and every entrepreneur you know a groundedness not achievable otherwise. To paraphrase Brené Brown, the only guarantee you have when you step in the arena is that you will get your butt kicked.

So when one of the most successful women in the world talks about her failures, it is wise to listen.

In 1998, Oprah Winfrey's big-budget movie *Beloved* was set to be her splash into Hollywood. Her agent called her the day after opening night and told her it was already a flop. She was devastated.

Two decades later, she is even more powerful than before. How does that happen? There are three telling quotes:

Gratitude

"That's when the gratitude practice became really strong for me, because it's hard to remain sad if you're focused on what you have instead of what you don't have."

There are volumes of anecdotal and scientific evidence showing that gratitude for what you currently have leads to your getting more of what you want. Your brain focuses on what you focus on, so concentrating on what's missing will only show you what you lack, not the new opportunities available.

Service

"It taught me to never again--never again, ever--put all of your hopes, expectations, eggs in the basket of box office. Do the work as an offering, and then whatever happens, happens."

Your job is to create something that the world needs -- and that's it. Profitability comes from prioritizing your employees and your customers, not from prioritizing profitability. Market share comes from creating a service of value, not from focusing on market share. In Oprah's case, she gives and gives, and her customers choose to give their financial, emotional, and mental support in return.

Presence

"There's not a human being alive who doesn't want--in any conversation, encounter, experience with another human being--to feel like they matter. And you can resolve any issue if you could just get to what it is that they want--they want to be heard. And they want to know that what they said to you meant something. Most people go their entire lives and nobody ever really wants the answer to 'How are you? Tell me about yourself.'"

It is ridiculously easy to depersonalize people because of your goals: networking with someone just to get something out of it, manipulating customers to reach a new milestone, or simply not taking the time to take care of the people who gave you success in the first place.

Gratitude, service, and presence can bring you to your goals -- and help you overcome the many failures it will take to get there.

6
DO GOOD ENOUGH
Perfection prevents greatness

We have a cultural obsession with extreme experiences: Things have to be uber or incredible or outstanding or breathtaking. The obsession pours into our expectations of ourselves, as it isn't enough to get funding, but to be a unicorn, and being a simple company is inadequate compared to being a grand disrupter.

It also means we tend to kill our ideas, if not our own success, before they have a chance to be great.

In praise of good enough

The best thing you can do is go for good. It doesn't mean settling for good when great is available. It means understanding that good is actually good, and that everything you do is intended as a start, not as a permanent state.

Ironically, while Silicon Valley is focused on "crushing it", the popular Lean Startup model is based on the very idea of good enough. In short, you take your idea, create it with as little resources as possible and get your good enough take - your minimal viable product - to your intended audience as quickly as possible.

The problem with high expectations
The feedback from your audience takes your idea from good to great. High expectations alone won't get you there. In fact, high expectations are likely to hamper your progress.

Ryan Holiday and Stephen Hanselman's *The Daily Stoic* explains that most of our frustration isn't with our progress, but with our expectations. We could have extraordinary success yet, if we are expecting an unrealistic amount of progress, that rare success won't even feel like an accomplishment.

The success trap
An excellent cautionary tale is iconic performer Michael Jackson handling the success of his breakthrough album *Thriller*. The late icon worked with megaproducer Quincy Jones and essentially redefined R & B - *Thriller* is still one of the top 20 selling albums of all time. The problem? Jackson wanted to do it again.

According to Jones, he spent the rest of his life, album after album, trying to create something bigger than Thriller. As a result, he never felt quite satisfied.

Keep in mind, Jones wasn't saying something equal to *Thriller*. Something more successful than *Thriller*. One of the best-selling albums of all time.

The Atlantic explained the challenge during the 25th anniversary of *Bad*, the critically-panned *Thriller* follow-up:

Jackson in interviews more often expressed Olympian commercial goals of breaking the sales records of his previous album than he did of pursuing new musical territory. And very much like how many filmmakers of blockbusters beef up defining fight scenes and plotlines, Jackson conspicuously restaged and amplified Thriller's signature moments with perfectionist's precision, making Bad sound sterile in too many places.

It is an amazing trap: You naturally hit a home run and, next time up to bat, you're checking wind conditions, wearing a lucky hat and trying to recreate the previous experience.

The rub is that what you did - the success you had - wasn't just based on your actions. It is both timing and inspiration, too. The sales success of *Thriller* could not be recreated because the whole record industry sold less records, as we would see with Napster and iTunes and Spotify. The needs of the listeners changed (ironically, because of *Thriller* itself), so doing another *Thriller* wouldn't recreate the same sea change. And Jackson was arguably in a different place, as he now had ridiculously high expectations of himself and a new set of pressures.

Lightning won't strike in the same place twice

Sometimes we expect to do the same amazing work twice, so we get sloppy the second time around. Just as often, though, we can give ourselves too much credit for our success, overanalyzing what we did initially as if our win was completely based on our actions.

It is wiser to be humble and focused rather than just expecting an unlikely win. And in a true Zen way, setting smaller, realistic goals leads us bigger long-term success.

7
MAKE YOUR SACRIFICE WORTH IT
Know when you're going to quit ahead of time

We have a cultural obsession with extreme experiences: Things have to be uber or incredible or outstanding or breathtaking. The obsession pours into our expectations of ourselves, as it isn't enough to get funding, but to be a unicorn, and being a simple company is inadequate compared to being a grand disrupter.

It also means we tend to kill our ideas, if not our own success, before they have a chance to be great.

Quitting is severely underrated. If you've been following entrepreneurial leadership, then you know that everyone from Steve Jobs to the Google founders built their success on quitting. So why are we obsessed with making things work instead of just accepting that some of our ideas have run their course?

On its decade anniversary, it is worth taking another read of business maverick Seth Godin's classic *The Dip: A Little Book That Teaches You*

When to Quit (And When to Stick). I just rediscovered *The Dip* on audiobook, and perhaps the biggest insight we can all use is this:

Write down under what circumstances you're willing to quit.

To explain, Godin quotes ultramarathoner Dick Collins: "Decide before the race the conditions that will cause you to decide to stop and drop out. You don't want to be out there saying, 'Well, gee, my leg hurts, I'm a little dehydrated, I'm sleepy, I'm tired, and it's cold, and it's windy...' and talk yourself into quitting."

If you're making a decision based on how you're feeling at that moment, then you will probably make the wrong decision.

You don't quit when the going gets rough. You quit when you know you've invested more than you'll get out of it. You need clear, measurable metrics to know when to give up on your big idea or business.

Here are a few I've recently used:

I'll spend this much money

I self-financed *The Bite-Sized Entrepreneur: 21 Ways to Ignite Your Passion and Pursue Your Side Hustle*. I set a budget and a timeline to recoup that money. It hit the Amazon Entrepreneur book Top 10, which helped me reach the goal and do a follow-up book, *The Productive Bite-Sized Entrepreneur: 24 Smart Secrets to Do More in Less Time*. If I didn't recoup, then there would be no follow up – and you wouldn't be reading this book right now!

I'll spend this much time

I spent a good amount of time on a side hustle and gave myself a few months to make it work. And, with no fanfare, I recently shut it down. Why? Come to find out, no one wanted it. To paraphrase Godin, the temporary pain of giving up is better than the slow death of mindlessly continuing.

I'll spend this much effort

I love working on new ideas, and there is one that I had been toiling away on for years. Within the last few days, I realized that the effort is too great to make it real based on my current time, priorities and resources. It sucks, but moving forward with it begs the question: How much of my life would I have to upheaval to make this thing a reality and, if I see myself at the finish line, would it have been worth it?

Give yourself permission to say, "No, it isn't worth it." And give yourself permission *before* you actually start.

8

THE ULTIMATE TIME LIMIT

Always remember your time can end at any moment

There is a simple reason why we procrastinate: We assume we will have more time. There is more time to make it perfect, more time to connect with others and more time to pursue that brilliant idea. But success lies in knowing that time will run out - and that we will die.

In two decades, successful entrepreneur Ricardo Semler turned Semco Partners from a four million dollar company to a 212 million-dollar company - namely by creating an intuitive, innovative work environment, shared in his best-selling book *Maverick*. Semler is also a very happy man, but he says it has nothing to do with his financial or business success. As he recently explained to Tim Ferriss, Semler's real secret is treating each day as his last.

I kept thinking 'Geez, I don't want to be in that situation where suddenly now I have to go to ballgames with the kids and I have to travel to places I haven't been and I have to write that play that I never wrote.' That's crazy. Let's do something else... So, on Mondays and Thursdays I have what I call 'Terminal Days', the two days a week in which my schedule is completely clear and I do on those days what I would have done if I heard this conversation from my oncologist.

This habit isn't just for show. Semler says melanoma runs in his family, so most of his relatives have had a sudden death. He himself has had multiple cancer surgeries that, fortunately, caught the melanoma before it spread. Even though he is 57, Semler faces his own death every day.

Semler sets aside two days a week to do exactly what he would do if it were the last day of his life. It is easy to assume that his work would suffer, but, in fact, he is regularly setting himself up for career greatness. Think about it: If you actually carved out time for personal fulfillment every single week, imagine how focused and productive you would be during the remaining days?

For the ambitious among us, our problem isn't saying "Yes" (as Shonda Rhimes said in her TED Talk), but in saying "No". You have to close a number of doors to truly do what you desire - and material or worldly success only increases the choices over time, making the process even more difficult.

Start making tough decisions now before they get tougher over time. What should you be focusing on today?

9

THE BIGGEST CHANGES

*Like icebergs, most of our growth happens
below the surface*

It has been a summer of transitions for most people I know, myself included. My family and I recently moved to the Midwest after spending a dozen years on the West Coast. I'm fortunate that my focus, on helping potential and current entrepreneurs reach their best without burning themselves out, only gets richer as I connect with new communities in the Toledo/Detroit area.

Any transition takes a great deal of energy, no matter how advantageous or exciting it may be. It is like what writer Elizabeth Gilbert said in one of my favorite talks I've ever seen at TED: Her stratospheric success with *Eat, Pray, Love* caused the same performance anxiety as when she was a waitressing wannabe writer collecting hundreds of publishing rejection letters. Both felt like a foreign place. Her way back to sanity? She started writing the next thing. She did the work.

The key during transitions isn't just to keep your focus, but to realize that it will take you more energy to do so. Like moving to a new town, previously unconscious acts like going to the grocery store or remembering a neighbor's name now require thought, rigor, and presence. You are building the foundation for your next chapter. Most importantly, you are given the opportunity to think about the things you previously assumed to be true and can make a structure better for you today.

All this takes time, all this takes energy, and all this takes patience. So, I'm allowing myself a few extra minutes of meditation each day, an additional breath or two before returning an urgent phone call, and considerable thoughtfulness in my workday strategy. The best gift you can give yourself is the space to get the inner work done to make a stronger you - even if you are the only one who can feel it. You are doing more work than you think.

II: TAKE IN

"For every single thing you want in life, there's a price; a price that has to be paid. And nature always demands that the price be paid in advance."

-Brian Tracy, How to Start and Succeed in Your Own Business

10
EVERY SINGLE DAY
Habits become your life

It's been proven that rituals and habits are the key to success. I meditate nearly every morning. I listen to something thoughtful daily, most recently *The Daily Stoic*. I always walk as much as possible. Still, the rapid evolution of my career gives me days where I question the very point of having these routines. I'm still struggling.

If you can relate, then it is key to remind yourself that practices are the foundation for those very times when you feel like things are going out of control. It is the structure upon which your stability sits.

I often think of an old *SPIN* magazine article featuring River Cuomo, the self-described temperamental leader of the alternative band Weezer. The feature talked about Cuomo taking up meditation, going deep into self discovery and so on. When asked about how he changed, a band member captured the general sentiment well. To paraphrase:

He's still a [explicative]. But imagine how much of a bigger [explicative] he'd be without doing this?

It's not that waking up early, always making your bed or writing down your gratitude will make you transcend disappointment, heartache and failure. It's that your routines will make you more *resilient* to face those obstacles. And, over time, it makes a cumulative effect on your life, like compound interest in the bank.

Pause before you consider subtracting habits out of your life because the results seem invisible. Instead, they could be keeping you afloat and keeping you from going further off your course.

11

CARRY ONE THING AT A TIME

Guilt over focusing on one thing will make you useless at all things

I remember the moment I realized it wasn't going to work. I was in New York, visiting to support a local TED conference, and it hit me that I would not be able to fulfill my new desire: Becoming a worldwide public speaker. My newborn son was at home, along with my toddler, and we crammed together a patchwork of support to cover my absence as the primary caregiver. It required a redeye to even get my day in Manhattan. I'd be flying home that same night, hopefully getting some shuteye at the airport while I waited to board. My boys needed me. My heart needed to be on the road.

Before I left, I had a tea with my friend and mentor, artist Leida Snow. I talked about my ambitions, my opportunities, and my conflict. She smiled, and talked for a bit. This is what I understood:

Balance isn't doing everything at once. Balance is

doing what is most important at the time. Sometimes you'll be super present as a dad. Sometimes you'll be super present as an international speaker. It's OK to put one down and pick the other one up. But you can't be both at the same moment.

It reminds me of Buddhist monk Thich Nhat Hanh, whom often talks about anticipation and anxiety for the future (which is the same thing) robbing the pleasure out of an experience when it actually does happen. Or my own research for my book *Our Virtual Shadow: Why We Are Obsessed with Documenting Our Lives Online*, where we pull ourselves out of the moment to capture the moment and, in a sense, don't experience the moment at all.

Bifurcating myself would make me a bad father and a bad public speaker, as I wouldn't be fully invested in either. Instead, when I was at home, my family would have my love and attention, and when I hit the stage, my audience would have me totally engaged in the conversation. It honors me, it honors you, and it honors my family.

Or, as Hanh puts it, "Do one thing at a time. Do it deeply."

12
BUILD LIKE YOU'RE ALREADY THERE
Focus on the small and the big will handle itself

The late, powerful speaker Jim Rohn helped guide Tony Robbins' early career and, as you can imagine, was a force into himself. A quote from one of Rohn's classic talks is still relevant, if not more so today:

"You say, 'If I had a big organization, you know, I'd really run it with a strong hand and I'd be a fabulous leader. But I've only got a few (followers) and I don't know where they are.' See, that's not going to work. If you wish to preside over a lot... you have to be disciplined when the amounts are small."

What Rohn is talking about is *systems*: A system to master your emotional intelligence so you can handle the power; a system to handle your relationships so your management can scale; and a system to organize your resources so you can use them most effectively in high numbers.

The thing is that those systems can most easily be put into place when the overhead is as low as the stakes. Ironically, as Rohn mentions, it's easy to not take the systems seriously when the rewards are weak, yet this is the very time you should be thinking about long-range goals.

It's kind of like wishing to win the lottery, but not actually thinking about what you would do with the money: The chances of you wasting the money if you got it are extremely high. And even if you did have a plan, if you didn't manage things well on the small scale, you certainly wouldn't have the discipline to do it with millions!

Entrepreneurs often learn this the hard way. How many companies end up growing faster than expected, becoming worth billions in a few short years, only to do expensive fixes because they didn't take the time to consider details that felt virtually inconsequential when they were small?

Instead, take a step today - even a small one - to put a system in place so you will be able to better emotionally, relationally and financially handle your business if and when it does reach new heights. It is often more dangerous to prepare for failure than it is for success.

13
THE 20/20 TECHNIQUE
Make the most of your time and of others

The further you get in your field, the more thoughtful you have to be about the time you spend. It often means saying "No" more than you would like. Former Googler Jenny Blake, author of the best-selling book *Pivot*, has a great way to defend your time and help other people.

When someone asks for a brain picking session, Blake instead suggests they do a 20/20 meeting (I interpreted it as 20/20, but the numbers can be higher or lower). The meeting is 20 minutes talking about what you care about and then 20 minutes talking about what the other person cares about.

I love this method for many reasons:

Eliminate the one-way conversation
Blake has a best-selling book, a significant career at the most envied startup in the world and a reputation for helping people get their businesses to the next level. You have

your own expertise, too, and it would be too easy for you to give and not receive, especially as you gain prominence in your field. By splitting the time evenly, you remove potential one-sidedness.

Prevent takers from monopolizing time

There are many reasons why people may feel comfortable monopolizing your time, from feeling like you owe them to listen to being just thoughtless about your other obligations. By declaring a split meeting, you create equal expectations from the outset and make it clear that you expect to be receiving value from the meeting, too. Their reaction to your suggestion makes their intentions clearer and can help you decide whether you want to actually spend more time with the person.

Smooth out the power dynamics

Everyone you meet has a piece of insight that can help you or has access to people or social circles that can be beneficial to your business. How do you know if you're the only one giving insight? Instead, the 20/20 rule gives you and your companion equal footing, potentially staving off weird power dynamics and giving both of you an opportunity for growth. And after the meeting, they don't owe you anything, just as you don't owe them anything either.

14

THEORY IS JUST THAT

Don't mistake an idea for a solution

You'd be forgiven for not immediately associating former heavyweight boxing champion Mike Tyson with emotional intelligence, especially if, like me, you remember his more ferocious years. However, he's always had a strong sensitivity and insight under the tough veneer, as shown in documentaries like *Tyson*.

He also has one of the wisest quotes you'll ever hear on how to make emotionally intelligent decisions as an entrepreneur, if not as a human being.

Everybody has a plan until they get punched in the mouth.

Accurate. His famous quote obviously leans on the ring analogy, but it applies well to your business strategy. Here is the two-part blow-by-blow.

Assume you will fail

Tyson is talking about the hubris behind our strategies. We've got millions of dollars in investment from the top VCs? That doesn't mean you go on cruise control. (If anything, as Mark Cuban says, you've just made the road to success longer) We raised a ton on Kickstarter? That's just the first step of many - and one misstep could knock us off balance.

The best defense is to assume you will get hit: Critics will drag you, ideas will fail to launch and burnout is real. Your strategy isn't a bulletproof dome protecting you from crisis, but rather a foundation that allows you to keep it together during the inevitable challenges.

Plan to the end

Tyson is explaining that you need to have a strategy deeper than the one in your head, as you are going to get frustrated as soon as you hit a stumbling block. Have you ever prepared for a confrontation by guessing what's going to happen? We're usually way off, as we are skimming over many different chaotic factors like the environment and our opponent's state of mind. Worse, by planning too much ahead of time, we are closing ourselves off to potentially better plans we can come up with based on insights we only see once we get in the proverbial ring.

The best plan is to focus on outcome. How do you want this thing to end? By focusing on the finish line and the important milestones along the way, you give yourself the latitude to get there based on the most practical moves of that dynamic moment. Think about boxing, where a quick hit could swell your eye shut, weaken your arm or literally take your breath away. The ability to pivot quickly without going over the emotional deep end is vital to your success.

There is a reason why every classic strategy book from *The Art of War* to *The 48 Laws of Power* emphasize planning to the end as well as assuming you will not always win. As Tyson knows, the ultimate personal emotional intelligence happens when you accept you don't know what's going to happen next.

15

DOING THEIR BEST

*When we undervalue others, we inevitable
undervalue ourselves, too*

Every entrepreneur learns quickly that creating your own path doesn't make you less reliant on others. In fact, it is the reverse: While a traditional corporate job may hand you one boss, entrepreneurship requires building and maintaining a healthy relationship with co-founders, customers, funders, mentors, and many others.

And the truth is that you won't always like the people you need. Emotional intelligence guru Brené Brown has a quick way to help you get even the most challenging relationship back on track:

The most compassionate people ... assume that other people are doing the best they can. I lived the opposite way: I assumed that people weren't doing their best, so I judged them and constantly fought being disappointed ...

The next time you get frustrated with someone, ask a simple question: Do you believe the person is doing the very best that he or she can?

What often happens is that we realize how much we are judging someone on the basis of our own skills, experience, and strengths. For instance, I have spent decades doing non-traditional work, so I have the discipline to stay focused in unusual work environments such as my home office or in an airplane while traveling. Some people fall apart under the same circumstances, either because they are new to the situation or just have a different personality. Are they doing the best they can, even if the results are poor? In most cases, yes, they are.

Try applying this simple question to the co-worker who always seems to fumble, the family member who regularly disappoints you, or the customer who seems rather dense. As Brown points out in her book *Rising Strong*, the result is empathy--empathy for the fact that they, too, are doing the best they can with what they've got. It opens up possibilities that you would be closed off to otherwise.

And while becoming a more empathic person is a smart relationship builder, the biggest impact may end up being on you: If you are more accepting of others, then you inevitably become more gentle with yourself.

16

IT ISN'T YOUR MONEY

More resources will just make you more of what you already are now

Podcasts to me, like for millions of people, have become an amazing staple this year. Forget TV: Podcasts are my episodic content. Jenny Blake's *Pivot*, Whitney Johnson's *Disrupt Yourself* and Oprah's *Super Soul Conversations* have transformed my business.

One of the most valuable podcast episodes you can listen to, though, is Basecamp and Ruby on Rails founder David Heinemeier Hansson on *The Tim Ferriss Show*. It is a monster of a conversation, clocking in at 3 and a half hours and touching on everything from smart productivity to brilliant learning strategies to startup mistakes.

The absolute best reason to listen is this gem:

Expectations, not outcomes, govern the happiness of your perceived reality

The line is originally from Heinemeier's own stellar piece about becoming a millionaire in *The Observer*. He and Ferriss spend a significant amount of time breaking down exactly what it means.

Here are three high-level lessons, though you'll want to listen to the whole discussion:

Develop skillsets necessary for after you "make it"

If you are doing 100 hour weeks, sacrificing time with friends and family and not developing any other interests aside from your business, then how do you expect to be happy once you sell your business and suddenly have a life composed of only undeveloped friends and family relationships and withered interests?

Maintain your outside pursuits, however minor the effort. In my own case, selling my first startup didn't land me in early retirement, but it did bring up many emotional issues on how a major part of my life was now gone. Imagine if it had been longer than a year of my life - and imagine if I had sacrificed being a present father, husband and friend along the way.

Your sacrifice now doesn't increase your chances of happiness later

Heinemeier notes that he and Basecamp co-founder Jason Fried manage the wildly successful company on a 40-hour a week schedule. Forty hours! There are administrative assistants that clock in more hours. Heinemeier, Ferriss and even I have met many an entrepreneur that believe sacrificing everything for seven to 10 years means that you'll find success and the ever-elusive happiness at the end. But there is no guarantee that you'll live to see it, nor that it will actually be there when you get there.

Now is all you've got. If your quality of life sucks now, then, after a decade, you'll be in the habit of burnout, hypertension, depression or any other aliments your body become accustom to. Better to take things day by day and pull in as much enjoyment within the time you have, which is a major premise of Heinemeier and Fried's wonderful title *Rework* as well as this very book.

Focus on process, not success

Success is often a deceptively vague outcome. If your goal is to be rich, then do you have a number in mind, and rich compared to whom, exactly? If your goal is to be famous, then is it to the world, to strangers on the street or to a handful of people who matter to you? And, as I've confessed recently, reaching goals is elusive because ambitious people always move the goal post as soon as they near meeting it.

Focus on the parts of the journey/struggle that motivate you, as they will be the same whether you have financial success or not. Heinemeier says that he enjoys himself the most when nurturing his now-ubiquitous programming language Ruby on Rails or working with his long-time business partner Fried - just like, as he notes, when he was broke living in a tiny Copenhagen apartment. The happiest among us do what we love now because we recognize where we feel the most alive, and, for better or worse, recognize that money won't change that basic principle.

17

YOU ARE ALREADY SUCCESSFUL

You're making more progress than you think

Many of us sit in one of two types of reality-distortion fields. You may think you are more successful than you really are, which means you're in danger of not accomplishing much. Or you may think you aren't doing enough, which means you may burn yourself out because you think you have farther to go.

If you are an ambitious businessperson, then by definition you are the latter. It fuels you. It also can destroy you.

I and long-time author Jeanette Hurt have talked about this for years: We are driven to an incredibly high goal, and just as it is clear we will reach it, we move the flagpole further down the line. Unfortunately, that means never quite being satisfied, nor actually giving oneself credit.

Your insatiable appetite for goal setting may drive you forward, but there's no danger in tempering that trait with some checks and balances. Here's what you can do.

Celebrate every victory

For my latest books, *The Bite-Sized Entrepreneur* and *The Productive Bite-Sized Entrepreneur,* I actually wrote down simple rewards I would give myself at certain sales numbers. I initially had super high markers, but I forced myself to make the victories low. It forced me into the routine of celebrating even minor wins - making the book process even more joyful this time around.

Lean on others

It is essential that you have a small group of people who know your intent and are invested in having you reach your goals. I call them a brain trust, as I've talked about before (Jeanette Hurt is part of mine). When you're not recognizing the success you've made, your brain trust will bring you down to earth and remind you that you did reach your goal - you just decided to move the flag.

Make realistic goals

The further the space between you and your goal, the longer it will feel like you aren't achieving much. Realistic milemarkers not only give you a system to recognize your success, but they also increase the chances of you reaching those momentous goals - since you will have the motivation to complete them from all the minor successes along the way.

18

MIND THE GAP

The space between giant leaps makes the giant leaps happen

Silence often breeds discontent, then enlightenment. I've found that the best thoughts aren't in the hectic speed of the day, the pushing towards bigger ideas or the relentless drive towards superior results. No, the challenge isn't doing the grind for another day – at least for me. The real discipline comes with navigating the space in between, the netherland between doing and not doing, the uncomfortable area that shows no results nor failure.

That uncomfortable space could be when you stop talking about your idea, between the newlywed excitement of a new idea and the actual prototype that you have to share. It can be the time between you launching a rough sketch and you refining the next version, since you have nothing new to show. It could be after your big success and, alas, your next idea is still a sketch on an index card, a document or even just in your brain.

What matters is persevering within that area, that gap, until you make it to the other side. Grinding it out is really easy. So is quitting. But both are smart when done in moderation, but foolish when used as a rule, as either extreme will not get the job done. Instead, it is a matter of breathing in, taking in the vagueness, and accepting that the gap, too, is an equal part of the process.

Sometimes taking a breath isn't a limbo before your next act. Sometimes taking a breath *is* your next act.

MORE FUEL

"You might dread the writing or the running or the leading, but it's the key step on the road to becoming. If it's easier, remind yourself what you're about to be."

-Seth Godin, About to be

1

DO LESS TODAY TO DO MORE

Sometimes the minimum is the best strategy

Giving it 100 percent every entrepreneurial day is an excellent goal, but it isn't realistic. There are days when I easily give 150 percent, while there are others when I struggle to do 80 percent. We talk about always showing up, but rarely address the fact that low energy, decreased time, or scattered focus can make some days better than others. It's just part of being human.

You are sometimes going to have a Minimum Viable Day -- and it is much more fruitful if you actively enter it. Inspired by the Minimum Viable Product approach to shipping enough of a item to satisfy consumers without depleting limited resources, a Minimum Viable Day means doing only the essential work and actively facilitating a slower day with the promise of more productive iterations tomorrow. We talk about products and working with the limited resources we have, but we rarely apply that to our lives.

A Minimum Viable Day should be simple and it should be rare. There are three solid guidelines to actively creating a Minimum Viable Day:

Ship, or it is a day off
Like a Minimum Viable Product, the whole point of a MVD is to "ship" by using the smallest resources necessary. Remember, this isn't a vacation day, nor is it a blank day where you make room for strategic development. I usually set one simple, yet significant goal for the day and use that as the compass for success.

Cut the to-do list in half
Feature creep is real, whether you're talking about adding "must-have" details to your bloated product or squeezing "necessary" meetings into your schedule. Here's a test: If you had a suddenly had a personal crisis or became ill, what items would drop off your calendar in a heartbeat? Take those goals off.

Plan to iterate
Your Minimum Viable Day should help create or build on the foundation of your work, but it

absolutely should not be considered the completion of your work. Instead, view it as a basecamp day between long stretches of mountain climbing or as a pit stop through a Grand Prix: It is a necessary pause that will not become the standard for your progress.

A slow day can make us feel guilty, but it is worth putting that aside. By stripping down your day to the essentials, you can differentiate between second-tier priorities and pure fluff. After having a MVD, you may be surprised at how inconsequential certain goals seem in the new light -- and how your productivity goes even higher in the future.

2

THE HOURGLASS PRINCIPLE
Focus on the small and the big will handle itself

The big picture is too much. To paraphrase Tony Robbins, people often overestimate what they'll do in a year, but underestimate what they'll do in five years. The more fully present we can be in the now, the more we can take advantage of any opportunities, and, conversely, slow us down enough to think strategically into the future. Our visions can be mighty, but our milestones should be small, and that is how we can reach our ultimate goals.

The big-picture focus is super common among ambitious people, especially entrepreneurs. It's the founder creating an ad campaign or renting office space when the product hasn't even been finished yet. Systems, as we talked about, are essential to your growth, but you also need to pace yourself so that your most valuable resources, like time and money, are put where they are most needed now.

Rene Rojas, founder of the HubBOG Accelerator in Bogota, Colombia, calls this the hourglass principle. When you first start, focus on the smallest, most doable part of your idea: getting a prototype or early version to your target audience; talking to an agent or editor about your great book idea; doing a quick-and-dirty website to see if there is interest in your side hustle. It is like sand going through an hourglass. And, like the slow drip, your focus will naturally expand to take in even bigger challenges and ideas. It isn't a matter of running straight into the big picture, but evolving into it based on your feedback, energy, and resources.

3
COMPLETING IS MORE IMPORTANT THAN STARTING
Finishing will give you the energy you're missing today

It's tempting to take nibbles at different activities on your to-do list. If you actually want to be productive, you're better off dropping the multitasking and getting one thing done. In fact, there is a nearly-century old theory that explains why.

The Zeigarnik Effect is named after Russian psychologist Bluma Zeigarnik. In her most famous experiment, she found that waiters were more likely to remember incomplete or unfinished orders than fulfilled ones. It was so extreme that they often could not remember any details of the finished orders.

Her further research supported one simple idea: Completed tasks are rarely remembered, yet incomplete tasks dominate our minds.

The problem is that having several sort-of complete things on your to-do list will make you less productive, as it will require more brain power for you to actually focus. However, if you actually complete the items one-by-one, you are more likely to forget about the finished tasks and give more attention to the important remaining items.

Here are some ways to boost that productivity and fight the Zeigarnik Effect:

Put only one thing on your to-do list

Here's how it works: The night before, decide the one, and only one, thing that must absolutely be done tomorrow. If you're having a hard time figuring out your priority, you can, to paraphrase Warren Buffett, make a list of 10 priorities in order, then eliminate the bottom nine.

The next morning, concentrate on the one thing you have to get done.

For me, the results were spectacular. First, I would almost certainly get the one thing done. Second, it would get done early. Third, it would give me the confidence to go on to the next activity. Fourth, it would bypass all the stress caused by having too long of a to-do list. Lastly, I'd move through each task so fast, I would inevitably get more done than if I focused on the entire list.

Choose a theme for the day
Focus your energy on one particular theme. For instance, you may designate Mondays for correspondence (which, as we talked about in The Bite-Sized Entrepreneur, is a good call!) and Fridays for planning the following week. This would inform how you schedule your phone calls, so you'd be less likely to get interrupted on, say, a Tuesday when you'd like to do your deeper work since your calls and emails would be designated to the previous day, Monday.

And even if you jump around tasks, you'll still be in the same wheelhouse.

Reward every completion
Give yourself a minute to appreciate a task when it is done. A brief walk, a coffee break, or another simple activity can help you complete whatever is at hand. It also may encourage you to get more stuff done.

The self-imposed reward provides a built-in break, too, which gives your brain the time to recoup and relax, allowing you to focus even better when you need to handle the next task.

4
IS IT REVERSIBLE?
Know the difference between challenging and fatal

Here's what is going to happen when you push yourself: The margins are going to become razor thin. Your emotions will have to expand to new boundaries, your resources will end up being utilized in ways never conceived before, and your management of yourself will have to upgrade to unforeseen heights. "To have more, you simply have to be more," Jim Rohn once put it.

In the process to become more than you currently are, to create a path more extraordinary than average, you'll spend time at the edge of the proverbial cliff looking, if not teetering, towards the drop. It will happen.

And when it does happen, you absolutely have to ask yourself "Is it reversible?" Not "Can it be fixed right now?" or "What can I do to feel less pressure?". The question has to be, "Is what's happening going to be permanent?" Money can be earned again, confidence can be rebuilt, and companies rebirthed from difficult histories.

The panic button is overrated. Your ability to overcome rough patches often isn't based on the toughness of the circumstances, as any unique path *will* be tough – that's why not everyone goes on it! No, your ability to overcome rough patches is usually based on how centered you can remain in the face of chaos. Forget bravery: it's about clarity. It is a scientific fact that the emotional part of your brain will short-circuit your intellectual and creative parts of your brain, the commonly known "Fight or flight" mode where fear and survival drives your decisions. Fight or flight is not strategic, nor is it considering the long-term effects. It renders you incapable of making creative, thoughtful decisions that could not only help you survive, but prosper.

It starts with acknowledging that the work you put in today doesn't go into an empty vacuum. It adds to your momentum and, like a slingshot, all that energy will propel you forward when the moment is right. You just don't know when that moment will be.

Find your treasure

One of my darkest career moments was in 2009. I was fresh home from a self-funded book tour and, based on the five years of work I put into my book *Porn & Pong: How Grand Theft Auto, Tomb Raider and Other Sexy Games Changed Our Culture*, I assumed the offers would roll in from publications eager for me to write for them. I was wrong, and instead I came home to crickets. More significantly, the print industry suddenly fell off a cliff. Stable, century-old publications, magazines that provided my bread-and-butter, were laying off their entire staffs. Long-time editors were contacting *me* asking if I knew of any work. My relatively reasonable San Francisco rent suddenly felt like a ridiculous fortune. I had no money coming in and, with my most reliable editors gone, no prospect of more on the way.

Joseph Campbell called this "the dark night of the soul", when the hero is lost, confused, and seemingly optionless. It is there, too, in this dark night of the soul, that the hero finds a treasure that cannot be gained by any other means. The rest of the hero's journey is spent mastering the newfound treasure and using it to come out of the darkness, bringing the treasure back to the rest of the world like Prometheus returning fire from the gods.

In my case, I heard a strong rumor that Steve Jobs was going to announce a giant iPhone, sort of like a laptop without a keyboard. I talked to a book editor about a simple guide to the device, and the editor loved it. The problem? Internet writers would be covering the gadget as soon as it arrived, and a traditional publisher, at best, would have my book out four to five months *after* the launch. The book would fail.

I then realized there were new options in self-publishing and, after some quick research, learned that digital books were growing much faster than physical books. What if I published my own digital-only book? I rounded up my dad, David Brown, who is an artist, and my colleague Jeanette Hurt, who is a freelance editor, and asked them to help. Sure enough, Jobs announced the iPad in January 2010. It launched April 3rd, and my friends and I stood in line all night to buy one. I spent the following three days exploring every nook and cranny of the device, writing down everything I thought would be useful. *Damon Brown's Simple Guide to the iPad* arrived on digital bookstores exactly a week after the device launch, well before any traditional publishers or even other self-publishers could get their books out. The book went to number one, my rent was comfortably paid into the near future, and I discovered a way to make a living independent of both the capricious print media and traditional publishing industries.

I found my treasure. I wouldn't have been looking for it without the pain. And my previous situation, however dire, became completely reversible.

Develop that muscle

Spirituality teacher Dr. Michael Bernard Beckwith asks this question:

If this experience were to last forever, what quality would have to emerge for me to have peace of mind?

He adds, "I may need some strength or something… name whatever quality. And what happens is your attention starts focusing on that quality rather than resisting the dark night, then the process is sped up. You move through it faster."

Consider that the same thing can happen to you and to me, yet your experience may feel much, much more difficult. It is because I may have a certain learned skill or attitude allowing me to float through the same situation you may consider a crisis. What if the point is for you to learn that skill, too? And, if the situation is reversible, then whatever happens to you may not even do any long-lasting harm.

I have had a few dark years in my career, and without 2009, I wouldn't have developed my voice outside of the traditional publishing industry, which led to several independent books, most recently the very one you're reading right now. I couldn't have known the profound impact my difficult time would have on my career, nor that the financial hardship I experienced would be made up for many times over based on what I was learning. And I didn't have to know.

All I needed to do was ask my favorite question to myself every single day: "Is it reversible?" I'd realize that it was. And, as I realized it, I would feel OK again.

5

RUN PARALLELS

The secret to your success probably isn't where you expect

Entrepreneurs cherish focus. It is what we search for during all-nighters, seek in that third cup of coffee and run after when we pursue extreme goals. But too much focus can kill your productivity.

Here is how less focus can make you even more powerful when you do focus.

Do sprints

Sportsman-turned-entrepreneur Lewis Howes calls it doing sprints, as in focusing on something intensely for a short period, then stopping to reassess. It helps keep your energy and, ironically, help you be more attentive when you do focus. I've been a long advocate, albeit from another angle: Implement palate cleansers between intense work and minimal viable days to give your brain a chance to rest and assimilate information.

Do mindless activities

Greg Mckoewn's *Essentialism* breaks down the process well:

But in fact, we can easily do two things at the same at the same time: wash the dishes and listen to the radio, eat and talk... and so on. What we can't do is concentrate on two things at the same time.

We can use this to our advantage, though: As I explain in *The Bite-Sized Entrepreneur*, our brain actually continues to work on our problems when we stop "thinking" about them. So-called mindless activities gives our mind space to think and create creative solutions. My preferred activity is walking (as it was for Steve Jobs), but it could be going to the gym, cooking and cleaning, or another simple, easily achievable act.

Do parallels

Working on other projects in parallel helps you see things you didn't see before. Consider Archimedes's Eureka moment or Newton's gravity-defining apple while he sat under the tree.

Personally, I gained insights into my last startup, Cuddlr, when I spent time parallel time working on my other startup, So Quotable, just as reading a book on warfare recently helped me understand how to be a more deliberate person.

Everything is connected; everything is useful.

6
WHEN IT COSTS TOO MUCH
*Sometimes a little investment can protect you
from a much bigger cost*

Maximizing your time is one of the tenets to
success. It is the reason why you hire other
people to do things outside of your most
productive areas. You can learn a lot by doing
the detailed, uncomfortable work, as I talk
about in *The Bite-Sized Entrepreneur*, but most
often it is like Bill Gates mowing his own lawn:
A waste of time, talent and opportunity.

I recently revisited Gay Hendricks' best-
seller *The Big Leap: Conquer Your Hidden Fear
and Take Life to the Next Level*, and he describes
the issue succinctly:

*The best way to do things within your zone of
incompetence is to avoid doing them altogether.*

A colleague of Hendricks spent hours trying to
fix his new home office printer. After 13 (yes,
thirteen) hours, he finally gave up and hired a
neighborhood college kid to set it up. It took
him an hour and $100.

How much does Hendricks' colleague get paid for his business? About $1,000 an hour. His colleague wasted the opportunity to make another $13,000. This is the zone of incompetence.

Apply it not just to your career, but your life

Emma Johnson talks about smart delegation in her best-selling book, *The Kickass Single Mom: Be Financially Independent, Discover Your Sexiest Self, and Raise Fabulous, Happy Children*.

Despite watching her money and raising two children alone in New York City, Johnson still swears by outsourcing her housekeeping and her laundry. Why? She knows the financial sacrifice to unload those tasks pales compared to the stress and exhaustion they would cause - and that time, like Hendricks' colleague, could be used to actually make more money.

Cost is not price

Seth Godin once put it extremely well in his piece, "Price vs. Cost":

Price is a simple number. How much money do I need to hand you to get this thing?

Cost is what I had to give up to get this. Cost is how much to feed it, take care of it, maintain it and troubleshoot it. Cost is my lack of focus and my cost of storage. Cost is the externalities, the effluent, the side effects.

This is why doing one thing in exchange for another is called "opportunity cost". And it is not just the missed chance to do something else, but the additional energy and effort it may take for you to follow through on your choice.

It is like the frugal consumer driving several extra miles to a distant gas station to save a few pennies per gallon. It feels great to be that thoughtful, but, in the end, it becomes an actual loss. Focus on being practical, not just *feeling* practical.

One big exception

You do not want to skip an experience that will actually make you better at your main competence. For instance, founding, programming, and bootstrapping the app So Quotable taught me a breadth of tough skills, and, without those skills, I'm positive I wouldn't have led my following app, Cuddlr, to success.

More importantly, though, is you should not offload less meaningful activities if they actually help you think through your best ideas. *The Power of Onlyness* author Nilofer Merchant swears by walking (as do I), Arianna Huffington absolutely needs naps and Richard Branson works half days to be his best.

Do not feel guilty if doodling with the new home printer or cutting the proverbial lawn provides space for you to think about your next great strategy. Just make sure you're not wasting your time out of austerity, stubbornness or habit, as it may be more costly than you think.

7
YOU HAVE TO BELIEVE YOU DESERVE IT
You won't make it if you aren't convinced you should have it

When it comes to pop television, VH1's biographical *Behind the Music* was a great way to better understand how to be successful. From rap to rock to Top 40, every group featured went from barely getting by to phenomenal riches and admiration to a seemingly inevitable downfall. And every crash proceeded with some quotable, like "We were loved by the whole world! We couldn't believe our success!"

Foreshadowing at its best.

There are two issues to unpack here. First, the entire world cannot love you, just as, at your very worst, the entire world cannot hate you. Both are an illusion based on your own inner stuff. A good portion of the world is in relative poverty – they're just trying to get their next meal. They are not thinking about your creative success.

Second, if you don't believe in your own success, then it isn't going to last. Consider why million-dollar jackpot lottery winners, on average, end up losing their money within a few years and often end up in massive debt worse off than before. Or why creative overnight successes rarely stay on top after getting into the spotlight.

The key is to actually prepare for your ascension as much as possible. How many lottery winners have an action plan *in case they actually win*? The fact is that they say they want to win, but don't actually believe it. You may want a best-selling novel or a white-hot startup or an amazing financial fortune, but unless you create a sound foundation, you wouldn't know what to do with it or even how to handle it, if you actually got it.

The Big Leap author Gay Hendricks calls this an upper-limit problem: You have the desire for something, but you don't believe you actually deserve the success. It is often built on beliefs we don't even realize are blocking us. For example, if you believe "Money is the root of all evil," and you also say you want to be a millionaire, what is going to happen when you actually get close to your goal? You will likely self-sabotage your potential success, as you don't want to be evil. Or you could change that long-held belief enough so that you allow yourself to succeed. The latter is a little harder, as it requires knowing yourself.

A classic Zen belief is to understand your desire and then to let it go enough so that it can come to you. Passion, patience, and persistence do not guarantee success, but you are guaranteed to not be successful without them. This means that, by focusing on working on yourself, your best life is yet to come. It also means that the best way to get and stay successful is to get out of your own way.

8

KNOW WHO IS AT THE WHEEL

Understand your drive and you'll avoid more accidents

I started speech therapy when I was around four, the same age my eldest son is now. I vaguely remember having a heavy lisp. I clearly remember the emotional frustration of people not understanding what I was trying to say. I began reading when I was around two, but I couldn't communicate well with others until much, much later. The conflict was not easy for me.

By age 21, I had a bachelors and a masters in journalism. By age 31, I had an intense journalism career and six books under my belt. Today, at 41, I've written 21 books in a dozen years and make a living speaking on stages, including at TED.

The ultimate fear? We're talking a year from now, in November 2018, and I'm doing the *exact* same thing I am doing at this very moment. It makes me feel physically ill.

I assume there won't be another time. This is the last moment. The window is closing *fast*. It is time to act! I have to get this out before it is all over. It needs to exist. I have to say it now.

This is my wound.

The wound is that place where you always feel just one step away from fear closing in. It is the place where a seemingly unlimited amount of passion keeps you moving forward. It is the place that drives you. And it will never completely heal.

Spiritual teacher Caroline Myss talks about bringing your wounds to the forefront so you can nurture them and understand them. She says when she helps people, "they can often see how they have lost their energy or power through their overidentification with these wounds or experiences."

At its best, your wound will act like a slingshot: Whatever you think held you back before will give you more momentum than others who aren't fighting the same fight. I just recently noticed the breadcrumbs trailing back to a frustrating early childhood. It is why I must talk to *you*. It is why I do not take it for granted.

Why are you reading this book right now? Why do you need to be something more than you already are now? Find your wound and you'll find your answer – and your ultimate path.

9
BE A GOOD INSTRUMENT
Showing up is the only universal secret to
success

Something happens when you think you've got the formula to success: You guarantee that your next effort will be mediocre at best. The cliché term "sophomore jinx" exists for this very reason.

Paulo Coelho, author of *The Alchemist*, one of the most successful books of all time, said this about his masterwork:

Did I write The Alchemist? I'm not sure. I'm sure I was a good instrument... One day, I wrote a book that is, let's be honest, much better than I am. So, one day, you manifest something. This is the real alchemy.

It *is* alchemy. Paulo doesn't know how this stuff works! And neither do I. Whether it is Elizabeth Gilbert personifying genius ideas floating in the air or Steven Pressfield talking about a visiting divine Muse, it is clear that we do not know the source of unique brilliance, excellent timing and, ultimately, phenomenal success.

One thing is clear, though: You can't have a feast on an unprepared slab.

How are you setting the table?

10
THE STREISAND EFFECT
Focusing on your weaknesses will only make them worse

Isn't it funny how if you are thinking about something, like having a child or buying a new red car, suddenly you see the desired thing all around you? There is actually a term for it: Baader-Meinhof phenomenon. Your brain is built to pick up patterns, so it will naturally pull out perceived repetition based on your focus.

There is a more popular, if caustic description of this idea: The Streisand Effect. *The Economist*, out of all places, explained it recently:

[Barbra] Streisand inadvertently gave her name to the phenomenon in 2003, when she sued the California Coastal Records Project, which maintains an online photographic archive of almost the entire California coastline, on the grounds that its pictures included shots of her cliffside Malibu mansion, and thus invaded her privacy.

That raised hackles online. The internet's history is steeped in West Coast cyber-libertariansim, and Ms

Streisand (herself generally sympathetic to the liberal left) was scorned for what was seen as a frivolous suit that was harmful to freedom of speech. As the links proliferated, thousands of people saw the pictures of Ms Streisand's house—far more than would otherwise ever have bothered to browse through the CCRP's archives. By the time a judge eventually threw the suit out, Ms Streisand's privacy had been far more thoroughly compromised than it would have been had she and her lawyers left the CCRP alone.

And we can totally Streisand our flaws: Focus on your weaknesses and you will see more and more of your flaws in your work and your life. Unfortunately, this will make you more likely to beat yourself up for minor mistakes and you may even emphasize your weak spots to potential coworkers or clients rather than highlighting your capabilities. There is little constructive that can come from blowing up your issues – and there's nothing you can do with the little information gained.

Career strategist Jenny Blake talks about it in her book *Pivot*:

Often the more stuck someone is, the more they tell me what is not working and what they don't want... [and] although it seems like they are clear on some aspects of how to move forward, this information is not all that useful.

It's pretty clear what you don't want to feel. But what do you want to have? To paraphrase another business strategist, Nilofer Merchant, a rebel rallies against something while a leader takes you to a better place. Fussing about your position in life is terribly easy. Clearly expressing where you would rather be takes more effort.

Focus on raw skills

Understand what you bring to the table. A photographer might not know accounting, but she offers the ability to take in both the big idea and the details – a rare ability necessary to either profession. Write down the most basic traits you take for granted. For me, I have spent years explaining complicated, often abstract ideas to the general public, and making it entertaining to boot. How many other ways can that raw skill be valuable? How can it launch me into new directions?

Write down your path

Create an exit plan for your current work, which is an entrance plan to your big goal. The first step or milestone should be relatively small. If you are a public speaker, then the first goal may be someone agreeing to have you speak for free. The next goal may be someone actually asking you to speak. The goal after that could be having your first paid gig.

Make room for greatness

Develop the habits that support your strengths. If you an ambivert (a person who alternates between introvert and extrovert, like myself), then you can structure your career to support both private time and social time. A so-called weakness may be just the personal system that allows you to function at your highest potential.

Author Louise L. Hay said it well: "Remember, you have been criticizing yourself for years and it hasn't worked. Try approving of yourself and see what happens."

Today is the time to start.

11
YOUR WORK WILL NOT ALWAYS BE YOUR PAYCHECK
True power comes from knowing who you are no matter the environment

My real journalism career started in a copy room. I just finished my Master's in Magazine Publishing, lost a job offer the day of graduation and, three months into freelance journalism, became an administrative assistant to make ends meet. When I met someone new in the office, I'd say "Hey, I'm Damon, assistant to so-and-so. And I'm a journalist." Note: This place wasn't a newspaper. It wasn't even remotely connected to media. It was an office downtown. This was two decades ago, so I can't remember specifics, but I do know my new coworkers were looking at me like I was crazy.

One day I was making copies, again, and someone came in to use the tiny station. I introduced myself my usual way. Their eyes lit up: They happened to be in charge of the publishing arm of the company – which I didn't know existed. They wanted to work together. Suddenly, I was really a working freelance journalist.

Here's a hot truth I still remind myself today: How you make your paycheck has nothing to do with how you make your *work*. I don't mean work as in the classic grab the briefcase, "time to make the donuts" way. It is your life's work. It is, as Oprah would say, "work with a capital W".

What's going to happen is that you're going to stretch, and sometimes that stretch means being between the old way you made a living and the new way you are stepping into. There is a gap. Your job is to fill the gap and keep your vision no matter how your money comes in.

I still go through this periodically, as I've moved from newspaper reporter to magazine reporter to published author to blogger to self-publishing author to entrepreneur to consultant to public speaker. Each move to the next level, each move closer to my core intention, is bridged by money and momentum served by my previous identities.

Don't hate the job that gives you funding to fuel your dreams. And don't disavow amazing work you've done in the past, as those raw skills will translate into something you need for your future.

Cuddlr, my app that connected strangers for hugs, succeeded because I knew how to talk to media and, after writing several books on tech and intimacy, I knew what we culturally needed to give users. Would it have gone as big without my years as a journalist? I doubt it, but imagine for a second if I did want to escape my past or not utilize my hard-earned skills in my new role.

And an amazing thing happens when you stop worrying about your past: You give the future time to grow. By getting money from stable, if less glamorous areas, then you don't force your Work (capital W) into something it is not. You can focus on understanding your audience, not on making a profit. You can create without fear of repercussions on your daily life. You can experience the joy and, ironically, from that same joy eventually comes income. As I've said in the past, my co-founders and I didn't intend for Cuddlr to be a money maker. For me, I just wanted to move the cultural needle and change how America looked at platonic intimacy. We focused on *that*, and that pure intention led to us making a profit. If we had quit our day jobs and were desperate for money, then the experience for myself, my cofounders, and for the users would have been entirely different, and the success would have been muted, if at all.

Motivational speaker Jim Rohn once said, "If you work on your job, you'll make a living. If you work on yourself, you'll make a fortune." The fortune to be had here isn't just money, though, but the personal fortune of self-knowledge and passion well beyond those living their lives just to get a paycheck.

You don't have to choose. The wisest among us take both the money and the joy.

12

ACT LIKE YOU MEANT IT TO HAPPEN

Unexpected events can become windfalls when you give up resistance

Chances are you didn't expect to be where you are right now. The place you live, the people you spend time with, and the work you do is likely not what you envisioned as, say, a 10-year-old or even as a college-age adult. The randomness of life – or, put more plainly, just *life* – will give you circumstances well beyond your scope of comprehension. Some people believe it is to test you, but it really doesn't matter why. Unpredictable is just what life is.

The best way to strive every day is to actually dive into new circumstances as if they were on your agenda.

Chris Jones, food entrepreneur and co-founder of ChefSteps, explained a similar philosophy his dad handed down to him:

Growing up, my father told me 'Don't worry about what you're going to do' because the job I was going to do hadn't been invented yet... the most interesting jobs are the ones that you make up."

What a breathtaking approach: Uncertainty is your ally. The tools, the skills, and the circumstances you need to make your mark on the world may not even exist yet. You cannot be certain of what's going to happen next. An event that happens in the next 24 hours could change the course of your career and provide a quantum leap in your understanding. It will not be something you can predict, and it will not be something you can control. It will be something that you will have to accept. The less resistance you have to your next adventure, the more you will gain from its arrival.

The philosophical book *The Daily Stoic* refers to this as a "reverse clause", meaning that we make the best out of any event:

If a friend betrays us, our reverse clause is to learn from how this happened and how to forgive this person's mistake... When a technical glitch erases our work, our reverse clause is that we can start fresh and do it better this time. Our progress can be impeded or disrupted, but the mind can always be changed – it retains the power to redirect the path.

It means having faith, religious, scientific, or otherwise, that there is a bigger puzzle at work here. It allows you to show up in the arena, every day, as if it was what you've been preparing for since the beginning of your life. And perhaps you have.

13

YOU ALWAYS HAVE TO COME HOME
Assume you will come back to where you started

Here's what happened the day I was wired the money for the acquisition of my hit app, Cuddlr: Nothing I can remember. Actually, I can remember checking my bank account online at the dining room table and softly saying to my wife in the kitchen, "Well, it's done." Paparazzi wasn't waiting outside, nor was there a big noise coming from my computer. Me and my two co-founders, Charlie Williams and Jeff Kulak, created one of the most popular apps that year, hitting the cover of the *Wall Street Journal* and countless other publications. After my bank notification, I vaguely remember talking about what I was going to make for dinner.

When you get success – and you will get success – the biggest mistake you can make is identifying with your newfound prosperity and assuming that the old you is done.

We've all been in a similar situation: Think about when you dated someone new and became so immersed in the relationship that you stopped calling your friends, family, and other loved ones. The problem, of course, is that the obsessive feeling will be over shortly thereafter, whether you break up with the person or simply began to normalize having this other person in your life.

And what happens after that? You call the people you care about to catch up or, worse, get support after a breakup. The thing is, you haven't maintained those vital parts that helped get you there in the first place. Remember, your loved ones helped make you this wonderful person who was worth dating. They have been busy living their lives and, for that time period, you weren't even keeping a relationship with them.

As I've told my toddler, "I'm glad you feel better, but just because you feel better, that doesn't mean that everything else is OK."

In fact, that may be the most important reason why I wrote this book you're reading right now. The year of my life spent nurturing Cuddlr users, guiding leadership, and putting out fires ended as abruptly as it started. During that same year, good friends got married, close family went through big changes, and my first-born went from baby to toddler. I'm thankful I was there for all of it, but what if I missed these moments in pursuit of the brass ring? The strategies in this series helped me know, in a deep way, my priorities, even as my co-founders and I were the media and late-night talk show darlings, busy fielding business opportunities that we wouldn't have imagined in our wildest dreams. *The Bite-Sized Entrepreneur* ideas made the foundation that helped me stay grounded, remembering, always, that the fame was fleeting and my life, my real life, was continuing independent of any business success I was experiencing. In fact, without my real life, I wouldn't have withstood our 11-month rocket into momentary stardom. It fueled my career, not the other way around.

Your rollercoaster ride will end. Your bestseller will eventually drop off the *New York Times* list, your album will be replaced by another new classic, and your *Forbes* cover will be off the newsstand in a month. You will have to look into the eyes of the people you love and, at worst, justify to yourself that your time in the spotlight was worth sacrificing your connection with them. The trick is that there is no ultimate justification, which becomes clearer as those accolades, no matter how high, inevitably fade into the past.

For each decision you make, remember you will eventually have to come home.

BOOK II:
BRING YOUR WORTH
LEVEL UP YOUR CREATIVE POWER, VALUE & SERVICE TO THE WORLD

To Papaya

"You must be selfish enough to be in alignments with your true self before you have anything to give."

Esther & Jerry Hicks,
The Vortex

How to Bring Your Worth

Why does the market not value my true worth?

Why does my bank account not reflect my true worth?

Why does the world not understand my true worth?

The more unique your voice in the world, the more difficult it may be to see your true worth in the marketplace, in your bank account, and in the world. If you don't feel like you are receiving what you deserve, then perhaps it is not a reflection of the world, but a reflection of how you truly feel about your own worth.

You have to bring your worth to make your mark on the world.

Did you ever try to believe that things are how they are supposed to be? The chaos, the pain, and the challenges in your life are supposed to be there. It hurts. Open up to that possibility for a moment, though, and you begin twisting the things in your world from different angles.

Life isn't a flat board, but more like a Rubix Cube, and the more sides you view, the more of the puzzle you see, and creating a bigger discussion, and, for you, a bigger life. But, again, that requires accepting where you are. That's the hard part.

Unfortunately, you cannot truly make an impact on the world until you believe you are where you are supposed to be. Resenting your station only makes you misunderstand your gifts, if you see them at all. Fighting the life you have now only tires you out and distracts you from the real fight to become your truest self. Bitterness costs you opportunities. This presents a real, yet silent, problem.

For a period of time, my toddler would just say "No" to everything offered to him. My partner and I would eventually stare at him with puzzled expressions, and he would become increasingly frustrated. He made it clear to us of what he didn't want, but he wouldn't actually say what he *did* want. We couldn't help him. It might sound ridiculous, especially if you've never raised a toddler, but we do the exact same thing every day. We get tired of shitty-paying clients, we loathe that organizations hold all the power, we feel downright mad that the world doesn't recognize our genius. But what are we bringing to the situation?

You have to bring your worth to the table to get your worth from your partnerships and then serve your worth to the world. Step into your role, and the world embraces you on that level. It is made just for you. It cannot be taken away. You cannot be replaced. It means only you possess the puzzle piece fitting uniquely, snugly, perfectly into that role. You cannot be replaced, but you also do not have a back-up. There is no understudy for you.

It is a three-legged stool: Your worth to the marketplace, your worth to the bank account, and your worth to the world. Bring two of these to the table and you may keep going for a little bit, but your career won't persevere. Bring only one to the table, and you're not going to make it – you'll topple before you even sit down.

Base your worth only on what the market desires, then you're following the current trends – which is what everyone else is doing. You're on a race to the bottom, as Seth Godin says, making your products and services cheaper than the competition, as that's the only bargaining tool you'll have to offer. You won't be original. Worse, since you're eager to hop onto the next trend, your community will feel abandoned, and in time, they likely will stop following you because they know you will eventually leave them.

Base your worth only on what the bank account needs, then you're putting getting paid over serving your community. One of two things, and likely both, will almost certainly happen: Either you'll get sloppy at your work because you're prioritizing the money, or your customers will recognize that you're just in it for the money. They will recognize you just don't really care about them. People are always more perceptive than we think.

Base your worth only on what the world needs, then congratulations: You're a starving artist. This is perhaps the saddest outcome, as there is no relationship between the quality of your work and you actually getting paid for your work. They are not inversely proportional. And if there were any inkling of an argument, it would be for the reverse. I've been a starving artist, and if you have been as well, then you know there is a significant amount of brain power dedicated to just figuring out your next meal.

Personally, I serve everyone better on a full stomach.

If *The Bite-Sized Entrepreneur* helped you with its tactics to fulfill your creative destiny, then *Bring Your Worth*, its spiritual successor, will aid you in living a more authentic (and valued) life.

Bring Your Worth is the live album as much as *The Bite-Sized Entrepeneur* series was the studio sessions. Inspired by my Create Your Worth keynotes, my TED Talks, and the many worldwide conversations I've had with you, my readers and listeners, this book breaks down the three legs you need to bring your full innovative value, power, and service to the world. You're not trying to create your worth, find your worth, or build your worth. You just need bring the strength you already have.

You need to recognize it first, though. Consider this your first step.

-Damon
December 2018

I
BRING YOUR WORTH
EVERYTHING IS A PARTNERSHIP

"The artist is afraid of finding out who she is. This fear, I suspect, is more about finding we are greater than we think than discovering that we're lesser.

What if, God help us, we actually have talent? What if we truly do possess a gift?

What will we do then?"

Steven Pressfield,
The Artist's Journey

There's confusion to valuing our own worth. No, it isn't just a job. The sensitives got it right: Your work isn't just an exchange of goods for services. It is the representation of yourself to the world. Aside from neighbors, friends, and loved ones, no one knows you beyond what you put out into the world and, more importantly, what impact you leave behind after you go. The demand for your stuff reflects what you are contributing to the conversation and how much you are committing to your unique perspective. It doesn't make sense to go after something just because it is the new hot thing. The trouble with trends is that other people spot them, too, with the same intention of riding the wave. Everyone else recognizes what is a hot thing, and, unless that hot thing matches your voice, which, if you are lucky, happens once or twice within a lifetime, then you strip away any original proposition you have.

When the trend does match your unique intention, though, then you can drive the market. The goal, then, is staying committed to what you know is important. Not think, but know. It is what Brene Brown means when she says "Braving the wilderness." It is lonely, and it has to be, because being your original self means having no duplicate. The wilderness can be strictly psychological, watching the rejection letters pour in day after day for your ideal project and having the wherewithal to keep going, or it could be financial, pouring your hard-earned pay gained from another, less exciting, path into something you know is your next calling.

Most of all, this knowledge stays silent. It may even be painfully quiet. And, no matter how much you shout, no one will be able to understand you, as if you are speaking Greek on the Roman Isles. This is how it should be. Hearing the thumbs up, the nod, or the go-ahead from anyone is a false positive, particularly from people in control of the market. The voice you begin hearing becomes theirs, not your own, and it is painfully easy to catch amnesia and start forging a path for them instead of a path for yourself. It can be a cruel fate. I've seen it: Brilliant, driven creators, machete in hand swatting through the proverbial Amazon to the sound of their calling, and, in a glimmer, they are just as passionately going in another direction, instead of listening to a gatekeeper's faint promise of security, fame, or money. I know I have succumbed to that siren call myself.

Know this: Gatekeepers themselves don't have security. Gatekeepers don't have the power anymore. They are our partners, your partners, as they should have been all along. The insight garnered from so-called gatekeepers is inversely proportional to the power of technology, which means the vision of, say, a publishing house in the 1960's would have compared to a new author would be much, much further than the same house would have today. We are reaching an inflection point where things are so inversely proportional, creators have a greater vision than those up on high. We are the ones on the front lines. We are the ones connecting with our audiences. We are the ones with the social media followings, the DIY opportunities, and the ability to continually iterate our ideas based on instant feedback. We don't need them. They need us.

ೞ

Alarcity is today's default setting. Entrepreneur Jason Fried reads the news in a newspaper once a day, saying it is the perfect delivery vehicle, as the things that are most important are curated and mentioned and stick around for the following day. It avoids the hyperbole of things seeming important at the moment, and everything can't be important at the moment, for, at that point, then nothing can truly be important at that moment. It is why we suddenly regain balance when we are with very young people, or with kind animals, as they truly are of the moment, not of the overstimulated moment, but of the hyperaware moment. All that matters is now. It is instinctual for them, as they haven't learned to see otherwise, to be concerned with tomorrow and to regret what was done yesterday like an infinity loop. Therapist Esther Perel's family and other European Jews survived World War II, yet Perel says most every individual was either disillusioned for the rest of their lives, which she calls "Joining the walking dead", or focused on making and enjoying every day to the fullest. They had to choose. It is why New Yorkers found clarity in the weeks following 9/11. Traumatic events propel us into hyperawareness. They remind us that we have to choose every day – because that choice was almost taken away from us.

You never know what is at stake. It is more than "Today's intern could become your manager in the future." It is of your intention. The small act magnifies, and how you do one thing is how you do everything. From the universe, sure, you are spiritually showing that you can handle something bigger. That's not the point. The point is the muscle memory, the knee jerk reaction you train yourself to have in the situation when the risk was more minimal. Archilochus said in moments of trouble, we don't rise to the level of our expectations, but we fall to the level of our training.

Picture scaffolding, but instead of from the inside out, picture it going from the outside in. It is our bones, our literal integrity, which difficult times test and fortify. Without challenging ourselves, we do not know if the values we created are really what we believe. The universe, which really means *you*, since you are one with the world, does not create struggle to punish you, but to reconfirm what you actually believe. The confidence to know what you believe isn't complete until you are given ample opportunity to disregard it.

The advocates will come. But first, you need to start.

You want your purpose to be as transparent as a drop of water: Only take a sip, and you are completely understood. You don't need anything deep or heavy, any dramatic pronouncements. Marcus Aurelius said that your truth should be clear as soon as you step into a room, like a smelly goat. That strength is undeniable by the many, even by your detractors, and it is unattainable by the masses, even by the envious. It is pure and unyielding. Once you uncover it, then it can no longer remain buried. This is a gift and a curse, as you cannot unknow it, either, and you will have to do something with it for the rest of your life. Other people will recognize it, too, and those who care about you will dog you to fulfill it, while even those who just met you will know when you are in alignment with it. They will see it in your eyes. Do you ever look at someone and know they are living their truth?

It could be ugly, it could be disagreeable, but it always means something higher than just muddling through life. They light up. It is undeniable. It is understood without saying a word.

⊂₈₂⊃

Words exist, but putting them in a certain order, in a particular cadence, changes the culture. Only a few musical notes exist, and yet, in the right hands – your hands – they number plenty to make a dent in the universe. Your work has value. The rub is that your work may not be tangible. That is, the world at large doesn't see your tangible work. A financial broker makes money moving money around, putting her in the same capacity as a three-card Monty hustler on the boardwalk. And yet, becoming a CPA may be more celebrated than becoming a poet because the path is clear. It is safe.

Get closer to your creative truth, though, and you'll get further from safety. You were never meant to leave the world the same way as you came into it. You know it. That's why it hurts.

Taking a leap rarely hurts, even when you fail. The pain arrives from the separation between who you are being and who you really are. Bonding with your truth is inversely proportional to clinging to your safety.

This value question isn't just yours, though, but everyone else's, too. Being closer to your truth makes you shine, and when others connect with you, they recognize their own gap between being and self. They feel your power. It triggers their own choices between safety and truth. They have to raise their own awareness, stop interacting with you anymore, or remind you of the futility of your path. Or they could do all three. Responses always reflect other people's view of their worth. Always. This is why bringing your worth is essential to any relationship, whether invoicing a client or pitching an idea or launching a service or explaining what you do at a cocktail party. Every interaction is a building block, and you're either adding or subtracting to this foundation to get closer to your true self and, therefore, your true worth. I have done lateral moves and even some steps back, and they serve as reminders of what I am not. As many wise people have said, setbacks are not failures, but information: Data on what you are not, figures showing your real path, live feedback on your pain points. The times when you undervalue yourself - and actually get what you asked for! - are just as valuable as the times you are able to reflect your true worth. It all depends on what you do with the insight.

 CR&O

Your longing for success creates enough fuel to draw in the right clients, build the best career, and create a higher opportunity for you. Drop the dialogue on crushing the competition, because when you are in tune with your intention, then there is no competition. There doesn't need to be concerns about the timeline, as things jump into place when they line up, not when you hit a time-based milestone. And frustration over your current situation should be acknowledged, but only as a barometer for what you don't want in the future, as your disdain for today will keep you focused only on what you lack now rather than what you desire tomorrow. Be as clear and as transparent and as honest as possible about what you want, regardless of your current moment, as the more visionary you become with your future, the more you will, knowingly and unknowingly, start to build systems to make it real.

One of the best ways to make your best work for the world is to create without the intention of shipping, launching, or selling. It doesn't mean working for free. It means working without expectations. Our biggest ideas are as fragile as a Parisian croissant, and the pressure of projected success can make them crumble before we even have the opportunity to see what they will become. They are too abstract to handle the stress test. It is why we should create pilots, just simple, minimal viable products that can get our ideas out. It is why we should do side hustles, fun pursuits we do outside of our 9-to-5 during, as entrepreneur Chase Jarvis says, our 5-to-9. It is why we should build support networks, so we know there are other people trying to make something out of nothing.

All these solutions have one thing in common: You are sharing and, then, listening. Pilots give you feedback from the people you want to serve, side hustles give you feedback from the financial realities of your pursuit, and networks give you feedback from your peers. Our biggest problems come when we are using our will rather than our intuition or, simply, our ears.

Do not get a win and attribute it to just your will, as if our anger or our frustration bended the universe to our desires. More often, though, we have our major breakthroughs, our quantum leaps, and our milestone moments when we are on our knees. The darkness before the dawn, the opening right in the nick of time, and so on, are cliches for a reason. It's high drama, sure, and gives us survivors a story to tell. But it also reflects that moment when we are ready to give up, because when we are ready to give up, we are the most open to aligning rather than maligning the future.

II
GET YOUR WORTH
DON'T WAIT FOR PERMISSION

"But this payment goes well beyond my generosity," the monk responded.

"Don't say that again," said The Alchemist. "Life may be listening, and give you less next time."

Paulo Coehlo,
The Alchemist

We are magicians. Our best work is creating something out of nothing. It is all binary. It doesn't matter if you are a writer, rearranging the same words that have existed well before your grandmother's grandmother was born, or an architect, turning scribbles written down from your mind's eye into a physical space, or a priest, literally calling upon the heavens which no living man has set foot in. Our best work is always invisible, as even the most physical acts have an alchemy that happens behind the scenes, a chemical reaction that happens within you, transforming what once was into what was never before. This is yours and yours alone. And this is yours to keep.

The challenge happens when we measure our work based on society standards instead of actual impact. For instance, a mason would be one of the most revered, well-paid people in our community in the 19th century, fashioning the bricks building our homes, kilning the shoes carrying the horses we ride, and finishing the weapons protecting our lives from harm. Today, masons are respected, but they aren't deemed as important to the general public. They are not as valued. Computer-aided design, smart cars, and equally smart weapons have taken over their role.

Now, take this idea to the small scale. Bring this paradigm to what you believe in. Pursuing something because it's the hot thing today makes sense in the short term. You aren't terribly interested, and you may even hate it, but you know that's what sells, and that's what the market seems to demand. Worse, you may get your first paycheck for it, and you can mistake something as a calling because someone is willing to pay you for it. The problem is two fold. First, if you're jumping on the bandwagon, then other people will be or, more likely, already are getting into that same competitive space. That's the very definition of bandwagon. You are almost certainly going to lose. Second, and more importantly, you are creating something that is unsustainable both externally and internally. You are doing something that you don't really care about and you are doing something that, almost inevitably, the market will stop monetarily valuing. You get the worst of both worlds.

It is wiser to trust the market cycles to do just that: cycle. Staying steadfast to your particular thing actually builds more security than hopping from trend to trend, as you build momentum, you build reputation, and you build community based on that very thing you care most about. People who give a shit about that thing will recognize your craftsmanship, or your dedication, or your commitment, and will reward you with their attention. Attention, not money, is the most powerful currency one can give you, as money is renewable, but time is not. And once the sun shines on your particular craft, then you will rise like cream to the top, as much as we're obsessed with science, technology, engineering, and mathematics (STEM) today, just as we were focused on web developers at the turn of the millennium, and on Wall Street whiz kids two decades before that. The biggest influencers of every era blaze brightly based on those proverbial 10,000 hours of study, and that doesn't happen, and can't happen, because the market is interested in what they care about. They have to proceed well before the market approves what they value. They cannot wait for the world's seal of approval.

Unmistakable author Srinivas Rao compares business to surfing. When you are looking for a wave to ride, you don't go after the beautiful, fully-formed ones. They are in the distance. Remember, you have to recognize the opportunity, direct your board, and create momentum to head there. By the time you get there, the wave will crash, likely on top of you. If you see the white caps, though, where new waves are forming, then you start heading in that direction based on instinct. It isn't obvious. It is likely only seen by you, based on your own viewpoint, experience, and eyesight. The wave is yours and yours alone, and, as it crests, you ride it as if you own it, because you do. Others may view you as an overnight success, as a visionary, or as a lucky bastard. You just got quiet enough to pay attention to your own voice.

And no matter how they feel, they will happily pay you what your insight is worth. But first, you have to know *yourself* what it is worth.

೮ঙ৪ড

There is always an intention tax: Are you willing to face your issues to move forward? In Paulo Coehlo's *The Alchemist*, the hero's mentor says he needs a tenth of his sheep to help him on his journey. The shepherd spends a pensive evening thinking about the request and, suddenly, realizes that a tenth of his current livelihood is worth fulfilling his destiny. The mentor, adorned in a gold breastplate, says that he didn't really need the sheep. He needed to make sure that the hero was committed to the journey. Not that the mentor knew he was serious, but that the hero *himself* knew he was serious.

When a family member or friend lends you money or other resources, the first question from them is not, "When will you get it back to me?" Even the bank doesn't ask you this first. The first question is, always, "What are you going to do with it?" The universe is the same way. It wants you to commit, then it will open up the doors. You can fill out the forms, you can say how much you want it, and you can sit in bitterness because you don't have it, whether it is the million dollars in the bank, the right job, or fabulous fame, but without knowing how you are going to use it – knowing your "why?" – then the chances of it arriving are as slim as a toothpick. It is intention, not desire, that puts the wheels in motion.

I don't like owing people. It's like a nervous tick that bypasses my thoughts, an automatic reaction. I chose to be an independent creative, and we always owe someone. This is a personal dilemma. We owe our family and friends the time they gave us to work on our craft, and that is time we didn't spend with them. We owe financial commitments, particularly when we first start out, as others have to have flexibility as we discover how to bring in income, and that journey is often an infinite one. We owe ourselves, the indebtedness of the aforementioned time, the opportunity cost of stability, and the weight of believing our trek is worthwhile to ourselves, which is why, if we don't understand why we do what we do, then that weight becomes guilt or shame or hopelessness. We owe, we owe, we owe.

So when I have had lean times, usually marked by a pivot to another world, the investment of, say, previous capital to new ventures, working hard at an old discipline to help fund the new discipline I care about more while phasing it out and seeing the old money come less and less while the new money hasn't quite come yet, then I see myself facing my fear: Asking for support. Could I get latitude on this bill? How can we barter for this necessity? What ways can we get this commitment down to something more manageable?

It feels like drowning.

And then I make the first step for support. Then the second. I begin breathing. I realize my ability to function independently is directly tied to my perception of self worth. I'm afraid admitting things are not going how I expected, that I have been hit with the unexpected, that my master plan needs deviation, makes me less of who I am. The cycle of independence and dependence, the wheel of fortune on which we all ride, brings me closer to acceptance.

It's like coming up for air. The lungs get bigger over time. It stops feeling like drowning. And when the current does change again, you'll be prepared.

I ask, "How would it feel if the lost check arrived or if the delinquent client suddenly direct deposited my money. I'd feel a sense of release, as if the birds began singing and everything, and I mean everything, was suddenly right in the world. But real pain doesn't shut off that quickly. It lingers, and leaves slowly, like a swelling going down. That's when I know it's not real pain, but circumstantial pain. It is temporary. That's when I know I'll get through it fine and, a year from now, I will not remember the circumstances of this all-consuming moment, if I remember it at all. I know I was in a financial bind exactly a year ago. I couldn't tell you its face, nevertheless its name.

The opposite is true, too: Just like blurry, scary faces in a nightmare, our own desires remain ethereal until we pin them down. The worst thing you can say is, "If I had a million dollars." It points to two negatives. First, a lack of gratitude for the resources you currently have, the very resources, fortified with luck and grace, that brought you to this point to even have this moment of thought. You aren't maximizing what you've got now, because you don't even consider your current resources worthy of your attention. It's smacking the universe in the face.

Second, you don't achieve your goals with round numbers. To paraphrase the late motivational speaker Jim Rohn, how can you handle $1,000,000 if you don't know what happened to the $5 in your pocket? You need specifics to do great works. If you're going to be rich, then what is your definition of rich? If you need money to get your idea started, then how much do you need and, more importantly, where will each resource go? It is the exact same thing with time, as if you need time to create, then how exactly will you use that time?

My turning point came reading Mike Michalowicz's *Profit First*. He recommends independents and small business owners put their money into buckets – the same, classic grandmotherly concept of putting cash into different envelopes or coffee cans. You get a check and it's automatically split into the predetermined groups. As an independent creative, you may get a big check today… and not get another one for weeks, if not months, and may have a completely different pattern next year, so creating your own system is crucial. It's worth reading for this discussion alone.

But what if you applied that same principle to all your resources? "Where did the time go?" is just as deadly to your career as "If I had a million dollars." I don't know where your time went. It was your time! Those specifics become your currency, not only to yourself, but to others, too. Venture capitalist Arlan Hamilton says she's more likely to trust a single mom with her investment money, as the woman would be adept at maximizing her resources every day. This is the key: You can charge what you want, if you make sure that your customer – the investor, the buyer, the public, whomever – knows that you will give them many times the value. The only way is to know what you're going to do with the extra resources you desire.

Sit down and figure out what you need to achieve. How much does that certification cost? What time would it take to learn how to code? Where are your potential customers and what would it require to meet them? Write it all down. We usually don't need a million dollars, nor do we need a week of solitude to get stuff done. We usually just need a few hundred bucks and 30 minutes a day for the next week. This is both inspiring and terrifying, as you'll realize you already have everything you need and the real block or challenge isn't in your resources, but in your mind.

ભ્રૠ

The people you owe are not your adversaries. They give you the privilege to do what you do. The car note. The credit card bill. The grocery budget. *The Soul of Money* author Lynne Twist recommends putting "Thank you" on the notes section of your checks, giving the universe a humble nod for allowing you the opportunity to have the thing you are paying for. If you resent paying for and having the responsibility of an economy car and a low-rent apartment, then how can you set yourself up for something more? You can't. You want protection from that resentment, that pain, and in doing so, you block out everything. You're trapping yourself in a cycle, for when you ask for money, price your products, or are asked what you charge for your special gift, then you're going to undercut yourself to stay safe from that resentment, that pain, that burden of living at a higher level than you do now.

You decide what you're worth based on how you accept things as they are now. It doesn't mean you have to be happy with where you are now. It is appreciating what you have within the context of your current life. This isn't a nicety, or a treatise on gratitude or thankfulness. You resent people not paying top dollar for your work, setting the expectation that everyone will pay up to *this* much for your type of work, so when you are setting your price, being asked what something is worth, or sitting at the negotiation table, you are less likely to give a number reflective of what you could and should be getting, and more likely to acquiesce when someone gives you a low ball number because, in your mind, that is just what people do. The only thing you can change, the only thing you need to change, is what you do. The people around you, everything around you, will respond accordingly.

Your worth is like a star. The stars you see in the sky tonight are based on light that's taken a long time to travel, so long, in fact, that some of the stars that you see in the sky have actually burnt out, collapsed, and died years ago. What you are witnessing is an afterglow, the last gasping shadow of a structure. What you are witnessing is the past. So, if you act according to what you see at the moment, then you are building your life based on signals that are no longer accurate. It also means new, budding structures, growing just outside of your point of view, will be decorating your future, but they are happening on a level you can't see just yet. It could be a new client who has been quietly watching you and thinks you can handle a serious job for a serious budget. It could be a great opportunity at the true stature of what you can contribute to the world. It could be a dynamite partner worthy of your current and future potential. And like an external star, bound by the properties of astronomy, your opportunities will react to you based on the bounds of your own internal belief system. A new-to-you client offers a budget ten times what you're current getting, but you offer your services at a fraction of the price and worth based on your own past beliefs. A giant opportunity rolls right up to your doorstep, but you go for the small ideas instead because it enables you to stay comfortable. A collaborator creates a rare chance for you to be pushed, challenged, and motivated to be a better creator, yet you suddenly find many reasons not to move forward. Your reasoning may be sound, maybe even right, but they are right based on the wrong system. They are based on what was, not on what is. They are based on the past. It is us looking intensely at the night sky, searing the visual into our brains, and making decisions based on our old view without ever looking up at the sky again. To move forward, to move closer to your greatness, you simply need to stop for a moment, take a breath, and look at where you truly are. In this case, your potential new opportunities, outside partnerships, and self-generated ideas are your constellations.

People cannot help you on your journey when you don't communicate what you desire and what you deserve. If you're not honest about what you really want, you can't help you on your journey, either.

What you "owe", then, isn't money, time, or sacrifice, but to turn what has been given into something greater in the world. Like alchemy.

It's replacing weight with levity. Weight is the burden, the pressure, and the fear of what lies ahead based on what has happened before. Levity is taking the reality seriously and making the best decision at the moment. One paralyzes you. One enables you.

☙❧

Honor your beautiful commitments, and they are all beautiful. They are your stake in the ground, your anchor of certainty, on which you build your life. They are to be adorned like tapestries and obelisks on which you fashion your foundation. If you listen, they bring the jewels and the surprises. Every day.

The circumstances delivering you pain will eventually recede, through time or through tolerance or through insight, but the wisdom gained will remain, glistening on the shore like seashells. The pain will go away. Do not be angry at the circumstances, or at the situations, or at the luck. You cannot be angry at a particular moment in your life without being ungrateful for the riches it gave you. One cannot exist without the other. They are one in the same.

The Greek and Chinese words for chaos are virtually synonymous with another term: opportunity. We can make the most progress when things are uprooted and previous boundaries blur, It just doesn't feel like it. Our perceived loss requires us to reach higher than before. We now have no past to defend.

The dying are often thankful for the experience of dying. They suddenly have clarity of purpose and firmness of priorities elusive to us during our regular lives. Why? It's not from being afraid or delusional, but being grateful for having life in the first place. I had an unexpected bout with cancer in my early thirties and, in short order, my perspective changed, just as it did a few years later finding out I was going to become a father. They are the same experience: Realizing everything is finite. What is forever? Love is forever. Knowledge is forever. Your tough time is not forever. Your wisdom will be. If you choose to take it.

Trust the Wheel of Fate, for it is what brought you here.

The chess pieces are **exactly** where they are supposed to be. You would never say that the game was unfair, that it robbed you. You would never throw the game away, flipping the board and starting over again. You would never say that it, or you, were broken. Players do their best when they trust where things lay. Time management expert and long-time jogger Laura Vanderkam says she had no problem committing to running every single day when she stopped asking *if* she was going to run today, but *when* she was going to run today. Same with your life. Throwing fists at the walls of unfairness is a full-time job better spent working within the circumstances, rules, and borderlines in your given life. You're able to soar, because only then you can maximize the resources you have available by having appreciation and gratitude for what you have at hand. Ironically, you have to create love, acceptance, and reverence for where you are at now to change your situation. Lynne Twist put it well: "When we let go of the chase for more, and consciously examine and experience the resources we already have, we discover our resources are deeper than we knew or imagined. In the nourishment of our attention, our assets expand and grow."

The trick is to fully participate in your life, even when your life isn't where you want it to be. It is to be fully present when you don't want to show up that day. It is to be here.

III
SHARE YOUR WORTH

YOU HAVE A LEGACY

"Think of your work life, therefore, not as separate from your spiritual life, but as central to your spiritual life. Whatever your business, it is your ministry. Every relationship, every activity, every circumstance is part of your ministry, to the extent that you think of it that way. Such devotion uplifts the vibration of your thinking, thus improving the experience others have of you and that you have of them… Energy can create wealth, but wealth itself cannot build energy."

Marianne Williamson,
The Law of Divine Compensation

The easiest motivation and the laziest shield from harm is anger. It is also the most treacherous. We're taught to show the world that it can't hold us down. Show them who's boss. I *will* make an impact today and you can't stop me! Best case scenario, one day, you would have shown the world how much of a bad ass you are, and there will be no more battles to fight, no more prizes to win. The most driven people can find themselves miserable in their mansion or their private jet or their worldwide TV show or whatever trinket of personal success. When they get to the so-called top, they realize that they were motivated by winning, which means, by their definition, someone else has to lose. What happens when you do win? Many of us don't think that through. And that vengeful, prove 'em wrong attitude doesn't just dissipate when you achieve what you say you want. It doesn't have a release, so you begin creating adversaries because you need enemies to stay motivated or, worse, subconsciously plot your own downfall so you can have another mountain peak to reach. *The Big Leap* author Gay Hendricks calls this an upper-limit problem, meaning you aren't comfortable with your success because you feel like you don't deserve it or you realize your motivation is going away. So you sabotage it. I'm tired of the accomplished entrepreneur, the established politician, or the amazing athlete share their take after a public, avoidable downfall, finally excited with a glint in her eyes, a conviction in her voice, talking about proving all the doubters wrong and loving being the underdog and envisioning herself back on top, when her drive was missing moments before she made the foolhardy decision in the first place. The only person that didn't believe she would stay on top was her.

The original reason you do things goes away, which is why you can't be motivated by anger.

You should be the same to whom you serve no matter what your circumstances. The trials seem frustrating, if not insurmountable, when we begin a new journey. For a while, I believed we were tested by a vengeful god, a tough universe, an omnipresent bootcamp sergeant wanting only the strong to survive and have the spoils. It is hard to earn.

I've learned differently now. The treasure is initially denied because we need to learn how to show up even when the rewards feel out of reach, when the tangible rewards are questionable at best, and when we aren't sure there will be a payoff at the end. It isn't a test of your ethics or grit. It is guaranteeing that you discover the real treasure: Serving others to your highest capacity.

Delayed gratification means showing up in a consistent manner, whether fiscally rich or broke, impacting audiences large or tiny, or being a best-seller or a minor seller. I worked on my first major book, *Porn & Pong: How Grand Theft Auto, Tomb Raider & Other Sexy Games Changed Our Culture*, for five years, and remained antsy about getting it out into the public after many rewrites, much agent drama, and different personal challenges, until various veteran writers pulled me aside and said my reward wasn't getting it published. I was *already* experiencing my reward: Creating my first manuscript outside of the scrutiny of the public. No one knew who I was and no one cared. There would only be one first book, and, no matter what the success of the book, I would never experience that solitary practice again. My voice was at its purist. They were right. My effort since has been to get back to that essence, to give you my clearest voice, and to serve you my best expression, regardless of how many copies my books sell. I've written best-sellers and I've written just as many flops. My intention is always the same, though, and I could not promise that the intention would have been the same if my first book had earned a six-figure deal before it was done (it didn't) or if I came from the public spotlight (I didn't).

Your core ideas, those core intentions as a creator, are all built in the struggle, not in the feast. The biggest danger, then, isn't missing your opportunity to shine brightly, to create wealth, or to impact the world, but not allowing the life experiences to prepare you to do those very things. The circumstances will come in disguises, cloaked in a frustrating situation, a setback, or an unexpected development. Your life is tailor made to develop the muscles you need to succeed.

અ૪૪

The universe doesn't want to punish you, which is as preposterous as believing gravity dislikes skydivers or flames hate firefighters. It is just physics, science, and nature. And, the universe knows exactly when to give you what you need, like a flower always blossoming on time. Your gifts are never gone, nor do your efforts die unspoken for within a vacuum. There is a wonderful deluge of opportunities on their way to you, with a proverbial hand holding the pressure-pushing door for the right moment to let go. "Hold on, she hasn't figured out this belief yet. Wait, she has to understand her worth before we give her the riches. Let's pause, because if we give this to her now, she won't have gratitude for the success. Not yet, as she doesn't know why she even desires these amazing things in her life." It is not punishment. It is timing.

We may respect the timing, but we almost certainly do not know *why* the timing. It could be something for us to learn or, potentially more maddening, it could be something that someone else must learn or an environmental change that needs to happen first. Have you ever had a desire that wasn't getting fulfilled and frustrated you to no end, and then circumstances change, you receive what you want, and you notice how it would have been unremarkable, if not impossible for it to happen any other time? When we say, "The timing was perfect.", it's not a parlor trick we pull on ourselves. No, within that **bundle of gratitude** is knowing the event, the thing, the idea appeared just on time – not too early, not too late – like the evening train. That's why gratitude speeds up the journey to your next best life. You are focused on the beauty coming your way, which means you aren't wasting time, energy, or emotion questioning the process.

Energy is more eager to fill an area where a space has already been carved for it. Giving gratitude for your next wonderful opportunity is not just good practice, but makes room for the event to happen. It's not trying to occur in a life that doesn't have space for it to happen. You've been saying this for years without directly saying it: "I began focusing on the wonderful friends, career, and health in my life and, of course, that's when I met my soulmate.", or "I began taking care of my customers instead of trying to make a quick buck, and that's when my business really took off.", and so on. Think about your life. Every example holds complete acceptance and unflinching gratitude, twin emotions that give us joy today and space for beauty tomorrow.

The universe doesn't care if you do "right" or "wrong". It's not testing you. It is confirming you want to behave based on your previously stated thoughts, desires, and intentions. Hypocrisy doesn't stand a chance. This is good news: You are empowered to create your own destiny – and have it supported organically by your environment – by being clear about what you really want in your life. There is a classic computer programming saying: "Garbage in, garbage out". In other words, you build the framework for whatever experience you are having, which is why we are handed some of our toughest battles and, if we survive, we have the indestructible resilience we desired in the first place. If you don't like your settings, then change in which you align.

⊂⊃

Spiritual author Caroline Myss compares our ever-winding success path to hitting road construction. We have a full tank of gas, we got our destination set, and we are eager to arrive. Then detour street signs appear, or perhaps our GPS beeps warning us of upcoming delays, and we realize we have to take a different way. We follow the signs and take the detour. The detour could be for a quick moment, it could be for several miles. It really doesn't matter. We watch the signs and keep an eye on our GPS *until it tells us to get back on the original track*. In the interim, we don't question if Cleveland disappeared. We don't wonder if we deserve to make it to Cleveland. We don't ask if the car is broken, the GPS is wrong, or the signs are incorrect. We just trust the process and know that the original path, now fraught with incomplete bridges, fresh tar, or other hazards, isn't our best way. You don't skip the detour signs and try to cross a broken highway anyway.

Questioning is the source of our grief as well as the source of our insight. The difference is in the questions we ask. "Why isn't this happening yet?" or "Why are they successful and I'm not?" creates a different context than "Why am I on this particular road?" or "How can I make the world better from this viewpoint?" We always choose how much we learn from our circumstances.

The best approach to your goal of career prosperity is to act as if it isn't coming. That doesn't mean it isn't coming. It means if someone says they are going to come at 10:30 a.m., then you're not standing there at 10:29 a.m. with your hand on the doorknob. Trust.

The mistrust doesn't come from not believing that we will reach our destination. That is a misnomer. Our mistrust comes from not believing we deserve to reach the destination. Why should you have the power to influence millions of people? Why should you have enough money to live a comfortable life? The answer, of course, is another question: Why not? Legendary marketer Seth Godin talks about the origin of the word "genius", which initially was used to describe your unique gift to the world, but, about a century ago, became a way to separate "gifted people" from the rest of us. We think we are being humble honoring

other people when we call them "geniuses",
but are subtly deifying what are just ordinary
humans with the same hours of the day. The
pain comes from the separation, the thin line
between us and them, that shoots down our
vision before it even has a chance to come
through.

CᴙᴞꙨ

My colleague got a surprise offer to do a new
kind of job. They already had a stable, long-
time career with another, more traditional
organization, and was fine with what it had
delivered, but was still intrigued by the new
opportunity. It was based on their hard-earned
skillset, but still out of their comfort zone. It
would be a risk. I recommended having a
conversation with the agency the upcoming
weekend, but warned that they would forever
be changed by the experience. Once you view
yourself in an expanded way, which
sometimes happens when we listen to how
others describe us in an expanded way, then it
is impossible to go back to your previous view.
It is a rubber band that cannot be unstretched.

They had the conversation and decided against pursuing it.

Walking into their current job on Monday morning, though, was like going into a totally new organization. They said it was like seeing the truth for the first time. Of course, the organization didn't change overnight. They did. More specifically, their own value of self raised because they heard and accepted that their worth was more than just this one opportunity at this one organization. You can be sure that the organization recognized their shift, too, and treated them with more respect because it knew that *they* knew how valuable they were, and were more eager to make opportunities to show them how much they were valued within the organization.

That's what happens when we see our true worth within the world: Everything seems new. It is like you found the cheat code, or in the climactic *The Matrix* scene when Neo sees everything for what it truly is underneath the intimidating surface. There is a system in place, and it reacts to how you show up. On better days, I can feel, and almost see, the exchange between you and I, between one and another, as we are contributing to the flow of life, and responding to our declarations, and fulfilling, or not fulfilling, our needs from moment to moment. We are all attached, like some complex, infinite game of Cat's Cradle, with you determining what kind of world you want to live in.

When we believe that we have no impact, we do damage to our potential power, value, and service. As a long-time freelance writer, I connect with people who believe they are a mercenary, a hired gun that churns out hit after hit, and, like a ronin, silently takes his or her reward and moves on to the next proverbial village. There is no sentimentality and, seemingly, no reflection. It is a much easier perspective to have as you juggle the daily needs of the creative business and of your health and of your loved ones and of your personal life. It is safer to feel removed from the rhyme or reason or even impact of your work to focus on a so-called higher order of being a worker. But it just *feels* like you are extracting love from the labor. There is still a reason why you do a particular line of work.

You could be an insurance salesman because your dad was one, and even if you hate it, you still are involved because of a love or, at minimum, respect you had for your father and any impressions, however forgotten or repressed, of him while you were young doing that same work that you do today.

I realized my own history just a year ago. I was in Detroit supporting Chris Guillebeau's book *Side Hustle*, and I ended up chatting with a Michigander afterwards. He shared how his whole family had side hustles, but no one called them side hustles – I first heard the term myself in Silicon Valley around 2009. But this guy's family wouldn't say side hustle, but they would say "I know a guy…" or "Talk to Uncle Charlie, he does this thing…". "This thing…", the guy said, ended up helping his family keep food on the table. It wasn't Mafia talk or anything deep, but just relatives who were good with cars or could bake a damn tasty cake and so on. We laughed about how amazing it was, and how perceptive it was of him to realize it. Driving home, I suddenly realized he and I were one in the same: My dad has been an independent cartoonist and publisher since I was a child, my favorite uncle has owned his popular tire shop for decades along with doing a full-scale, mobile carnival ride business during the summer, and my grandfather on another branch of the family owned a series of bars and tire shops from when he was in his twenties until his death in his sixties. His son, my pop that raised me, started his own mortgage business and did quite well until wrapping up after the 2008 housing market collapse. One random day, I remember coming home from high school and seeing my pop beaming about a big check he received. He was proud, and he wanted me to be proud of him, too, though, as a teen, I could only understand so much. I didn't know, or couldn't concieve the work that went into that five-figure check, or that things were tight just the week before, or that he may have thought about giving up on that very deal, or on the business itself, when things suddenly came together.

But I understand now.

Not one of my African-American predecessors called themselves an entrepreneur. I don't recall ever hearing it come out of my family's mouth. Back then the word was still French, as in used primarily in France. And yet, it planted seeds in me, watching each and every one struggle and beam and fight and declare themselves, through action and persistence and vision, saying "I'm here to make my mark", These ideas, like me knowing what to charge the market for my services, or being able to negotiate based on some seemingly invisible service I provide, or even me knowing the value of what I bring to a world that isn't ready for it today, but will be ready for it tomorrow, I do not and cannot take full credit for that. I watched them, just like you watched others. But it was up to me to toil that soil, and that process begins with even recognizing that the seeds are there.

This is why you cheat yourself when you don't connect the dots. There is always a pattern. You may not even like the pattern, and that's ok, for you can change the pattern of your future, and no time, no matter how frustrating, is wasted time. And often, without that previous time, you wouldn't have came to this moment when you realize what you must do next. There is no one without the other.

When did you start this path? When was the first time you were paid to do what you do to pay you bills? Start at the beginning. Dig out the contract, if you have it, and see how they describe you, and how you describe your services. Is this you? Is this still you? As I said in *The Ultimate Bite-Sized Entrepreneur*, if you haven't created a new baseline for your market value, what you're worth, and how you serve in five years, then you are making decisions based on who you were five years ago. Picture my Kindergarten child holding the same values as an infant, or your 30-year-old self making the same choices as your 25-year-old self. It is ridiculous, at best. And yet, we create these magnificent, epic careers doing our thing, and do not take the time to actually see why we're doing this thing, how we are being valued for doing this thing, and what we're contributing by continually doing this thing.

Your monetary lack is a direct reflection of you not knowing the purpose. "To put food on the table" is a purpose, but that doesn't prevent you from spending 15 minutes a day working on a side hustle you really care about, or watching a YouTube video that will educate you on making your big idea a reality. But all that is unhelpful until you actually get still enough, you stop enough, you value your life enough to reflect on what you really want. To paraphrase *Pivot* author Jenny Blake, you can have the joy and the money. I would add, though, you first have to know what brings you joy. These dots, from your family, from your childhood, from your career thus far, clue you in on what brings you joy. There is a reason why you do the work you do – otherwise, you wouldn't be doing it.

Poet Mark Nepo says when we immerse ourselves into our craft, then, for that moment, we are connected to everyone else who has ever done it before. How honorable is that? You are not a struggling artist, but someone participating in the same actions, and perhaps facing the same feelings, as Michaelangelo and Picasso and O'Keefe. By doing what you are called to do, by doing what you do best, by doing what only you can do in your special way, then you are not just honoring yourself, but you are honoring those that came before you and the sacrifices they made to make your profession even valid. Edison is equal to Jobs is equal to you. This is your ancestry. They have probably felt the pain you feel now. They probably conquered it, too. That means you can as well.

It means that bringing your true power, value, and service to the table is up to you. To paraphrase James Baldwin, your crown has already been bought and paid for – often in blood. Isn't it time you wore it?

CONCLUSION
BECOME YOUR OWN PATRON

"Failure has a function: It asks you if you really want to go on making things."

Elizabeth Gilbert,
Big Magic

Well before becoming an author, or even an adult, I spent years studying esoteric histories. I was fascinated by astrology and astronomy, Tarot and crystal balls, and Jungian arguments and Hero's Journey theories. People often described me as a laidback, light-hearted kid, but internally I was, and still am, fascinated by the shadow, the parts that we don't know of ourselves. As a late teen, *The Complete Jung* and the *Classical Mythology* textbook were regular, comfort reading.

In one non-fiction book, I read about highly-spiritual monks investigating potentially dangerous religious areas. It may have been a temple thought cursed by a dark entity, or a church that needed to be blessed by a grounded, focused force like themselves.

The monks, however powerful, never go it alone, though.

Instead, one brave monk leads the group into the dangerous area. The other members begin tying a rope tightly around the waist of the leader and then, ever so carefully, cinching their hands around the lagging rope and bracing themselves as the leader opened the door. They remain outside as the brave monk goes inside.

The theory is this: If things get out of hand, then the group pulls the lead monk back to safety. He had an out. And the monk felt more free to explore, as he knew he could be pulled out of a jam.

He relaxed.

From my reading, this is why certain monk sects to this day still wear frayed ropes around their cloth. It's not just practical to keep their loincloth intact, but a subtle reminder that they are always protected by the group. They are never lost. They are alone, but never abandoned.

CB80

As I'm finishing this book, on New Year's Eve 2018, I feel the weight, not the levity, of my progress. The pieces don't feel like they are coming together or, more accurately, the parts are not coming together as quickly as I want or need them to be. It is one thing to not be sure what needs to be done. It is quite another to not be sure if you have the capacity to make the journey.

It is in these moment you have to become your own energy source. No one cares about your particular mission, desire, or impact as much as you do. Recently, an entrepreneur confessed her frustration not finding employees as passionate as she was about her business. She will probably always be frustrated, as she will never find someone as passionate as she is – otherwise, they'd be starting their own business. Your momma, your partner, and your advocates hopefully have your back. You need to man the front.

Moments like my New Year's Eve will always happen to you. They remind you that you are the ancient monk, in your new, dangerous, highly spiritual place, and you are alone. You are always alone.

Your safety rope is your own awareness.

Sometimes others won't treat you at your true worth, often because they are holding more financial or veto power and abusing the imbalance. You need to build great partnerships not just based on the needs of the money or of the ego, but on how positive you feel working with the other. That positive feeling will naturally create creative, emotional, and potentially financial prosperity. Everything starts with a feeling. The energy from the feeling opens up the new opportunities.

Sometimes the ends will not meet. The resources you get from a beautifully-done endeavor may be a great contact for future ideas, a cool story to tell people later, or a brilliant vision of what could be next for you. In the meantime, get your bread. There is no shame in that. I love Elizabeth Gilbert's take, in *Big Magic*, about keeping a day job for years after becoming a professional writer, saying "I was always willing to work hard so my creativity could play lightly, and, in so doing, I became my own patron."

And sometimes, the world won't seem to see your purpose. The worst way to create is to say you want your thing to be embraced by the world. It is too earnest. You open the door to grandstanding and preaching. And what if your thing isn't embraced by the world? The bitterness will leach from your skin, and others will probably sense your resistance even before you give them the thing, as they recognize it in you when you share the idea and they don't have an immediately positive reaction. Instead of being embraced by the world, how do you want to transform one person? Literally, just one. Make the goal of serving one and, when you do make an impact, your appreciation will shine and nourish you when you have those dark, cold nights.

All successes are based on quantum leaps, be it having a fabulous business partnership, a highly profitable business, or a true appreciation by the world. It isn't there, then it is. You don't know when the switch will flip. As Deepak Chopra says, "When and where will bubbles appear in a pot of boiling water?" It is binary, and sudden, and unpredictable. We know that it *will* happen, though, providing we keep the pot on a consistent source.

Understanding your creative power, value, and service is your consistant source, your monk's rope, your allies on this journey. It is the ouroboros, the mythological snake eating its own tail. It is nourished forever. Imagine never retiring, not because you need to work to live, but because you live to work. You live to serve. You feed it, and then it feeds you. Forever.

Your job, then, isn't to predict the leap to success, nor to wait for success before you begin. Your job is to serve, and in serving, your true worth will always come to you.

It begins when you bring your worth to the table.

It begins with you.

BOOK III:
BUILD FROM NOW
HOW TO KNOW YOUR POWER, SEE YOUR ABUNDANCE & NOURISH THE WORLD

That which we do not bring to consciousness appears in our lives as fate.

Carl Jung

I
AN OUTSIDE JOB

THE LOW END OF THE SOUP BOWL

The function, the very serious function of racism is distraction. It keeps you from doing your work. It keeps you explaining, over and over again, your reason for being.

Toni Morrison

Your 24 hours a day are not the same as mine.

There are headwinds that push against us. They are invisible, pervasive, and constant. Like air. They wrap around us and try to hold us tight. They want our resources. They want our strength. They want to keep us where we are.

The headwinds are as man-made as Hurricane Katrina. The storm was happenstance. The slipshod levee system is what created the damage. The barriers were made for cheap to better line government pockets. They were considered less consequential because the breach threatened poor, minority communities the most. Leadership already knew about the levee danger when I lived in my New Orleans apartment, as I biked thorough the nearby, beautiful 9th ward, eating, drinking, and bonding with the local artist community who had been there since Napoleon's troops stomped through.

This systemic neglect was a conscious choice. Certain people and their culturally-rich resources held less value than other neighborhoods and their populations. Therefore, they were starved of additional resources, such as peace of mind. It remains expensive to be poor. As I lived there in the year leading up to Katrina, literally everyone I met damn well knew we were in danger. "We are in a soup bowl," they'd tell me again and again. The French Quarter loomed as a raised lump in the middle. The upper-crust Garden District stood protected, too. The rest was fucked. How much extra effort does it take to do to, well, *anything*, if you know you're already fucked?

Nature designed New Orleans. Systemic choices designed the headwinds.

Not all headwinds are some natural phenomenon. Women are not born inferior leaders; in fact, New Zealand, Germany, and the handful of women-lead countries showed amazing guidance and smart containment during the 2020 coronavirus pandemic. Minorities are not naturally less-educated; recent studies show diverse C-suite leadership means better profits for businesses. And LGBTQ people are not culturally unsound;

non-heteronormative-led family households create an environment as stable as, and often even more stable than heteronormative-led homes (Remember the oft-cited high American divorce rate was established well before gay marriage became legal. That's on straight people.).

These headwinds are formed by prejudice, guided with malice, and protected and maintained by systems. In Silicon Valley, they called it "pattern matching." Walk into a venture capitalist investor office looking like a young, straight white male, both cocky and antisocial, wearing a well-worn hoodie and ripped jeans, and freshly dropped out of an Ivy League school. As such, you look like you're cut from the same cloth as Mark Zuckerberg, Elon Musk, and the late patron saint of Silicon Valley, Steve Jobs. You don't need to keep explaining your reason for being. You don't need to allocate your precious resources to proving why you *belong* in the room. You can just be the best at what you do – and walk into the room. That's enough.

I founded my first startup in 2014 in San Diego, shortly after living as a tech journalist and author in Silicon Valley. It's not an exaggeration to say I was one degree away from all the active black founders in San Francisco. This culture was small and rich. We'd meet informally every Wednesday at our favorite watering hole. My friends, colleagues, and I would meet to share stories, support each other, and seed potential collaborations for the future.

In a CNN interview at the time, Silicon Valley tastemaker and TechCrunch founder Michael Arrington said, "I don't know any black founders." When pressed further, he said, "There's a guy, actually, his last company just launched at our event [TechCrunch Disrupt], and he's African American... But he could've launched a clown show onstage, and I would've put him up there, absolutely."

Ironically, as journalist Violet Blue wrote at the time, that *guy* was Clarence Wooten, whom sold his company, ImageCafe, for millions in 1999, well before Arrington and TechCrunch were even known quantities.

But Wooten didn't pattern match.

Since then, the number of black founders has grown considerably. Still, though, we get less than two percent of Silicon Valley investment. And that's now. Not ten years ago.

Today, they call it "culture fit." You don't match the pattern of those of us already in the room, so we do not trust the worth you bring to the table. You don't seem to culturally identify with what we've experienced, so we do not see the value of your contribution.

The pendulum swings from explaining your reason for being to proving you actually belong in the room beyond the scope of other's limited view of you.

If you don't match the pattern, if you don't fit the culture, then you are paying a resource tax. It is invisible, pervasive, and constant. Like air.

When I say I bootstrapped my two startups (building them from scratch with no outside investment) and sold the second one at a profit, it means something different as a thirty-something African-American stay-at-home dad with two college degrees. I paid and still pay a resource tax – a cut taken right off the top, like FICA and Social Security – before I even show up. It is remaining focused as people who look just like me are killed in front of their children on camera, their soul trapped eternally in a hashtag. It is adapting as the opportunities for myself and people like me narrow within an increasingly corrupt system. It is maximizing time as I untie emotional trauma passed down from generation to generation, cleansing my soul of unconscious biases to not cap my own two black and brown sons. It is finding energy as I fight against what others believe are my limitations simply because of who I culturally am.

Chances are, your 24 hours a day are not the same as mine.

This is also why believing you can accomplish as much in 24 hours as any said celebrity will corrode you like rust. Rust cannot begin on the outside. Rust always starts on the inside. The crack in your own worth lets the productivity virus in. The compare and contrast will drive you into the ground.

Where our resources need to go matters as much as how many resources we need. It is pure mathematics: for the average American, making $100,000 annually would be enough for a comfortable life (the average American household brings in around $60,000). But what if you live in San Francisco, where, when I was there in the late aughts, I paid four-figures for a tiny studio? Or if you were plowing through hundreds of thousands of dollars of debt, where the interest alone would be your monthly take-home pay? Or if you had family, friends, and loved ones dependent on your paycheck because of systematic circumstances beyond their and your immediate control?

Money is the most tangible example, but, of course, I'm not really talking about money.

I'm talking about weight.

There is a mental, physical, and emotional weight we carry when we face an undiagnosed health issue, when we feel guilt for a taking a sorely-needed break because of required responsibilities, and when we struggle with not reaching our potential because of on our seemingly too limited resources.

But to give yourself grace, you first have to recognize the battle.

Systematic oppression hums along in the background like an air conditioner. It is on when you enter the room and, after an almost imperceptible adjustment, its buzzing in the background becomes the norm. (Now, imagine if you are born in the air-conditioned room.) You fight to block out the noise. You work twice as hard to progress half as far. You don't see this resource tax. You are just used to paying it.

But what if the air conditioning suddenly turns off, as it did for all of us in March 2020? We realize how loud we had been talking just to be heard, how distracting the noise had been to our focus, and how much long-term planning we gave away just to get through the day.

"As I make my suffering conscious, less is passed on to others," says spiritualist Chani Nicholas. "As I come to understand what was personal, what was systemic, and what was familial, I get closer to the truth; I am more than what hurts, but I am not above being taught by the process of pain relief."

We're angry at 2020, not because it is a bad year, but because it has woken many of us up from a long slumber. We realize how autocratic our democracy really can be. We realize the system will automatically continue to chew up and spit out black and brown lives, even as we sleep peacefully in our own homes. We realize how quickly our financial security can be shredded to pieces, as if we're sitting in the low end of a soup bowl.

We realize how long we've been fighting upstream every day. But the river isn't directed by nature, but by man.

Which means we can change it.

SALMON

By default, you bring your previous system with you to the next experience.

Esther Perel,
Steal the Show with Michael Port

We believe our personal GPS is broken. We don't trust it anymore.

We think we're asking for too much, when we have hardly been compensated enough. We feel like we're being extra or unreasonable fighting for basic rights, when others don't have to validate their existence at all. We feel like we just need to work harder, when we see others moving forward faster seemingly with ease.

We often move against our instincts even when, especially when, the world itself is upside down.

Women have been labeled naturally giving and self-sacrificing. This so-called compliment sets the expectation that they should be happy to put themselves last, not have their needs fulfilled, and accept having their credit taken for brilliant ideas. It isn't a mistake: white women still make 78 cents on the dollar compared to white men in the same job, and black and brown women are closer to half a dollar to that same dollar. That resource tax is passed on to the very corporations that employ them. Literally pennies paid on the dollar.

The LGBTQ community may get married, but doesn't have the rights to have anal sex in many states, even if it may be a part of adult intimacy. Black people may legally have a gun permit, but will still get shot by the police for having a firearm, as Minnesotan Philando Castile was in front of his young daughter in 2016.

We are traveling upstream. Even when we lean in, even when we follow the rules, even when we are being a "good citizen." Even when we are told and believe that we'll do better when we do better.

We are traveling upstream simply based on who we are.

The secret is we may be more prepared to nourish the world than the dominating voices.

You are ready for the more equitable world. This has all been training for you to usher it in.

"We have to look at it with the mindset that we're equal. Shit, we're not only equal, but we had to live at the bottom. There are parts of us that are superior because we've had to live underwater damn near and we can hold our breath longer than you," comedian Chris Rock said on *The Daily Show*.

I come from a long line of hustlers. My father as well as my stepfather (whom I call Pop) are freelancers and entrepreneurs, as is my closest uncle. My Pop's dad was an entrepreneur, too. But my grandfather never subscribed to *Inc. Magazine*, my father never sat me down to talk independence, nor did my stepfather say he was an entrepreneur. As I share in *Bring Your Worth*, "Not one of my African-American predecessors called themselves an entrepreneur. I don't recall ever hearing it come out of my family's mouth." No, my grandfather, born in North Carolina in the thirties, began opening his own speakeasies likely because he and his people weren't comfortable, or even welcome, in the white bars. My father became an independent artist after he realized corporations would steal his ideas while simultaneously downplaying his contribution in ways not seen with his counterparts. My Pop launched his own mortgage company when he accepted that his white partners would never share equity based on his work.

They discovered the resource tax – the bifurcated focus between who they were and how they were perceived, the adapting from their cultural needs to conforming just to operate in mainstream white America, the time spent building their own insights and proving why it matters to those in charge, and the energy being true to their vision while being blocked from expressing it. It was an additional layer of friction, a resource tax they ponied up as soon as they showed up as themselves.

And, one day, they decided to stop paying it.

The cost were conditional relationships, perceived security, and stable money. The reward was freedom.

Award-winning filmmaker Ava DuVarnay put it like this: "My truth is I don't want a chair at the table. Or even three or even half anymore. I want the table rebuilt. In my likeness. And in the likeness of others long forced out of the room."

We go upstream because we are fighting for a seat at the table. We go upstream because we want validation. We go upstream because we want to blend in.

But you weren't meant to blend in. You were meant to rebuild. Otherwise, why are you here?

"Sometimes it gets exhausting. Sometimes it doesn't feel fair. But the idea that you would just stop and give up is something that would be a betrayal to our ancestors." Barack Obama said in a recent interview. "The sacrifices [our ancestors] made did, in fact, make a difference. There is greater power, greater freedom, greater representation. This idea that somehow no progress has been made is mistaken. So, we have an obligation to do all the work now to make sure that our grandkids fifty years from now, they look back and they say, 'Y'all had to put up with that?' And the reason they won't is because we did the work."

We can have intense, often overwhelming clarity on the work ahead, but it can take us a while to recognize the work done by our predecessors before we got here. Like a child discovering something new and believing she is the first to find it, we don't always see that people have walked the path we're on. They may have made our path clearer. Without them, the path may not even exist.

As I share in *Bring Your Worth*, it took me decades to realize my lineage "planted seeds in me, watching each and every one struggle and beam and fight and declare themselves, through action and persistence and vision, saying 'I'm here to make my mark'. These ideas, like me knowing what to charge the market for my services, or being able to negotiate based on some seemingly invisible service I provide, or even me knowing the value of what I bring to a world that isn't ready for it today, but will be ready for it tomorrow, I do not and cannot take full credit for that. I watched them, just like you watched others. "

"When a young person tells his parents, 'This is my body; this is my life. I can do what I want with it' he is only partly right,' Buddhist monk Thich Nhat Hanh says in *No Mud, No Lotus*. 'He doesn't see that he is a continuation of his parents and of his ancestor before that. This body is not yours alone. It is also the body of your ancestors. Your body is a collective product of your nation, of your people, of your culture, of your ancestors. So you are not strictly an individual. You are partly collective... Even if you don't have a regular interpersonal relationship with your parents or your ancestors, your body and mind contain their suffering and their hopes as well as your own."

If you do not fit the straight old white male norm, then you are essentially multilingual. The more culture norms from which you deviate, the more languages you know. (In my community we call it "code switching", or using different words and dialects based on the culture you're trying to navigate. Proper English in the boardroom, while casual slang among friends.) These dimensions reflect your potential cultural impact. They are like sides of a die, different parts of your cultural depth, but all represented at once, and all representing you. And, just like my long-dormant New Jersey accent surfacing whenever I get excited, they are ever present. You bring your blackness to work. You take your queerness into every business relationship. You carry the femininity or masculinity you identify with into every room. It doesn't matter if other people acknowledge, identify, or respect it. This richness creates an abundance of insight, a well of strength, and a security of identity unavailable from the outside world. To paraphrase Julia Cameron, it is your vein of gold.

Mainstream America suffers because these other dimensions are being undervalued, underfunded, and otherwise dismissed. As DuVarney says, leadership has succeeded in keeping diverse voices from having a seat at the table. While living in Silicon Valley, my close friends, colleagues, and associates bootstrapped YouTube, Dropbox, and other companies that would eventually change the world. Before 2005, independent creators could not build their own following and needed to appease gatekeepers on the radio or on the television. Before 2008, it was impossible to do your hard work on one device and seamlessly keep doing work on another device, and now you could create without being tethered to a laptop, an office, or even a continent. But I was there: the establishment initially thought their ideas were crazy, or unrealistic, or impractical. The people at the table couldn't read the cultural vision. The cosigns from companies like Google, or the support from startup accelerators like Y-Combinator, would come well after they created power from their own viewpoint. In their own image. In other words, they shifted the point of power by building from now. They were the vanguard.

But more than a decade later, those investments and that support have become even scarcer. Most Silicon Valley-funded startups are led by white male founders, followed by Asian males.

Their pattern matching worked. Their culture fit is accurate. But it comes at what cost?

In Summer 2020, Donald Trump signed an executive order to ban TikTok. The short-video app had grown exponentially in users within a few short years. Facebook, LinkedIn, and Instagram started cloning its bite-sized content strategy, to the point where TikTok users would just slap their content onto Instagram – TikTok logo in the corner and all. It was so powerful, TikTokers systematically organized to buy free tickets to Trump's Oklahoma City rally – and then didn't show up, leaving potentially thousands of seats empty. The rally was a bust. Within a week, Trump said the app needed to be banned.

What was Trump's argument? The most powerful app in recent memory was not made in Silicon Valley. It was made in China.

What happened to the innovation? In America, everyone in power is looking at the same side of the die. It is the equivalent of neighborhood gentrification: the counterculture makes something out of nothing, the hipper mainstream kids pick up on it and share it with the masses, the masses absorb this cultural vision while intentionally or unintentionally pricing the counterculture out.

The price could be access to capital to make the vision real, the price could be being privileged enough to not have your contributions undervalued, the price could be being allowed to move forward because of the color of your skin, whom you prefer to sleep with, or where you are from.

And once the pattern matching is complete, and the cultural fit is executed, then the new leaders wonder where the magic went. Remember when this neighborhood was gritty? Remember when it had flavor? Remember the soul it had? They don't realize that the magic is in the diversity.

"We are culture," Jay-Z says. "Nothing moves without us."

What Jay-Z is saying, what DuVarnay is saying, what established creative are saying, is that we have the special sauce. We can and should be creating our own table. Technology affords us the power to share our music with the world *for free*, to telegraph our vision live to the entire planet *for free*, and to establish our own worth with our own community *for free*.

They don't have anything for us but a co-sign from a dying worldview.

Eventually, they will understand the power of your cultural capital. It may happen today. It may happen later in your career. It may happen well after you are dead.

Waiting for validation is a fool's errand, though. For every Watson and Crick, there stands a Rosalind Franklin. For every Jack Daniels, there is an Uncle Nearest. For every person, institution, or system that holds the validation you seek, there is an individual who gave their cultural capital to it and was simultaneously absorbed into and erased by them. Because on some level they immediately recognize and are afraid of your power. It is like a pig being eager to get to the slaughter so their value will finally be validated.

"Everyone has a voice in their head, and every one of those voices is different," Godin says in

The Practice. "Our experiences and dreams and fears are unique, and we shape the discourse by allowing those ideas to be shared. It might not work. But only you have your distinct voice, and hoarding it is toxic."

When we wait for the mainstream co-sign – the nod from a major influencer, the backing of an established entity, the acceptance into an exclusive club - and don't get it, it's not just depriving the culture at large. It is toxic to ourselves when we don't share it.

We automatically devalue our worth when we don't stand on our own.

"This wanting to be part of something, though, is bullshit," Chris Rock says. "Jackie Robinson got to play baseball, that's a great thing? No, those motherfuckers got to play with *him*! And you realize, when Jackie Robinson got to play baseball, it destroyed the Negro League – some of the only Black businessmen who were making real capital at the time. [It's about] having a stake in your own future."

You may ask yourself why you are so tired. For many of us, we have been creating what fashion icon Dapper Dan calls a parallel universe. The eighties legend handmade clothes worn by Mike Tyson, LL Cool J, and other New York elite by sewing together bootleg logos fashionable at the time. At his peak, Dapper Dan was raided, sued, and shut down. In a recent interview, he said traditional fashion business avenues weren't available to him.

"I entered the industry through retailing, but they denied me the right to buy luxury goods to sell. So I had no alternative, but to be creative on my own. I took a look at how we addressed this matter in history. So what I created was an 'alternative parallel universe'. If I can't be in their universe, I [will] create a universe of my own."

Decades later, in 2017, Dapper Dan was brought in to launch a fashion line – for Gucci. Their reputation wasn't as cool as it once was. It needed a boost.

We have to contribute, whether we bring our worth to the current systems or, as myself and my ancestors before me have done, create our own systems in our own likeness. As technology grows and the world gets smaller, we have more opportunities to do the latter than ever in history.

"Whenever I speak to young guy or gals with this frustration, what I say to them is, 'Don't let the frustration turn into cynicism where you just think nothing can change.' Because the truth is, things have changed. It's just that it's an ongoing battle. It is not just a one-shot deal where you kind of climb the mountain and you just stay there," Barack Obama said in an interview. "The roots of racism in this country are deep, the psychology of it has lessened, but it never fully went away, the legacy of slavery and Jim Crow means that we started the race behind with respect to the resources in our communities, the way the criminal justice system was set up, the lack of representation in corporate America. All those things didn't just go away: They built up over 400 years, and they weren't just going to go away in just 50 years, let's say, my lifetime. You can expect that each time we took two steps forward, there was going to be some pushback, because there are forces within our society that don't want to give up status and privilege. They don't want a level playing field. By the way, that's not just true for African Americans."

"Not just true for African-Americans" means people of color, folks in the LGBTQ community, the neurodiverse, and the physically different. It is anyone who can check a box that represents "Other". But now, more than ever, being the "Other" is becoming the norm. Which means your voice is necessary to represent not just you, but others within your distinct community.

Bringing your worth means recognizing that, under the veneer of toxic capitalism and xenophobic myopia, your power is equal to their power, and that everything is a partnership. It means not waiting for permission to envision, create, and nourish the world, especially when others don't see it, as that vision initially belongs only to you. And it means knowing that your fight against racism, sexism, and other isms, has turned you and your people, with you and before you, more focused, agile, efficient, and resilient, in ways that you would be remiss to not honor. If anything, the suppressions of the past have only better prepared you to lead in the future. And the future is now.

This is true even for some of the people holding on to the edifice of power. Staying in the room often means showing only the parts of you that match the culture. Keeping your seat of power usually means you aren't bringing your whole self to the table. Your privilege can become your cage. It's ultimately up to you to set yourself free.

"It was up to me to toil that soil, and that process begins with even recognizing that the seeds are there," I say in *Bring Your Worth*.

Externally, you can reach your audience, make your own money, and bring your own worth.

The first battleground, though, remains an internal one.

YOUR SYSTEM IS THE LOCK AND THE KEY

One dollar from your own system is worth a thousand dollars of another man's system.

John Henry,
Earn Your Leisure Podcast

Shame and guilt often walk hand-in-hand with your output of the day, the hour, or even the minute. To paraphrase Brene Brown, shame is when you feel like you aren't meeting the expectations of others, while guilt is when you feel like you aren't meeting the expectations of yourself. Both are intertwined, as you can internalize society's expectations of you and take it on as your own.

It wasn't always this way. For centuries, the main measurement of your worth was how your craft provided for yourself and your family. The concept of hustling every day wasn't a badge of honor – it was just something everyone did. The axiom "I'll sleep when I'm dead" wasn't a point of pride. If you were an early-to-rise farmer, hard-working craftsperson, or what in modern terms we'd call a day laborer, then you didn't have much time to sleep anyway.

You just did your job based on the resources you had at the moment.

Our biggest hurdle today isn't finding the right hack to more output, but realizing that accepting our limitations actually improves our results.

Years ago, my family and I went to Italy and ate our way through several cities, each meal seemingly better than the last. The food tasted both simple and rich. When we asked about the meal, even at most humble location, they would unfailingly say that the pasta was made in house, the wine harvested from the next door neighbor's vineyard, the fish caught by the locals this morning, and so on. It was odd coming back home, going out in our charming San Diego neighborhood, and paying a premium to have what we Americans call the "farm-to-table" experience. It was strange because we were paying extra to have an establishment maximize our experience with the local resources at the moment. Why does nearly every Venetian restaurant serve squid? Because Venice is surrounded by water. It is also why they don't serve a lot of chicken or beef. The restaurateurs respect their offerings and, because of the limitations, actually master the resources' they've got, honoring both the land and the customers they serve.

In conversations with hundreds, if not thousands of creatives over the years, I see many of us landlocked looking for fish. It is the new parent trying to find time to be creative. It is the senior citizen pushing to do all-nighters. It is the 9-to-5-ers believing the only way they'll have the energy to pursue their dream is to immediately quit the day job. We are not honoring where we are, who we are, and what we've got in this moment.

The problem is we mistake productivity, which is one of the most loaded words in modern history, with effectiveness, which is based on your own particular goals, resources, and abilities.

On productivity, the word has been redefined in ways that don't fit strong personal health, well being, or even output. It wasn't always this way. As recently as 2016, I published *The Productive Bite-Sized Entrepreneur*, on how you can maximize your time without burning yourself out. The operative word here is "your." Not how you can maximize the organization's time, the government's time or, more broadly, society's time. Your time. Being productive should be based on your own criteria. Thus, the personal productivity goals and expectations of, say, a 75-year-old retiree will likely be different than that of a 25-year-old grad student. Unfortunately, society's ruler of measurement is often the same. Check the ever-popular magazine cover stories featuring the next young, sort-of-proven entrepreneurial prodigy – like the now-disgraced Theranos founder Elizabeth Holmes – or celebrating how much venture capitalist money a startup got – even though, to paraphrase Shark Tank investor Mark Cuban says, you are essentially leveraging against your future.

"There are plenty of '30 Under 30' lists. I recommend '40 Over 40' and '50 Over 50.' And when we do that, let's celebrate the older people who are working and the older people who aren't working. Showcase this amazing talent that can then be hired instantly," says 60-year-old Make Love Not Porn founder Cindy Gallop. An ad industry veteran, Gallop wants us to question why we hold certain metrics dear and totally disregard others. "If you're told that the target is youth and millennials, ask why. My industry plays a powerful role in shaping the way people think and behave. Here is a way we can use this power for good. When we make age aspirational in advertising, we make age aspirational in real life."

The fact is your strengths – the powers you draw on to be an effective leader, citizen, or creator – will change depending on your circumstances. These changes can be slow, or these changes can be rapid. They are based on where you are in your life.

Our lives are like the grooves of a vinyl record. They begin smooth and impressionable, like a black acetate. Over time, the feedback of our environment and the call of our needs create habits. The needle falls into the groove, making the patterns more ingrained. Even when we direct the needle elsewhere, it naturally falls from the peak into the comfortable valley.

What we often forget is that our best grooves are ever changing. These grooves are animated, ebbing and flowing based on where we are and who we are. They are far from static. They are alive.

I call them the F.A.T.E.s: FOCUS, AGILITY, TIME, and ENERGY. These resources are our life force, neverending until we end. They are life itself.

Anthropomorphizing them helps us realize that they, truly, are not under our control. If you are hoping to will yourself to have incredible FOCUS, to become super AGILE, to make more TIME, or to have unstoppable ENERGY, then I have some bad news for you! Just as an octogenarian, no matter how fit, cannot match the ENERGY of a healthy teenager, we should not expect to will our best resources into some pretzel knot of power. In fact, most of our power gets wasted in trying to either utilize the same resource – or FATE – we had in abundance before that we no longer have now, or to make ourselves master a resource we have very little of now in hopes of it becoming our main resource tomorrow.

This remains wishful thinking at best.

Instead, you can look at these resources like levers: they aren't absolutes, and they operate independently of each other. You may have a brief period where all four are at their peak.

More often, though, one trait will run be particularly high and at least one particularly low.

Mastery isn't about keeping all four at their peak. This thinking is unrealistic, if not unhealthy. For example, surviving a serious health procedure or trauma and immediately pushing to maximize your ENERGY doesn't make much sense at all. You need space to heal, so perhaps TIME becomes one of your activated powers.

Instead, the goal here is to maximize whatever phase you are in your life. Each lever possesses its own different strengths and attributes.

If you are hyper-FOCUSED, then your view should be on big picture thinking. It's possible to be so myopic that you succeed at one narrow goal, but you miss out on the bigger win.

If you are super AGILE, then you should hone your consistency. Being flexible can become a weakness without having a set plan or commitment.

If you have ample TIME, then your main challenge is, as business leader Adam Grant calls it, attention management. The more TIME you have, the bigger danger you have of wasting it.

Lastly, if you have an abundance of ENERGY, then your main challenge is goal management. It is easy to waste plenty of ENERGY pursuing the wrong milestone.

Perhaps the biggest challenge in understanding your strengths is acknowledging what you *don't* have in your toolbox. This requires vulnerability. You may not have the ENERGY to help someone move their furniture or to help them fight their fight, but you might have the time to listen to them and give them the encouragement they need to fight that fight or to just move that furniture. You might not be able to physically be at an event for them because of previous commitments, but you can show up in another important room entirely and make sure their name is mentioned. You could miss the opportunity to be for someone at that moment, but you can show them in other ways that you care as much as do. You may not be able to take on their burden, but you can connect them with someone else who may help carry the load. It is being vulnerable enough to say, "I can't do that," or "It is not possible." It is learning to say "No".

When we show up no matter what, then deny our emotional, physical, and mental boundaries, and we go going upstream when we really should be acknowledging our current moment. The ego gets involved when we worry about our limitations: we're having a hard time focusing, so we beat ourselves up about procrastination, or circumstances give us a blank slate to work with, and we get mad about not being sure what to do with the sudden time we have on our hands. Instead, we have the opportunity to recognize our versatile, curious mind of the moment, or to honor our rare chance to do things at our own pace. But first, we have to understand, acknowledge, and accept our boundaries of the moment.

If you do happen to be hyper-FOCUSED, super AGILE, TIME abundant, and extra ENERGETIC at the moment, then that balance will likely last for quite literally that: a moment. Balance doesn't mean all cylinders going. Balance means knowing the strengths of your current life, embracing your place, and leaning into your flow. Balance means your abundance parallels your lack, and knowing that the cycle can and will change in the future based on the past. Balance means creating where you naturally rise, like a river automatically finding the subtle cracks in the basin created before the drought. You don't worry about the strengths you don't have for the moment, as you know, as long as you breathe, life can shift at any time and change where your abundance lies.

"There are people and organizations in our lives that we trust. How did that happen? We develop trust over time," Seth Godin says in *The Practice*. "Our interactions lead to expectations, and those expectations, repeated and supported, turn into trust. These organizations and people earn trust by coming through in the difficult moments. They're not perfect; in fact, the way they deal with imperfection is precisely why we trust them. We can do the same thing to (and with) ourselves. As we engage in the practice, we begin to trust the practice. Not that it will produce the desired outcome each time, but simply that it's our best available option. Trust earns you patience, because once you trust yourself, you can stick with a practice that most people can't handle."

Your purpose isn't to make things happen. Your purpose is to recognize the best timing to create. Part of that timing is based on how you create in the first place.

Your current strengths represent this timing. Your current strengths represent the fates.

Here's how you can embrace them.

UNDERSTANDING THE FATES

According to the creation story in the biblical book of Genesis, God said, "Let there be light." I like to imagine that light replied, saying "God, I have to wait for my twin brother, darkness, to be with me. I can't be there without the darkness." God asked, "Why do you need to wait? Darkness is there." Light answered, "In that case, then I am also already there."

*Thich Nhat Hanh,
No Mud, No Lotus*

In my research, I've found the very ways to maximize your biggest resources also match how you can best compensate for your lowest resources. For instance, if you have an abundance of TIME, then you can maximize it by setting clear, definitive boundaries and strong, strategic goal setting. How do you handle things when TIME is scarce? Set clear, definitive boundaries and do strong, strategic goal setting. As Wharton professor Adam Grant says, it's not about time management, but attention management, and we can use that whether we have a bunch of time or not much time to spare. They present different sides of the same coin.

Some guidance books recommend taking the knowledge specific to you and reading that chapter. This isn't one of those books. In fact, that would be a mistake. Your resources aren't monolithic.

We all have the ability to FOCUS, to be AGILE, to maximize TIME, and to use ENERGY. We do until the day we die. So each one of these resources are immediately relevant to you. They all are. Stories, examples, analogies, and contrasts between the different resources are woven throughout.

My recommendation? Read the book, *then* do the quiz in the back of the book or, even better, online at www.buildfromnowquiz.com. You'll be able to get a feel for different resources, which is important because your primary resource today is based on personal and professional circumstances that will likely change tomorrow. Remember, your resources are not fixed. If you take the quiz post-reading, you could be pleasantly surprised, too.

The veil between you and your subconscious self thin when you have an intense, life-relevant experience. A messy divorce, a painful funeral, or a child's birth don't automatically cause reinvention; two people may have the same experience, but one may seem unchanged, while the other utterly transformed.

Usually, though, the veil is too thick for us to be objective. Through reading this, I want us to slow down enough to see the patterns, feel the pain, and respect our past and present enough

420

to acknowledge our best strengths and limitations.

Your dominant resource represents what classic business theorist Chris Argyris calls your Ladder of Inference.

We go through five steps when we get new information:

- we select the data relevant to us;
- we paraphrase the data in language we understand;
- we label the data to describe what we believe is happening;
- we explain or evaluable what's happening;
- and we decide what to do.

Then we do it.

This would be less important if we looked at every experience in a fresh light. But we don't. We begin to see what we believe and experience things in ways that confirm the world to be.

This phenomenon plays into our FATEs. It is why we will keep doing all-nighters (ENERGY as our primary resource) even though we're way past a point in our life when it makes sense; It may be more efficient and comfortable stretching the deadline (TIME as our primary resource), but we're locked in the habit.

There are a few things at work here.

First, we have "confirmation bias", which means we're more likely to accept data that fits our world view and, frankly, our ego. We like *feeling* right more than actually *being* right. It gives us security. "We have millions of questions that need answers because there are so many things that the reasoning mind cannot explain. It is not important if the answer is correct; just the answer itself makes us feel safe. This is why we make assumptions," Don Miguel Ruiz says in *The Four Agreements*.

We can be so eager to create a narrative, we tell ourselves a story and commit to it before we even have all the important details. In *Rising Strong*, Brene Brown says about how storytelling could also be our downfall: "We're wired for story and in the absence of data we will rely on confabulations and conspiracies.... More information means less fear-based story-making." Filling in the blanks gives us comfort, not clarity.

Second, the more you think about something, the more likely you'll see it. For instance, if you worry about your ability to maximize your TIME, then you're more likely to be paralyzed when you have to decide what to do with it – and then end up wasting your TIME, confirming your own theory. Theorists call it the Baader-Meinhof phenomenon. (Pop culturalists call it The Streisand Theory, named after the singer who sued to get pictures of her secluded mansion off the web – and ended up drawing attention to pictures of her secluded mansion on the web.)

I talk about the Baader-Meinhof/Streisand trap in *The Ultimate Bite-Sized Entrepreneur*:

And we can totally Streisand our flaws: Focus on your weaknesses and you will see more and more of your flaws in your work and your life. Unfortunately, this will make you more likely to beat yourself up for minor mistakes and you may even emphasize your weak spots to potential coworkers or clients rather than highlighting your capabilities. There is little constructive that can come from blowing up your issues – and there's nothing you can do with the little information gained.

Third, Argyris' Ladder of Inference theory is the equivalent of an online "filter bubble", as your options begin to feel narrower and narrower because the framework is built to give you more of the same. Your mind works like a modern Internet browser, website, or social media platform: You liked this message from McDonalds? Well, let's show you an ad from Burger King, Wendy's and Jack In The Box. You bought this crib? Well, let's suggest you buy baby bottles, rompers, and a car seat.

And you like being AGILE? Makes you feel at your best? Feeds your ego, too? Well, we'll keep putting you in situations where you have to adjust at the last minute. Let's keep you feeling good.

The Ladder of Inference calls it a "reflexive loop" and it can have you leaning on a particular resource for unhealthy reasons:

Our assumptions, values, and beliefs influence how we select data, interpret what is happening, and decide what to do. Our interpretations and decisions then feedback to reinforce (usually) our assumptions, values, and beliefs. We act on the basis of our interpretations, and our actions affect what data is available to us. So our ways of understanding and acting in the world create a self-reinforcing system, insulating us from alternative ways of understanding.

As you look into your resources, do not believe one particular strength is the answer. Focus, AGILITY, TIME, and ENERGY are all necessary for you to make any sort of impact on the world.

More importantly, partnering and respecting the different dimensions of you – of all of us – raises the bar for all. If you lean into Focus, then you will be totally sure when you have to be AGILE, make the most of your TIME, and have your ENERGY be concentrated on only the most important goals. If you embrace AGILITY, then you won't FOCUS on ideas that no longer serve you, be less likely to waste TIME mourning the past, and know quickly what goals give you the most ENERGY. If you understand TIME, then you can FOCUS on the long-term, be AGILE enough to adjust to the culture, and build disciplined, consistent ENERGY. And if you respect ENERGY, then you can bring serious FOCUS, keep your passion even as you are AGILE, and make the biggest impact with your TIME.

You have a dominant resource, but it is never your only resource.

Your resource is the filter to your world. As the saying goes, if you have a hammer, then everything is a nail. But the most dangerous thing is not knowing you're using a hammer at all.

II
AN INSIDE JOB

HOW TO PARTNER WITH FOCUS

Your power is not measured by how many opportunities you can get. Your power is measured by what you have the ability to turn down... You have so much power, that [the opportunity] doesn't make sense to you.

Julian Mitchell,
The Business Behind Music and Culture
with John Henry

My dad left when I was very young: no doubt in part because both my parents were very young. As a career-driven new adult, my father told me later he wanted to establish himself first to properly provide for my mom and me (in retrospect, a very 22-year-old idea to believe). Of course, time waits for no man. My parents never reconciled, however cordial they remain. When I became a young man, I met the love of my life, courted her for several years, then got married and immediately had our first son – and launched my first startup at the same time. I was proving to myself that I could have a robust career and a healthy relationship with my own son. When I finally got to the TED stage, it was a talk about giving people – specifically children – attention. Overlaying my current FATE framework onto the past, my primary resource has almost always been focus.

That's because I believe focus is love. Giving something or someone your full attention changes it. I see it in my one-on-one coaching, looking my client right in the eye and letting them know we are on the journey together or holding on to one of my sons, afraid at the moment, and consciously calming my heartbeat so his will follow suit. My very ability to be highly driven, relentlessly strategic, and purposefully creating and needing intense connections to others is the result of my trauma.

These are the grooves in my vinyl record.

It's taken me years to not wear it as a badge of honor, saying that pain made me, or to argue that my childhood environment has nothing to do with the way I use resources today, plugging into some perverse, self-made man myth.

Instead, it just is. That, in itself, is freedom. That, in itself, is love. Self love.

GAMEPLAN FOR YOUR FOCUS

1. Show up with one goal in mind
2. Constantly remember your intention
3. Remember why you do, not just what you do

HOW TO STRENGTHEN YOUR FOCUS

1. As soon as you wake up, write down your number one priority for the day
2. Do not immediately say "Yes", but politely give yourself time to consider what it requires
3. Think about what you want to accomplish next and the singular action that will get you closer

BOUNDARIES FOR YOUR FOCUS

1. Create clear metrics on what you want
2. Establish early what you will or won't do to see the desired results
3. Check in often to make sure your idea, belief, or goal still serves you

FOCUS is nothing more than a decision. It is giving one solitary fuck, and making that fuck your objective at a specific moment.

FOCUS is not obsession. Obsessions are unconscious and, often, are the rooted in the avoidance of something else. Focus is not passion. As I wrote in *The Bite-Sized Entrepreneur*, "The truth is that passion will not get you out of bed every morning. Like love, it can be fickle and moody and fairweather." And FOCUS is not willpower. "The problem is that will and resources can never be equally prioritized," Simon Sinek says in *The Infinite Game*. "There are always circumstances in which one is pitted against the other."

FOCUS-rich individuals are not necessarily obsessed, passionate, or willful, just as FOCUS-low individuals cannot obsess, emote, or will their way to more FOCUS.

FOCUS is the act of consciously showing up at this very moment as well as you can. Being FOCUS-rich means choosing to show up again and again and again.

Award-winning author Ta-Nehisi Coates explains it this way: "It's not really that mystical. It's just repeated practice over and over again, and then suddenly you become something that you didn't realize you could really be. Or you just quit the field and realize you really suck (laughs). But hopefully, you have a breakthrough!"

But, how do you define 'breakthrough'? We can become too dependent or independent of Focus when we do not define our success. It is realistically navigating the gap between where you are and where you want to be, and what concentration it will take to get there.

Focusing on the process, Elizabeth Gilbert says, protects us from the extreme emotions of failure and success. "My point is that I'm writing another one now, and I'll write another book after that and another and another and another and many of them will fail, and some of them might succeed, but I will always be safe from the random hurricanes of outcome as long as I never forget where I rightfully live. Look, I don't know where you rightfully live, but I know that there's something in this world that you love more than you love yourself. Something worthy, by the way, so addiction and infatuation don't count, because we all know that those are not safe places to live. Right? The only trick is that you've got to identify the best, worthiest thing that you love most, and then build your house right on top of it and don't budge from it."

"There are three simple ways you can make [a change in the world] with more focus, energy, and success," Seth Godin says in *The Practice.* "First, you can embrace the fact that you can, in fact, trust the process and repeat the practice often enough to get unstuck. Second, you can focus on the few, not everyone. And third, you can bring intention to your work, making every step along the way count."

When my clients say, "I'm having a hard time focusing on this thing I really want," it really means they have at least one of three factors:
- Vague metrics of what they want; or
- Hidden assumptions about what they will or won't do to see the desired results

- Holding on to an idea, belief, or goal that no longer serves them

Ironically, it is also the very same factors when clients say, "I'm having a hard time letting this failing project go." Again, it is a trend I've seen in with folks having a surplus or a deficit of a particular resource: they can be in opposite situations with the same challenge.

First, what is the result you want?

If you're looking to get full, then it doesn't matter about the quality, health, or sustainability of the food. If you're looking to have a gourmet experience, then it may not matter how much it costs or how long you have to wait for the opportunity. We can expect to do a getting-full effort and unconsciously expect gourmet experience results. If you are FOCUS-rich, then you could be barking up the wrong tree and become increasingly frustrated with the progress. If you are FOCUS-challenged, then you could break your FOCUS quickly because you were expecting better results sooner.

Partnering with FOCUS means putting perfection on the shelf. Perfect is an ideal, not a goal.

I explain why in my 2018 TEDxToledo Talk, "Why You Should Strive for Good Enough":

Emotional intelligence pioneer Brene Brown says "Perfectionism is armor." It is different than an internal metric or standard that we have, as in 'I'll be better tomorrow than I am today.' That's good! That's growth. That's the way it's supposed to be. No, when you get into the perfectionist's mindset, it has nothing to do with internal; it is all external. And everything you do comes down to the same basic question: "But what will they think?" Capital "T" in "They". "Perfectionism," Brene Brown says, "is our way of hiding our true selves."

You can't focus on being perfect because it doesn't exist. That's why striving for perfection remains good for only one thing: burnout.

Knowing what you want, though, is entirely different. It is tuning out the noise and stating your intention as clearly and plainly as possible.

To contrast, AGILITY is utilizing and maximizing whatever is in front of you. FOCUS is removing and minimizing nonessential things around you.

It is taking a magnifying glass and concentrating the sunlight – your attention – on a specific spot. The sun could have been beating that same spot all day, but now that concentration is organized, uniform, and exclusionary. It is easy to forget that you, the chair in which you sit, and every single thing around you is made up of molecules. And even the most solid objects are constantly vibrating, however slowly. The higher the heat, the faster the molecules move. Our concentrated attention adds more heat.

Focus creates flexibility in an otherwise immobile situation. To FOCUS, we have to be still while others move. In stillness, we see the true, deeper dimensions of a situation. Only in FOCUS, in stillness, and in singularity, can we see the multitude of cadences around us.

Second, what will or won't you do to see your desired results? As Seth Godin says in *The Dip*:

"Write down under what circumstances you're willing to quit." I launched my first startup, So Quotable, at the same time I became the primary caretaker to my 3-month-old, Alec. He was my priority. If bootstrapping my first company ever prevented me from feeding, caring, or otherwise guiding Alec, then I would quit. No questions asked. Financial sacrifices, mental stress, and intense daily routines left me undeterred, as I could ask every morning "Am I doing right by Alec and, by extension, my family?" and confidently say, "Yes."

We don't always have these conversations about expectations and sacrifice, probably because we don't think about it until we have to. Scarcity breeds clarity. It is why we suddenly become specific towards end of life, become efficient when we take care of children or our elders, and become financially thoughtful when we get our first paycheck. The truth is that we always have these leaks – these minor incongruences that eat at our FOCUS, our AGILITY, our TIME, and our ENERGY – that become major misalignments as we continue on. Big life moments don't create the disparity. They just expose the issues we've had all along.

The late Stephen Covey's classic *First Things First* has my favorite FOCUS framework. The premise is simple: Your life has big rocks and little rocks. The size represents the importance and, essentially, what should be prioritized. They all have to fit into a jar. Pour the little rocks in first and you can get them all in the jar, but you won't be able to fit the big rocks in. Put the big rocks in first, though, and then the little rocks will naturally fall into the remaining space allotted.

Your rocks will evolve over time. My kids don't need me as much now. Alec was my big rock, and my fledging startups, So Quotable and Cuddlr, had to be squeezed within the space between. Today, Alec and his younger brother, Abhi, are old enough to be more independent. I have the space to do seven books in four years, build a healthy coaching practice, and do way more keynote talks. The rocks changed.

When I first started as an entrepreneur, a good friend said, perhaps, my family was my real startup: low resources, minimal TIME, and little guidance. It helped me accept that priorities would have to be juggled and to be realistic with what was possible. Realizing your true priority can be tough but, when you do, you can truly maximize how effective you are at the most important thing.

You can fit nearly everything in, if you take care of the most important stuff first.

FOCUS isn't just in your outward actions, but what is top of mind for you. It is remembering your intention within chaos, building connections as you rest, and working on your process to be ready for your next breakthrough. The results we desire often manifest internally before they create an external event.

Poet and Andrew W. Mellon Foundation president Elizabeth Alexander talks about how we can always be actively creating, even if our output fluctuates based on the season of our lives.

I would often send writing students to look at a retrospective of an artist's work [and] the thing that you learn is that there are fallow periods and there are incredibly generative periods. There are periods where you're trying to work an idea out so you're kind of stuck in a groove and there are periods when you have breakthroughs. If you look on the walls there will be years where there's nothing at all. And I think it's also really interesting when you learn about the lives of the artists and I think about this with women artists in particular. Where they, you know, had children in those years? What were the usually family forces or forces within the self. Were they in a depression? Were they struggling with their health? Or were they just, to use the fantastic expression that jazz musicians use, were they just woodshedding. Were they in the woodshed just working on their craft, biding their time, trying to work it out in private so that then they could come out – shazam – with something different and public?

"Woodshedding" is building towards tomorrow based on our intention today. You're still working, even if you aren't moving. Practice your instrument so you don't have to focus on the basics. Sharpen your vision so you

442

can focus strictly on your execution later. And, most importantly, build your systems so you don't have to focus on correcting sloppy mistakes when the stakes are higher.

In my coaching, one of the biggest dangers I see is wishing for a future you aren't prepared for. We can be so focused on what's next, we become myopic on what we can improve and control today. You want your product featured by Oprah, but have you tightened up your manufacturing enough to handle a 100x demand? It's cool to envision being a busy life coach, but have you researched and determined how many clients you can realistically serve?
Manifesting a millionaire lifestyle by age 25 is fine, but how are you going to serve the world in a way where you can financially there – and what personal cost are you willing to pay?

The late motivational speaker Jim Rohn explains it simply, as I share in *The Ultimate Bite-Sized Entrepreneur*:

"You say, 'If I had a big organization, you know, I'd really run it with a strong hand and I'd be a

fabulous leader. But I've only got a few (followers) and I don't know where they are.' See, that's not going to work. If you wish to preside over a lot... you have to be disciplined when the amounts are small." What Rohn is talking about is systems: *A system to master your emotional intelligence so you can handle the power; a system to handle your relationships so your management can scale; and a system to organize your resources so you can use them most effectively in high numbers. The thing is that those systems can most easily be put into place when the overhead is as low as the stakes. Ironically, as Rohn mentions, it's easy to not take the systems seriously when the rewards are weak, yet this is the very time you should be thinking about long-range goals.*

"People tend to start with a business model and then become unhappy when their days are filled with tasks they don't enjoy," Paul Jarvis says in *Company of One*. "Instead of thinking, What product can I create? or What service can I offer?, [*Atomic Habits* author James Clear] believes that we should first think: What type of life do I want? And How do I want to spend my days? Then you can work backwards from there into a business model that allows you to create scalable systems to deliver your product to your audience."

These systems are built around our FOCUS. For instance, Andrew W. Mellon's Elizabeth Alexander says she thought, when she became a mother, her creative muse would leave. Instead, during the midnight breastfeedings, she'd envision poetic lines, scribbling them down with a spare hand. Her FOCUS as an artist didn't die; she just evolved the system in which she created.

She says, "Once I got old enough to start realizing that for every day of my life I would not rise with the dawn and write into the light and do that every day and thus there would be a book every other year. It just doesn't work like that. Things happen in life. There are stages. There are eras in life."

Lastly, are you holding on to an idea, belief, or goal that no longer serves you? Inertia is a hell of a drug. It is easier to keep our FOCUS on something we've outgrown than to find a new direction. It can feel like losing our identity, even though, like skin cells refreshing every seven years, we're in a constant state of perpetual growth, change, and evolution.

It reminds me of a long-shared Thanksgiving story I first heard from my mother. I later realized that other people heard a variant of it in their lives:

A couple is getting the Thanksgiving ham ready to put in the oven. Suddenly, one of them takes out a large knife and begins cutting off the end of the raw ham - a significant chunk of it. "What are you doing?" her partner asks. "I'm getting the ham ready to put in the oven." "No, I mean, why are you cutting the end off?" "That's how my mom taught me to cook it." "Why?" "Because... I don't know."

Now curious, she goes over to her mom's house. "Why do you cut the end off of the ham?" "Because that's how Nana does it."

Now both perplexed, they go over to the retirement home to visit the grandmother. "Nana, why do we cut the end off of the ham?" The grandma pauses, then a light comes on in her eyes. "Well, during our first Thanksgiving we didn't have much money, and it was a tiny kitchen with an even tinier oven, so the only way we could make our ham fit would be to..."

Even more to the point, spiritualist Jessica Dore recently shared a New York Native American story of the Icehouse. A witch puts a group of men into an icehouse to freeze them to death. She even included ice chairs to sit in when they inevitably get tired, pushing them even closer to their demise. Instead, the wise men dance and sing all night. The body heat begins to melt the house, making holes in the ceiling and, eventually, letting the sun in.

They are free.

"Icehouses come in many models, shapes and sizes. Some are internal monologues that run on loop, some are classical trainings or informal social conditionings, some are thought patterns so subtle you don't know they're there until one day someone looks you in the eyes and says hey, that's foolish what you're doing on account of some assumption you never bothered to question," Dore says.

The icehouse, she says, is "any place in life where you have chosen to siphon or partition off vital ENERGY in service of staying the same. Any place you've thrown up a barricade against pretty much the one truly un-interruptible thing in life, which is change." In other words, your FOCUS isn't on growth, but your FOCUS is on *not* growing. You can't hide and create at the same time. You can't be safe and improve simultaneously. You can't get there from here.

The word "siphon" is perfect here, as you're stealing FOCUS from potential future greatness and giving it to a past that no longer serves you or the world.

Think about the last time you spent an inordinate amount of TIME for an incremental improvement on a completed project. Now, imagine all the other things you could have been doing with that time. At a certain point, spending more TIME on something will provide significantly diminished returns. That inordinate amount of TIME can have devastating effects on your *big rocks*. It is better to ship it out, get it out the door, and move on

448

to the next task, as having the perfect little rock won't help you manage any of your big rocks – assuming you have any room left for your true priorities.

In *Big Magic*, Elizabeth Gilbert talks about ideas leaving when they aren't acted upon:

What was the idea supposed to do, sit around indefinitely while I ignored it? Maybe. Sometimes they do wait. Some exceedingly patient ideas might wait years, or even decades, for your attention. But others won't, because each idea has a different nature. Would you sit around in a box for two years while your collaborator blew you off? Probably not. Thus, the neglected idea did what many self-respecting living entities would do in the same circumstances: It hit the road.

You could be holding on to the corpse of an idea already past its time. You're focusing on an empty husk. Windows of opportunity don't always close, but they do have a shelf life. What opportunities are you missing when you're focused on an expired idea?

"Locate your icehouses," Jessica Dore warns. "You'll know them because they are the places that what was once supple, flexible and teeming with life goes to do its hardening, stiffening and waiting around to die. Now ask yourself this: What dances can I do, *will I do*, what songs can I sing, *will I*, in order to revive those things, in order to keep them alive."

The proverbial dance is simple: Remembering the weight of a bad goal far outstrips any benefits of persistence. "What should I give up?" is as essential of a question as "What should I begin?"

There's a wonderful urban myth about veteran comedian Bill Murray. For years, it has been said that he'll pop up to a stranger, or no more than a few people, at a random, unassuming moment, do something just odd enough to get their attention, and then say, "You can tell others that Bill Murray did this, but no one will believe you." And then he'd leave as suddenly as he came. It would be a benign activity, like crashing a small, public wedding happening in the park, or dropping in on a young rock band playing loud in their apartment. Many of these events reportedly happened before cell phones were common and cheap; the onlookers couldn't just snap him and capture him in a viral video. The Saturday Night Live alum is known for his straight-face, sardonic comedy, and the improvised moments always seemed to be hilarious to the people involved. But, as he presumably predicted, when they'd share these funny incidents, no one else believed them.

In 2018, new director Tommy Avallone made a documentary about the nationwide phenomenon, *The Bill Murray Stories: Life Lessons Learned from a Mythical Man*. It all turns out to be true.

But what happens to people in the gap between their Bill Murray encounter on, say, a golf course in Biloxi, Mississippi, and that moment when Avallone's indie movie shows *everyone else* that they were telling the truth all along? Did they spend the TIME trying to convince others in their lives that it really happened? Did they quietly cherish the thought, like a childhood memory only you recall? Or, after meeting skepticism, did they eventually convince *themselves* that it never happened at all?

What you know to be true, what you value as a FOCUS, could be a little fuzzy around its definition or as clear as the Sun rising in the East. Honestly, it doesn't matter. What does matter is how much you depend on someone or something else to validate your truth. The more important the change in which you seek, the more pressure you will be under to trade your truth for another person's truth. It is never a fair trade.

Your work may be seasonal. Your intention is not.

HOW TO PARTNER WITH AGILITY

We don't have a map, but what we do have is a compass. A map lays everything out for you. A compass says, "Go that way." … It doesn't care what's in your way, and, if you're following this compass, neither do you.

Chase Jarvis,
The Chase Jarvis Show, Creator Therapy with Seth Godin in New York

When my eldest son was young, he would get up in the middle of the night wide awake. I would want my wife to sleep, and, when we were at my in-laws house, not to disturb the rest of the household. So I'd put on my pants, search for my keys in the lightless house, and then grab him and hustle to the car in the dark.

Our summer baby must have been around 6-months-old, as I distinctly remember seeing my breath in the chilly California winter air. He may have fussed, but, once we started moving, everything would grow silent.

I remember the hallmark Southern California traffic would be virtually gone, aside from an occasional, fast-moving pickup truck or a slow driver with an out-of-state license plate. The stars would be clear and bright. I'd occasionally binge on a business podcast, as I was just getting into the pleasures of audio rather than reading – being a baby's primary caretaker means you can't just sit and read a book, as your hands have other immediate needs.

Often, though, it was just me, my thoughts, and the endless road. I imagined being a New York cab driver, an active participant in the scene, but still objective enough to appreciate the spectacle of the night, and tired from the time of day, but lucid enough to drive. It was like removing a filter from my emotional landscape. Odd memories from childhood, assumptions I suddenly realized were opinion, not fact, and new, seemingly obvious business ideas floated to the blank dashboard ahead.

It would happen anytime from 1 a.m. to 3 a.m., and, because he'd often wake up if I lifted him out, it wasn't unusual for me to drive until just before dawn. I'd come back tired, of course, but also invigorated, as if I'd taken a long, hot bath, or had an amazing post-coital moment. It was as if I discovered something that made everything clearer.

It took me many nights, though, to embrace this chaos. I remember being angry at my son for not sleeping, as if he were somehow doing it just to get under my skin or, perhaps, I was doing something wrong and was, despite my desire to love, just an ill-equipped father. I would feel bitter because it was my job to chauffeur him around, a job that no one else could do and a job that, when my wife and I decided to have a baby, I actually was stupid enough to elect to do. I sat salty, back sore from lack of sleep and arms tired from being at the 10 and 2, as I drove for hours with literally no particular place to go. I was being pulled in directions I didn't want to be, physically and otherwise.

Once I began to accept this interruption, then I started to relax. As an introvert, I realized these one, two or three hours of silence could be part of how I recharged, like a bonus solitude away from the daily fatherhood ruckus. I began to lean into these moments and, when he fussed hard in the middle of the night, I'd embrace the challenge.

The white space is, by definition, uncomfortable. It is the time before a decision is made. It is the gap from the first action to the next action. It is often without a definitive end and, sometimes, without even a definitive beginning.

It is also a gift. Floating between here and there, the white space gives us the objectivity to see how we operate. It exposes our systems. It widens the moment between response and reaction, as it doesn't allow us to jump to the next conclusion, and if we do, our reaction just sits in space, like a vacuum, for us to see and digest.

This clarity is a rare opportunity. All things eventually conclude, even the moments when we are too distant to see the shore and too far to see the destination.

My son turned seven this summer. His younger brother just turned four. The endless road has ended. And that white space now is becoming a distant memory in itself.

GAMEPLAN FOR YOUR AGILITY

1. Trust your curiosity
2. Lean into observing what's next
3. Believe every new experience will be useful later

HOW TO STRENGTHEN YOUR AGILITY

1. Let someone else take the lead in an area you usually control
2. Try making small changes in your habits to exercise your flexibility muscle
3. Learn a new hobby that will help you apply old concepts to new experiences

BOUNDARIES FOR YOUR AGILITY

1. Adding more because we can
2. Believing something needs to be changed when it just needs to be persevered

Busta Rhymes is a quintessential New York rapper. In fact, many fans – including myself – would put him among the Top 10 rappers of all time.. He began his career in high school with the short-lived, influential hip-hop group Leaders of the New School. What keeps him top of mind as a solo artist, however, is consistent AGILITY: His breakout hit, 1995's "Woo-Haa!! Got You All in Check," has him rapping at a stream-of-conscious, dizzying clip; his 1997 landmark song "Put Your Hands Where My Eyes Can See" is him flowing almost ridiculously low and slow, as if he's trying to match the level of the deep syncopated bass drums; and one of his biggest appearances, on Chris Brown's 2011 club smash "Look at Me Now", is rapped so fast that there are viral videos of listeners – and fellow rappers – attempting to following his lines. (They often fail.)

Now a middle-aged rapper, Busta just released his tenth studio album. He started as a teenager in the late eighties.

On Drink Champs, a video podcast hosted by fellow veteran New York rapper N.O.R.E. and

Miami DJ EFN, he explains what happens when he enters the recording booth.

On a deeper level, too, I don't think people realize how beautiful it is to be able to go into the studio as an artist and lock yourself into those four walls... You love your woman, you love your kids, your mom, your friends, everybody, but the studio don't argue with you. The studio don't ask you no questions. And the studio don't stress you out, bro... There's a lot of times when I go to the studio and I just sit there and I don't even create nothing. I just go in there for some peace of mind... but when I go in the studio, not only do I get the chance to avoid shit I don't want to be bothered with, but I can also become whomever I choose to be. If I think about becoming a fucking Avenger in the studio, I can become an Avenger. If I want to become The Incredible Hulk in the studio, I can be The Incredible Hulk. That's a fact. And you can freely share whatever those thoughts and feelings are and capture it. And there are no repercussions, because you can live with it for a week or two to determine whether or not you even want to share this shit. And the world doesn't have to give you criticism within that space of you trying to create it. And then you can go back and revisit it, and perfect it, and revisit it, and perfect it, and get it to a place where it is so impeccable that before you even share it a [playable] form, you've mastered the intricacies of this thing so phenomenally, you already know what it's going to be when they hear it, you already know what it's going to be on that stage, and you already know what it's going to be when it's time to compete.

AGILITY is play. You could do this. You could do that. The possibilities initially seem endless. When you show up in the arena, as Brene Brown might say, you don't know what mood you'll be in, what will be on your mind, or how your first action will land. It's like poker the moment right before you get your hand. And, like a card shark, Busta can anticipate how things may go ("You already know what it's going to be when they hear it, you already know what it's going to be on that stage, and you already know what it's going to be when it's time to compete.") because he's spent so much TIME in the arena. It's the same way I can envision how this book will land when I share it with my coaching clients, as I talk about it from a keynote stage, and, as we discuss in the

Understanding Your FATEs chapter, where it sits among other creative business books.

But notice that Busta isn't just saying what he can do. These four walls. Outside voices aren't let in. There are restrictions and boundaries to this expression. This, in turn, gives him the freedom to explore. When you're anticipating that five-stud poker hand, you know you're not going to get an UNO card. You know anything you get will be an Ace, a King, or something in between. Anything else would be shocking. Anything else would make you question fully exploring the possibilities. Anything else would make you feel unsafe to play.

The boundaries make us free.

Timing is different than TIME. As a resource, TIME is maximizing the literal moments you've got to make the greatest positive impact. AGILITY is timing: knowing when to move and, since the best opportunities usually don't give much notice, it about always being prepared.

AGILITY is trusting yourself to make the next best move. It is intuitive, fluid, and welcoming.

In her book *The Creative Leap: Unleash Curiosity, Improvisation, and Intuition at Work*, consultant Natalie Nixon describes the intuitive process in three steps:

Think of leading with intuition as three concentric circles. Wonder is at the core because stillness and observation are required for us to hear that little voice inside. The second circle is discernment – finding the strength to act on our intuition and speak up. Rigor often comes into play here as we dig deep to find the data to back up our intuition. The outermost circle comes from making a practice of listening to and action on our intuition.

Nixon's three concentric circles of reflecting, strategizing, and doing parallel my own cycle of renewing, pursuing, and doing. I broke it down in *The Productive Bite-Sized Entrepreneur* (now available in *The Ultimate Bite-Sized Entrepreneur Trilogy*):

I call the productivity process "pursuing, doing, and renewing." It is an infinite iterative flow where we research our interests, implement our theories, and assess our growth. It is not unlike Eric Ries' landmark Lean Startup method, in which you ship the 'minimal viable product,' or MVP, to get feedback from others as much as possible. In the case of productivity, we're getting feedback from ourselves.

When you think about it, we all do things this way: we think of something, we do it, and then we see if it worked out. When it comes to AGILITY, though, the difference is seeing the potential in something that isn't tied to previous actions. In *The Creative Leap*, Nixon says perspective is "mining the past in order to get insight into the future [while] forecasting requires the practice of inquiry, improvisation, and intuition; it necessitates an ability to toggle between wonder and rigor."

Perspective – seeing how to make the biggest impact because of your previous results – is offered by another precious resource: TIME. On the other hand, forecasting – taking an educated guess as to what should be next – is offered by AGILITY.

The agile-rich and agile-challenged alike do the same cycle of pursuing, doing, and renewing as everyone else, just at quantum levels. To paraphrase Nixon, AGILITY is the high-speed toggle between wonder and rigor, observing and doing, and even trying and failing.

AGILITY is not being paralyzed of potential failure, as you know you'll get another opportunity to choose tomorrow. AGILITY means the opportunity outweighs our sunk costs.

AGILITY assumes that the higher the inputs, the better strategy. Basecamp co-founder Jason Fried says, "In software, people often turn to Apple for design inspiration. It makes sense - the company is wildly successful, it defines trends, and it pushes envelopes. But copying Apple doesn't make you a trendsetter or a rule breaker. It makes you a follower. When everyone mimics Apple, everything tends to look the same. Apple's clean and simple aesthetic is Apple's - it's not yours."

Apple reflects not only the tech ambitions of the late co-founder Steve Jobs, but his time doing transcendental meditation, his time studying history, and his sixties' counterculture aesthetic. The groundbreaking fonts available on the first Apple computers? According to *Becoming Steve Jobs*, they were inspired by a calligraphy class he took in college. Outside influences gave him success in his main field.

Crosspollination adds fuel to the change you seek. I recently talked with serial entrepreneur David Krock. He is an accomplished drummer. When he considers getting involved with a new company, he looks for the rhythm of the business – just as he would anticipate the perfect high-hat or bass drum drop when onstage. I spent my college years DJing, and that pacing – knowing when to let the beat ride, when to let the anticipation build up, and when to change the direction with an entirely new tune – helps me now as a writer, public speaker, and even a one-on-one business coach. When you guide others on their journey, it is priceless to know when to let someone talk, allow an uncomfortable silence, or to ask a question to guide the conversation elsewhere.

There is no wasted experience. They are all valuable in our toolbox.

A great example is fellow DJ D-Nice. The former rapper came into the spotlight with his riveting music sets. The catch: His curated events were all on Instagram. It was Spring 2020, just as America started sheltering-in-place.

From *The Washington Post*:

Last week, Jones woke up at 4 a.m. and, instead of being crippled by the anxiety of the times, decided to throw a party online for his famous pals. With his laptop, signature wide-brim hat and view of Los Angeles ready to go, Jones played music he loved for an Instagram party of about 200 music-industry heavyweights. The next day, 2,000 people joined. Then 12,000. Then 25,000. By Saturday night, more than 100,000 people — including former first lady Michelle Obama and a host of A-listers — were jamming together in "Club Quarantine," the tongue-in-cheek shorthand for the hours-long broadcasts streamed live from Jones's kitchen on his smartphone.

How could he know a pandemic was coming? He couldn't. How could he know he'd become the premier virtual DJ of this era? He didn't.

And he didn't have to.

"I just wanted to do something good for people, and it turned into something really good. It was so unexpected," Jones said in an interview.

Jones' AGILITY wasn't based in the moment. AGILITY is never instantaneous, though it could feel like it to everyone else or even to yourself. It is always rooted in past decisions. I actually grew up with D-Nice. When I was in middle school, his first rap album, *Call Me D-Nice*, was a perennial favorite. As hip-hop eras shifted, Jones became an old-school set live DJ and, later, a professional photographer and music documentarian. Moving the crowd, reading the cultural pulse, and capturing the moment are skills Jones built over time. And when the "Club Quarantine" opportunity presented itself, he was ready.

For the agile-rich and agile-challenged, the boundaries can become blurred between curious exploration and avoidance of rigor. Two tough factors come into play:

- Adding more because we can, and
- Believing something needs to be changed when it just needs to be persevered

Adding more feeds the ego. Sometimes we can identify with the AGILITY and not the practicality of it. Does joining a new club when your dance card is full, being a shoulder to cry on when you don't have the bandwidth, or pursuing yet another creative opportunity when abandoned ones lie in your wake, actually help you nourish the world? Hell, are you even nourishing yourself?

Yes, you may proudly attribute serving others with your busy, hustle nature. Your busyness may also unravel any goodwill you've gained from those you serve. AGILITY can diffuse the impact of what you do.

In *Essentialism: The Disciplined Pursuit of Less*, Greg McKeown says "Essentialists see trade-offs as an inherent part of life, not as an inherently negative part of life. Instead of asking, 'What do I have to give up!?' they ask, 'What do I want to go big on?' The cumulative impact of this small change in thinking can be profound."

Public speaking coach Grant Baldwin puts it like this: "The longer it takes to describe you, the more your speaking fee drops." He's not just talking about money – he's talking credibility, he's talking potential impact, and he's talking your value to the world. The same is true for investors in your new idea, publishers considering your new book, customers thinking about switching to your new brand, or the community who you are building trust to serve.

The commonality is telling a new person why they should spend time with your vision. It is about getting people as comfortable with your big idea as quickly as possible. And that, of course, reflects the clarity you have with your own vision.

I call it the cocktail test: how would you describe your important vision to someone you just met at a party? I took this quite literally early in my career, and I'd find myself stumbling and fumbling over what, exactly, I was doing as a writer. Every year, though, the vision would get tighter, and before I knew it I could tell people about my intention in one breath. The process began again after I became an entrepreneur, and, after several years, my vision is clear: I'm debunking the myth that you have to sacrifice everything to make your entrepreneurial and creative mark.

Your product isn't for everyone.

Your services can't lift everyone.
And your voice doesn't resonate with all.

Not everyone in your life likes you. Why would what you have to offer be for everyone, either?

True AGILITY begins with purpose. Business coach Marie Forleo's multi-million-dollar empire is built on the first page of *Everything is Figureoutable*: "The power isn't out there, it's in you." Marketer and teacher Seth Godin simply says, "For more than thirty years, I've been trying to turn on lights, inspire people and teach them how to level up." His brilliant

Akimbo podcast, online courses, and classic keynote are all built on this simple idea.

Every thing I'm involved in – from keynotes to books to coaching – revolves around my short, focused entrepreneurial creed. This is why you're reading my 25th book. This is how I can make more with less. This is how you can partner with AGILITY. It is simpler for me to adapt, create, and take advantage of new opportunities because I'm providing the same discussion, no matter what the platform. It is also easier for investors, publishers, and communities to understand my vision, bringing better sales and higher investment because they trust my expertise and clarity.

We can also believe something needs to be changed when it just needs to be persevered. Pivoting to a new idea kicks in the adrenaline. It feels good. A pregnant idea is always more romantic than a crying baby. You can't have one without the other, though, and the follow through – what *The Creative Leap* author Natalie Nixon calls transitioning from "wonder to rigor" – is where you bring your worth.

"Your core ideas, those core intentions as a creator, are all built in the struggle, not in the feast," I wrote in *Bring Your Worth: Level Up Your Creative Power, Value & Service to the World*. "The biggest danger, then, isn't missing your oppportunity to shine brightly, to create wealth, or to impact the world, but not allowing the life experiences to prepare you to do those very things. The circumstances will come in disguises, cloaked in a frustrating situation, a setback, or an unexpected development. Your life is tailor made to develop the muscles you need to succeed. The universe doesn't want to punish you, which is as preposterous as believing gravity dislikes skydivers or flames hate firefighters. It is just physics, science, and nature. And, the universe knows exactly when to give you what you need, like a flower always blossoming on time."

We have been fooled into believing trying something new is a risk. It's not. Bravery is picking up the messy pieces from a failure, a mistake, a misstep, and continuing on the journey anyway because it fits, to paraphrase poet Mary Oliver, what you plan to do with your one wild and precious life.

As I talk about with FOCUS, giving up can be great. Giving in, though, doesn't ever make sense.

"The image of the tragic artist who lays down his tools rather than fall short of his impeccable ideals holds no romance for me," Elizabeth Gilbert says in *Big Magic*. "I don't see this path as heroic. I think it's far more honorable to stay in the game – even if you're objectively losing the game – than to excuse yourself from participation because of your delicate sensibilities. But in order to stay in the game, you must let go of your fantasy of perfection."

As a coach, I instinctively get chills when I hear someone talk about "starting over," getting a "clean slate," or "erasing the past." That isn't even possible. As the classic saying goes, "No matter where you go, there you are." Eventually, you're going to have to do that work.

There are things happening beyond your scope. It's not from ignorance or naiveté, but simply because you aren't meant to see them. Your name could be spoken in rooms. Your next best step could be materializing as you read this. Your co-conspirator in a game-changing partnership could be lining up to meet you at your level. You just won't know it until you're supposed to.

AGILITY is trusting you'll be ready when they appear.

HOW TO PARTNER WITH TIME

I'm bad with time management, but great with attention management. If I'm choosing people and projects that matter to me, then it doesn't matter how long they take.

Adam Grant, The Tim Ferriss Show

One day, I was having breakfast with a friend and they asked, "How do you know when to let something happen and when to *make* something happen?" *I knew* I knew, but I never really articulated it before. I sipped my coffee and paused for a minute. Then I could explain: "Personally, I don't focus on making things happen. I put all my focus on paying attention and watching for the right moment to do it. Then it takes care of itself."

I've created every day for decades, and yet people observing may not realize it is a daily operation – not just when I feel like it. I have a hit about every four years: I do a heavily-citied book, then a couple years pass, then I have a best-seller, and more years pass, and then I co-found a popular app, and so on. In-between those times are flops and duds, quiet work and self doubt, honest conversations with self and others. In-between is creating. In-between is time.

Time affords you the opportunity to think, to create, to fail, and to ultimately impact the culture. If Timing is knowing *when*, Time is knowing *it will*. If I embrace this experience bombing at my first book event, if I spend an evening exploring this thing I'm drawn to, if I give, give, give to the people whom I serve, then all those resources will be at my disposal tomorrow.

I have always been aware of my mortality, well before I experienced any life-threatening situations as an adult. When I wrote, I assumed it would be the last thing I would write. (Something I've found shockingly common among passionate creators.) When I talked to someone, I would sometimes think, "What if this was the last time we say goodbye?" Journalist at 14, high school graduate at 17, grad school graduate at 22. Running like a man on fire.

I understand something different now. Partnering with time isn't about the time you have left or even doing things as quickly as possible, but nourishing the world as much as possible with the time you've got. What this is *not* is public work. This is often silent work. This is often internal work. This is steadfastly building a skill, creating a service, or adding more love, trusting that, over time, your cup will runneth over. Now I can work quietly, with peace, as I know time will naturally accrue the power I need to nourish the world.

You actually have all the time you need. You just have to trust time will give you what you need to make the biggest impact.

1. Build a routine
2. Create boundaries. Artificial is fine
3. Set a timeline independent of outside judgment

HOW TO STRENGTHEN YOUR TIME

1. Focus on small wins that build on the results you want later
2. Make decisions based on an easier tomorrow, not an easier right now
3. Remember no matter how hard it is today, it will only be harder to start tomorrow

BOUNDARIES FOR YOUR TIME

1. Time is not something to fill, but something to leverage
2. Set a personal timeline independent of the time available

Alex Haley knew he had gone too far. Way too far. The late author stumbled upon his family heritage, tracing it all the way back to The Gambia in West Africa. He grew up sitting on a porch in Henning, Tennessee, hearing his Grandma, his Aunties, and other older relatives tell tales of royalty, slavery, and his ancestor, Kunta Kinte.

Fortunately, he listened.

Haley flew to The Gambia with some money he scrapped together and confirmed they were telling the truth: his family roots began there. He got a nice book deal through his literary connections and began writing. And writing. And writing.

He kept writing and traveling and researching until he was tired and broke. In his words, he'd max out all his credit cards and run out of friends to borrow money from, then he'd find a way to make more money and start the process over again.

He also ran faster than the deadline. By his count, he missed the publisher deadline six times. (Doubleday & Company's Editor in Chief Samuel S. Vaughan, in fact, said Haley missed the deadline *nine* times.) Unfortunately, he was no closer to completing his epic family saga. The last time he flew to New York for a deadline extension (and some more advance money), Haley just wrote the most eloquent start to the book, wagering the editor would intensely read the first few pages during his visit to see his progress, and then just trust the rest of the manuscript was coming together. He was right.

Now Haley had just a year – a final year – to complete the massive manuscript pulled together from an estimated 500,000 miles of travel across three continents, hundreds of researched books, and a seemingly infinite number of interviews.

"I could have gone on that way forever, never satisfied that I'd learned quite enough, always hoping that tomorrow I'd stumble across one more piece of evidence that I couldn't do without," Haley told *Playboy Magazine* in 1977, after his book, *Roots*, became the first book in history to sell more than a million hardback copies. "Finally, in exasperation, my attorney, Lou Blau, told me, in so many words, to just stop runnin' my mouth about it, take the research I had – *which was enough for ten books by then* – get off on some desert island somewhere and write the goddamn thing."

And it turned out fine. It usually turns out fine. As long as you actually start.

"It doesn't make any sense to not make something as good as it should be, but we will always be making things that are not as good as they could be, because if we have unlimited time and unlimited money, of course we would make something differently, but we don't have unlimited time and we don't have unlimited money and we must interact with the market," Seth Godin says.

For Haley and other journalists, TIME is our savior and our crucible. We love writing, and, if we find a story we love, we would write forever if we could, peeling away the layers of the onion and getting deeper into the real story. We need a barrier, though. For many of us, our first experience with limitations is the deadline. When does the story need to go to press? When do the editors need it by? When do I have to stop? And our approach becomes based on that limitation, that border, that proverbial stop sign.

But what happens, after years of TIME-based thinking, we are given an assignment that has no deadline? The story sits there. It becomes the neverending story. It will always be published tomorrow. I've been in many newsrooms, and each and every one of us have had at least one story that is important, that is close to our heart, that will absolutely get our full attention once we get the more pressing, deadline-driven articles out of the way.

It is the same for the retiree who no longer has the friction of work to keep him steady, or the long-married divorcee who can't make a decision because she doesn't have someone arguing against her, or the new college student who feels overwhelmed because their parents' rules suddenly don't apply.

We need the friction, the pressure, to perform. It is essential to create deadlines, even if they are artificial.

Before having children, I wrote a dozen and a half books over the course of a decade. After having kids, I wrote seven books in four years, bootstrapped two startups and sold the latter, Cuddlr, within a year an a half, and did my first, as well as my third, TED Talk. It isn't a coincidence. We create within the limits we set. It is just clearer when we have outside influences making this fact tangible.

Off the Clock: Feel Less Busy While Getting More Done author Laura Vanderkam has one of my favorite TIME management stories. A busy mother began tracking her time spent using one of Vanderkam's methods. Suddenly, her water heater broke and flooded her basement. The damage, cleanup, and replacement took several hours out of her week. To her astonishment, though, she still managed to get her weekly activities done – and then some. Somehow she found the time, as if it was lost change under the couch cushion. Necessity breeds efficiency.

TIME is less like a straight line and more like a curve, bending when we're doing something we prioritize. Maximizing TIME is knowing what is important and leaning into those curves. Those curves begin to compress and you progress towards your intention faster.

Vanderkam calls this TIME dividends: you start getting returns based on work you put in before and you are able to get more done faster. We talk about it in her book *Off the Clock*:

"I have been doing my most basic work [writing] for a quarter of a century, so I know exactly how much material and resources I need, just as a veteran craftsman knows the correct amount of wood and nails to build a table." Such knowledge accrues bit by bit. The brain develops muscle memory, which makes much of what would have required deliberation mindless. Brown's insight is this: certain things we do in the present can open up space in the future. These investments of time pay off again and again, much like a stock can pay an annual dividend. People who seem to have lots of time have often structured their lives to create time dividends; as money dividends make a person rich, so time dividends make you feel like this resource is abundant.

What matters isn't how much TIME you have, but what effort you are capable of doing within the TIME you've got. In short, TIME doesn't matter, but the results do. "You can learn a lot from billionaires," basketball-legend-turned-mogul Magic Johnson said in an interview. "The same amount of time it takes to make a million dollars is the same amount of time it takes to make $100 million. Time is key."

The TIME-rich and the TIME-challenged can have the same two blindspots:
- Feeling like TIME is something to fill, rather than something to leverage; and
- Forgetting to set their own timeline independent of the TIME available

The amount of TIME doesn't matter if you aren't building these proverbial muscles. If you want to learn an instrument and don't practice every day, then it doesn't matter if you have a few minutes or several hours available. Building from now means starting where you are with the resources you've got. The TIME-rich can believe they will always have tomorrow, while the TIME-challenged can believe they will never have enough TIME to start.

I learned long ago that it is easier to adjust an oven when you start it already. If I know I'm going to bake, I'll set it to 350 degrees, and then set up my mise en place and pour over the details. Why? Either way, you're going to have to wait for the preheat. You might as well get started. And it's much easier to turn the oven up a few degrees to 375 or down to 325 instead of getting there from a cold oven. And your preheat is the prep, the skills, the Work with a capital "W". "If you want to perform when the world is watching, you have to do the work when no one is watching," Farnam Street's Shane Parrish says. The behind-the-scenes work and details will come together, perhaps quicker than you expect. But you have to put things in motion to have a place to show up once you are ready.

Ironically, not worrying about TIME is the best way to partner with it. Worrying about TIME happens when we use comparative measurements like:

- how long it takes for you to see progress relative to cultural norms,
- how long others believe you should pursue your goal, and
- and how long it should take for you to have outward results.

Saying you have to make some amount of money by, say, age 30 or looking to one-up another peer based on speed are recipes for burnout. What happens if you don't reach these obscure, time-based goals, based on factors not completely in your control? Are you just going to throw it all away? The comparative approach leads us straight into extreme thinking. It's an easy trap to fall into: We have two choices and must absolutely go full throttle into one while leaving the other choice behind. We either stay in a job we hate or quit it to start our own business. We either get married and start a family or dedicate our lives to our careers. There is no flexibility. You're either all in or you give up.

And you must choose now!

Funny measurements pushes us into what psychologist Carol Dweck calls a fixed mindset ("I'm a winner or a loser," all or nothing, pass or fail) rather than a growth mindset ("I will learn from this experience," levels of success, seeing opportunities rather than competitions).

You need to create your own metrics.

When I work with people, the number one reason they are ready to quit isn't because their goal is unrealistic or that they are not ready to do what it takes to achieve it. It is because they haven't accomplished their goal, or made as much progress to their goal, as quickly as they expected. This expectation of TIME is often unconscious.

Motivational speaker Les Brown says you have to water the bamboo tree for years with no sign of life – until, overnight, it suddenly sprouts thick and tall. All the growth is happening underground.

Like your resources, your timeline should be completely based on your personal and professional situation. A side hustler with a 9-

to-5 and kids isn't going to create as quickly as an unemployed high school student or a retired grandmother. When I launched my first startup, I knew that my single, tech-inclined friends could do my app in a five-week sprint. My sharpest Silicon Valley friends could have done it in five days. It took me five months.

When you are TIME-challenged, then you need to stretch the timeline to give yourself a proper runway to create. When you are TIME-rich, then you need to shrink the timeline to give yourself a sense of urgency. Both need to create, recognize, and respect limitations.

And Winter 2020 made this abstract distinction very real for Americans. When the Coronavirus pandemic hit U.S. shores, there were immediately two outspoken camps in the creative world. On one hand, the capitalist hamster wheel was finally pausing. Rest as much as possible. No, you don't have to be productive. You can take a well-deserved break. It's a damn pandemic, for God's sake. You better stop while they let you! Otherwise, this was a waste.

On the other hand, the entire world was finally pausing. Get shit done! Yes, you have to be productive. I know you're not going to come out of these weeks, if not months without a new exercise routine (and summer body to go with it), a completed book manuscript, and at least one additional passive income stream. It's a damn pandemic, for God's sake. You better make the most of it! Otherwise, this was a waste.

You either rest like hell or be productive as hell. Any moderation is served with a side of guilt.

Journalist Nora Salem noted a particularly acidic social media message.

On April 2, 2020, Jeremy Haynes, owner of a marketing agency, tweeted:

"If you don't come out of this quarantine with either: 1.) a new skill 2.) starting what you've been putting off like a new business 3.) more knowledge

You didn't ever lack the time, you lacked the discipline"

She says backlash was immediate. "It could have been the timing: With most of the country less than a month into lockdown, and many unemployed or sick or both, Americans were not in the mood to be told that they weren't hustling hard enough… Everyone, it seemed, agreed that simply surviving the terrifying uncertainty of the moment with physical and mental health intact would be accomplished enough."

But it also speaks to a deeper issue of privilege. We aren't all running the same race. She adds, "[They] often see those who don't have the resources to ensure their health and well-being as lacking the motivation to improve their circumstances, as opposed to facing high structural barrier like lack of inherited wealth, food deserts, or environmental racism."

The truth is that there is nothing extraordinary about this creative time. There was an American pandemic, influenza, exactly a century ago, and at least a half dozen very recent pandemics, from Zika to SARS, that just didn't hit America as hard. The TIME you're spending giving yourself the rest you need, working on your craft, spending with your family, or rebalancing your life was always there. It wasn't given by a pandemic. It was given by you. You gave yourself permission to make the time because you didn't feel judged by others in the world making the same decision to stand within their own priorities.

And this rush to do something isn't because we suddenly have the gift of TIME, but from our fear that this TIME will go away: You will never get the opportunity again to uproot the political system, nor to create the life you want, nor to bring your neighborhood closer, nor to impact the world. You better act now, because you will never have this much power, opportunity, or influence again.

This simply isn't true.

You don't want to be building a cause in the moment. You want to be continuously creating, brick-by-brick, and have a full-blown blueprint prepared when the world is ready for your message. Those that are telling you to hurry up now are speaking from their own fear – and perhaps tapping into yours.

"We have to understand the interplay between intensity and consistency," says *Start With Why* author Simon Sinek. "You can't go to the gym for nine hours and get into shape. It doesn't work. But if you work out every day for 20 minutes, you will absolutely get into shape. The problem is, I don't know when."

It doesn't mean you don't build now. It means you create for the long game. It means Black Lives will Matter to you in 2030, or sustainable food will still be your intention after the pandemic ends, or the causes you trumpet in your social circles will blanket your timeline as their popularity ebbs and flows.

Yvon Chouinard, founder of the eco-focused clothing company Patagonia, said, "The faster a business grows, the faster it dies. We decided on a growth program so that we would be around 100 years from now. So all decisions were made as if we're going to be around 100 years from now." Frankly, it is far away enough so that you know you'll be dead. Your ENERGY has to lean into creating systems – of beliefs, of actions, of standards – rather than quick fixes.

TIME benefits tremendously from pulling your scope out to the bigger mission. First, it sharpens your intent. Choulnard said, "We slowed down our growth, said 'No' to a lot of opportunities, and became more responsible. In Patagonia's case, it has been a long-time advocate of the environment, supporting global warming prevention initiatives, and donating to aligned causes. Second, daily issues become a lot less petty. Will delaying an action affect your culture 100, ten, or even five years from now? If not, then it's much easier to bypass any hysteria that comes from a minor snafu or setback. Third, it simplifies any overcomplex mission. What basic statement embodies your very purpose? When you think about the next century, what you leave for the world well after you are gone, then the superficial steps, safe platitudes, and popular niceties fall by the wayside.

The spotlight is separate from the creation. Partnering with TIME happens when we remember the difference between the two.

Jay-Z, who began his career a quarter-century ago, explained it to *New York Times'* executive editor Dean Baquet:

The white-hot space is when it is fresh and new, and it's like [clap], "This is the hottest song ever." I stretched that window and I stood in that window for a very long time. [Now], people are not looking to me as 'the thing'... That white hot space, people think it is the biggest thing, but it is really small. It's almost like a trend. Would you rather be a trend or would you rather be forever?

TIME affords you forever.

HOW TO PARTNER WITH ENERGY

Stop measuring your strength by how much shit you can tolerate.

Josie Rosario

My name is Damon Brown, and I am a napper. It started when I finished grad school and became a full-time freelance journalist. It is an independent hustle, pitching publications and offering your services, and you can work from wherever you want. I liked that part. Something romantic about being able to turn in articles from New Orleans one day, then from Tokyo the next day, with my editors being none the wiser. Sure, I was too broke to travel, but I liked to plan. (It would pay off later when I did start world traveling and, much later, became a stay-at-home dad.)

The naps, though. I'm a focused guy, so once I got into the flow, it wouldn't be unusual for me to stay up all night writing or unplug the phone from the wall (as I said, this was a while ago) to go undistracted. I could lean into my biggest resource: FOCUS. Then, I'd go to rest, often with a strong mid-day siesta. On his podcast, Tim Ferriss once talked about a legendary martial arts champ who would take a nap on the sidelines – snoring and all – until right before his fight. Then he'd wake up completely alert and win the match. I felt seen.

But for years, I didn't tell anyone about my daily naps. I wouldn't tell my in-laws, as their tough immigrant culture didn't accept young adults taking siestas. I wouldn't tell my fellow freelancers, as it felt duplicitous to strategize about how to get above the poverty line in one breath and then talk about how refreshed I felt after I spent the afternoon being virtually comatose in the next breath. And I definitely wouldn't tell anyone who didn't believe working from home was an actual job. (This was before WFH, flex days, and the like became fashionable.) So I'd come up with excuses as to why I didn't answer the phone, had to disappear midday, or just wasn't available sometimes.

I knew, though, that napping was an essential part of my energy cycle. My thoughts were clearest mid-afternoon, post-nap, and on well into the night. When I finally moved to New Orleans, I'd wake up mid-morning, nap in the afternoon, and then write my first major book from late afternoon until around midnight. Afterwards, I'd often grab a nightcap with my fellow creative friends in or around the

Quarter. I did that for a year. My book manuscript was done shortly after.

I came out about my napping quite a few years back, even calling it essential in my best-selling book, *The Bite-Sized Entrepreneur*. Now colleagues are pleasantly surprised when they listen to their body, actually stop for a moment, and wake up more powerful than before.

Today, entire freaking studies are dedicated to napping. The British Medical Journal, the University of Warwick, and other medical experts found that sleep deprivation – less than six hours a night – can lead to increased heart disease, depression, and other undesired outcomes. A short, hour-or-less nap can help counteract these effects.

I had the wisdom to keep my napping habit for decades. I just wish I was wise enough to listen to myself more and let go of the shame. I'm sure I would have slept a lot sounder.

Gameplan for Your Energy

1. Always have a strategy
2. Choose your battles wisely
3. Use "No." as a complete sentence

How to Strengthen Your Energy

1. Journaling, meditate, or otherwise reflect on your actions
2. Cultivate moments of silence without tech to pay attention to your thoughts
3. Let go of habits that no longer serve you physically, mentally, or emotionally

Boundaries for Your Energy

1. Recognize leaks in your energy
2. Don't mistake stillness for death
3. Know when to let go of an intention

Essentialism author Greg McKeown says the origin of the word "priority" is Greek for "first" or "foremost". There cannot be multiple priorities. There can be primary and secondary, but saying you have a dozen priorities is like saying you are going in a dozen directions. It isn't possible.

It is possible to overanalyze every move you make to the point where you either give up or stop caring out of pure exhaustion. We assume that more choices empower us. In reality, each decision takes more ENERGY away – and can eventually create inertia. It is how you slip into autopilot, perhaps waiting for something big to happen so you can get energized again to take the wheel.

The Paradox of Choice author Barry Schwartz calls this "decision fatigue". In his popular TED Talk, he breaks down three effects of having (or, more accurately, giving ourselves) too many options. First, we tend to procrastinate decisions when the number of choices overwhelms us – and, I would add, the more important the decision, the more likely we are to delay it. Second, we worry about opportunity cost: we're interested in one action, but afraid that we'll miss something else that we can't do as a result. In more modern terms, we'd call this F.O.M.O., or the fear of missing out. Our ever-connected, social-media powered world is ripe with F.O.M.O. opportunities. (ENERGY-conscious folks have come up with one of my personal favorite acronyms, J.O.M.O., or the joy of missing out.) Lastly, Schwartz says we have an escalation of expectations. We made a decision and sacrificed all these other opportunities, so the one we chose *better* be damn good. Schwartz points out that we have more choices than ever, from what ketchup to eat to which type of jeans to buy. That paralysis of analysis has leaked into our personal and professional lives, making us too tired to make the big decisions because we've been, consciously or not, making dozens more little decisions every day.

Like many entrepreneurs and creatives, I hate saying "No". Why? Unlike scientists and other logic-driven people, we don't see the downside. We usually see the possibility.

Unfortunately, saying "Yes" to everything means eventually saying "No" to other things. This is one of the few times when the "scarcity mindset" actually comes in handy: You can't just *make* more TIME, nor can you just make more ENERGY. They will come from something else. You may as well make that a conscious process.

"Opportunities are just obligations wearing an appealing mask," Paul Jarvis says in *Company of One*. "There might be a positive outcome to seizing them, but they always come at a cost – in terms of time, attention, or resources. No matter how hard you try, you can't scale the amount of time in your day. And since you can't somehow buy more hours, you need to find ways to use those hours better."

Saying "No" is the closest thing we've got to creating ENERGY. We know that taking on less with automatically increase our power in what we *do* choose. And yet, we don't say it. In my research, we claim to avoid saying "No" for three reasons:

- We don't want to disappoint others,
- We don't want others to fail without our help, and
- We don't want to miss an opportunity

In reality, it rarely has to do with other people. It has to do with our fear of being free. Without a non-stop agenda, we can feel rudderless and out to sea.

We're in the middle of pandemic time: large swaths of Americans have more TIME than ever before. The same can be said for ENERGY. But we can't escape into social gatherings, we can't hop on a plane to change scenery, and most of us can't dive into our work in the same way. You may have complained about your work commute, doing business trips, or going to a wedding or funeral you would rather avoid. These basic rituals also filled up your day. They created a rhythm. One you don't have anymore.

We're all staring into the void.

"The more accustomed you are to solving problems, to getting things done, to having a routine, the harder it will be on you because none of that is possible right now," University of Minnesota professor emeritus of social sciences Pauline Boss, Ph.D., recently said in an interview. "Our [American] culture is very solution-oriented, which is a good way of thinking for many things. It's partly responsible for getting a man on the moon and a rover on Mars and all the things we've done in this country that are wonderful. But it's a very destructive way of thinking when you're faced with a problem that has no solution, at least for a while."

What is extraordinary about this mass experience is how quickly it exposed our long-standing silent pact: our perceived productivity is directly tied to our self worth. If we aren't busy, then we feel lost. And if other people aren't happy with their station in life, then they don't have the right to rest.

My 2016 book *The Bite-Sized Entrepreneur* was, in part, a reaction to Silicon Valley productivity shaming. You can do good work, serve your customers, *and* have a life. I saw lots of young men and women buy into the myth that your startup had to be your *entire* life. And then I saw them burn themselves out into oblivion.

Now, we've moved on from judging others on productivity to judging others on how they are productive. Right before the pandemic, there were a slew of thought leaders arguing everyone should wake up at 4 a.m. Apple CEO Tim Cook does it! So does the Seal Team leader who killed Osama Bin Laden! Unsurprisingly, I didn't find one article that gave scientific evidence as to *why*. At least naps have some evidence.

I got up at 3:15 a.m. every morning for two years to run my two startups – because I was primary caretaker of my baby. I still wouldn't argue anyone else do the same.

Seth Godin says culture simply means, "This is how we do things here… [and] what changes culture is each of us: what we expect and how we expect things to go." It doesn't have to make sense. It is just what we decide to believe. That means we can change our minds, too, beginning on an individual level.

"There are so many things that capitalism has stolen, and [one of them is] our dreamspace which is where our power lies," says The Nap Ministry founder Tricia Hersey. "You don't have to work like a dog to get to the end result. You should work towards your calling, but you can work within alignment. You can be balanced. When you're resting and sleeping, you get some of your best ideas for the next move you have to make."

ENERGY-full and ENERGY-challenged people alike can have the same three difficulties:
- Mistaking stillness for death,
- Recognizing leaks in their ENERGY, and
- Knowing when to let go of an intention

Pivot author Jenny Blake talks about being in a "goo" state: The liminal, unclear moment between finishing one action and taking another one. In my *Bite-Sized Entrepreneur* framework, it is the "renewing" part of the renewing, pursuing, and doing creative cycle, as discussed in the AGILITY section.

On her podcast, Blake and spiritualist Penny Peirce described the "goo" state:

Penney equates the liminal space to the time when a caterpillar has created and entered the cocoon, but has not transitioned into a butterfly. It is the space in which we are given the chance to rest, reset, and recharge before moving into the next phase. It sounds lovely when put that way, so why do we often want to rush the process?

But to the caterpillar, stilllness is *death*. Just as losing our inefficient routines, dissolving the toxic relationships sapping our ENERGY, and unloading our overbooked schedule feels like a loss of our identities.

The "goo" state – the necessary pause – helps us recognize the leaks in our ENERGY. In my coaching, I've found we usually waste our ENERGY putting the abundance we have or the little we've got into areas in which we have no influence.

We waste our ENERGY trying to gain validation of our work. Our work begins with putting your trust into your instinct, "This particular thing needs to be given to the world and I'm in the position to offer it," and then putting your trust into your audience, "And those whom I want to serve will show up." Doubt in what we instinctively know needs to be given to the world stops us from starting. Doubt in the audience actually showing up keeps us from finishing – and we begin to wiggle, evade, or otherwise drop our best intentions. We try to find ways to secure the win and guarantee our work will be accepted. It means wanting that extra degree or certification to have others take us more seriously (when we really want to validate ourselves), waiting for a major music contract before we take song recording seriously (when we could have been building an audience all along), or investing money in fancy business cards and other paraphernalia (when we haven't sold our first item yet).

We're effectively turning an inside job into an outside job. And we're scattering ENERGY all over the place.

"Our commitment to the process is the only alternative to the lottery-mindset of hoping for the good luck of getting picked by the universe," Seth Godin says in *The Practice*. "A lifetime of brainwashing has taught us that work is about measurable results, that failure is fatal, and that we should be sure that the recipe is proven before we begin. And so we bury our dreams. We allow others to live in our head, reminding us that we are imposters with no hope of making an original contribution."

This is a danger even when we have monumental success. It may even be worse when we have a significant social impact, as it is harder to tune out the outside voices from our inside instinct.

For instance, pop icon Michael Jackson became obsessed with topping his legendary 1983 album *Thriller*. Keep in mind *Thriller* was and is one of the top 20 selling albums *of all time*. As I share in *The Ultimate Bite-Sized Entrepreneur*, his long-time producer Quincy Jones saw him trying to top his record sales – something that was ultimately out of Jackson's control.

The problem? Jackson wanted to do it again. According to Jones, he spent the rest of his life, album after album, trying to create something bigger than Thriller. As a result, he never felt quite satisfied. It is an amazing trap: You naturally hit a home run and, next time up to bat, you're checking wind conditions, wearing a lucky hat and trying to recreate the previous experience. The rub is that what you did - the success you had - wasn't just based on your actions. It is both timing and inspiration, too. The sales success of Thriller *could not be recreated because the whole record industry sold less records, as we would see with Napster and iTunes and Spotify. The needs of the listeners changed (ironically, because of* Thriller *itself), so doing another* Thriller *wouldn't recreate the same sea change. And Jackson was arguably in a different place, as he now had ridiculously high expectations of himself and a new set of pressures.*

There is something unusual about the air on the mountaintop. I've felt lost twice in my life: The year escaping Hurricane Katrina and the year after selling my second startup, Cuddlr. In both cases, my identity – as a Crescent City resident or as a co-founder – and a home – New Orleans or with the Cuddlr community we cultivated – was suddenly gone. It didn't matter if one was by force and the other was by choice. And while I recognize now that the months following Katrina held me in a low-grade PTSD, our sale of Cuddlr showed me how much I identified with the 3:15 a.m. business meetings, constant limelight from the

New York Times, WSJ, and other outlets, and the potential of more growth, more community, more opportunities. Suddenly, the light switch turned off. I was no longer a founder. I was just a writer. And perhaps I'd never create again.

So I began to brainstorm new ideas – things I could spin up quickly. I still have a physical journal full of them and a bunch of iPhone notes to match. I'd come up with an idea that I knew would be the next big hit, share it with my confidants, buy the domain name, and so on. Then I'd lose interest. I'd do everything but complete the mockup version so I could actually see if it was worth going deeper on. And then I'd do it again. And again. This went on for weeks.

One day, a friend visited me and we caught up over a long coffee. I breathlessly talked about the Cuddlr experience, the acquisition, and lots of inside baseball that would eventually be shared in some way. Enough of that, I seemed to say, as I have this new idea that will make an even bigger impact. I'm ready to get back in the game.

It was late Fall, and Cuddlr had just sold the

previous Summer. I spent almost two years waking up at 3:15 a.m. every morning to found and lead my two companies, So Quotable and Cuddlr, while being a stay-at-home dad and active journalist. I was still primary caretaker of my first son, Alec, now also two years old. And I just found out that we had another son on the way.

"How about this," my friend said, pausing me after I shared my new idea. "What if your family is your startup right now?" It stopped me in my tracks. My family is and was my priority throughout, but I also needed something more. But what if this was my season to be still? Isn't that how So Quotable came about or, when I connected with the two co-founders, how I saw the potential in Cuddlr? It was ENERGY waiting for the best opportunity, not ENERGY scattered trying to make an opportunity. It was trust.

Come to find out, *Inc. Magazine* was looking for a columnist. It became a cathartic way to process my experience and pass along any lessons learned in the whirlwind journey. The column eventually became my self-published best-seller *The Bite-Sized Entrepreneur*. I was now a touring public speaker. And everything happened that brought me here to you right now. But first, I had to let go of my win – the past – and sit still enough to reassess where I should put my ENERGY – my future. I had to stop chasing success.

After her book sold an unexpected 10 million copies, *Eat, Pray, Love* author Elizabeth Gilbert found herself famous, financially secure, and, in her words, stuck. She explained it beautifully in her 2014 TED Talk:

For most of your life, you live out your existence here in the middle of the chain of human experience where everything is normal and reassuring and regular, but failure catapults you abruptly way out over here into the blinding darkness of disappointment. Success catapults you just as abruptly but just as far way out over here into the equally blinding glare of fame and recognition and praise. And one of these fates is objectively seen by the world as bad, and the other one is objectively seen by the world as good, but your subconscious is completely incapable of discerning the difference between bad and good. The only thing that it is capable of feeling is the absolute value of this emotional equation, the exact distance that you have been flung from yourself. And there's a real equal danger in both cases of getting lost out there in the hinterlands of the psyche.

But in both cases, it turns out that there is also the same remedy for self-restoration, and that is that you have got to find your way back home again as swiftly and smoothly as you can, and if you're wondering what your home is, here's a hint: Your home is whatever in this world you love more than you love yourself. So that might be creativity, it might be family, it might be invention, adventure, faith, service, it might be raising corgis – I don't know! Your home is that thing to which you can dedicate your energies with such singular devotion that the ultimate results become inconsequential.

Being famous or prolific won't help you succeed again. What matters is the work and your intention. Is your product or service being done with the audience at the forefront? Are you contributing something more to the cultural conversation? Ego-driven enterprises rarely rise as high as purely-motivated work –

and we are in the most danger of doing the former after a big win.

"At some point, the professional has to bring home the fish. That's the fuel that permits the professional to show up each day. But the catch is the side effect of the practice itself. Get the practice right, and your commitment will open the door for the market to engage with your work," Seth Godin says in *The Practice*. "You might seek a shortcut, a hustle, a way to somehow cajole that fish onto the hook. But if it distracts you from the process, your art will suffer. Better to set aside judging yourself until after you've committed to the practice and done the work."

We also waste our ENERGY trying to change someone's mind; it is more effective to change by example rather than argument. In coaching, they say that you can't want your client's success more than they do. A hallmark of my boutique coaching business is that I'm super selective of the people with which I work. I learned early on the cost of taking on a client because they had the money, but didn't currently have the mindset to improve themselves. In one instance, a referral said they wanted to leave their corporate position and launch their own startup. Great, I thought. But then they explained that they were determined to quit their day job as soon as possible, had no entrepreneurship experience, and had no interest in taking on a co-founder because – after I asked a few questions – admitted they wanted as much control as possible.

Let's briefly break down all the alarms that went off: You don't quit your day job based on the promise of potential income. Potential doesn't pay the rent. You cannot understand being a founder until you become one. That's like imagining being a parent when you don't have any kids or thinking what it's like to visit Japan if you've never set foot in Asia. And we co-found companies because it is often too intense to go about it alone and, as was this potential client's case, you need other people to balance your own skills or compensate for all you don't know. In the case of my most notable startup, Cuddlr, it had three co-founders: Charlie Williams as the programming veteran and initial founder; Jeff Kulak as the veteran artist; and me as the media and tech culture veteran. I was the sole founder of my first startup, So Quotable, but I am far from an expert programmer and couldn't draw my way out of a shootout. Our app launched to a 100,000 users in the first week, a quarter million at our peak, and was acquired in a cash deal less than a year after we started. A balanced team doesn't guarantee success, but not having one will almost always guarantees failure.

As gently as possible, I explained all the above to the potential client. They directly rejected each and every insight. This was different, they said. They had an extraordinary idea and the market would carry them where they needed to go, they said. Can I help them? "Not at this point," I say. "But good luck on your journey." (At the time, my bank account wanted to give a different answer.) And then I let them go.

Sometimes you need to let go when other people won't let go. Sometimes you have to protect your own ENERGY leaks when other people won't protect their own.

Several months later, they emailed me out of

the blue. They left their job, they built their startup, and, to paraphrase the movie *Field of Dreams*, the people didn't come. Could I help? I could not. As the Greek Stoic Epictetus said, "For it is impossible for a man to begin to learn what he has a conceit that he already knows." This isn't a slam on the potential client, and I did and do wish them the best. I also know that working with them would be a waste of my ENERGY. They are not in a place to receive what I am serving. We all do better when we give sunshine to the plants that are open.

We waste ENERGY building things that aren't built to last; something isn't worth the effort if we have to prop it up 24/7. It reminds me of the old-school Hollywood sets of New York, San Francisco, or a random Western ghost town. You may be able to fool some folks into thinking they've been magically transported to Manhattan, but people are always smarter than we think. And it isn't a passive act: we have to maintain that façade. Think about the one-hit wonder who engineers their entire career to have a big single, a best-selling book, or remarkable fame. The problem, of course, is that these rewards are not permanent, but fleeting. There will always be next week's Billboard chart, tomorrow's New York Times best-seller list, or the up-and-coming starlet taking your place.

"Your audience doesn't want your authentic voice," Seth Godin says. *"They want your consistent voice."* Your job is to keep showing up, and that's a lot easier if you are true to your own message from the start.

Being who we are is the ultimate ENERGY source. When people ask me how creators like myself can be so prolific, I say it is easier when it comes from the same center. And that center is me being myself. There is no façade. And when people like my work – as a coach, as a keynoter, as an author – then they recognize and trust the consistency across the board and support my work financially across all the platforms. It also means it requires less effort to deliver consistently.

"People can copy skills, expertise, and knowledge, which are all replicable with enough time and effort," Paul Jarvis says in *Company of One.* "What's not replicable is who you truly are – your style, your personality, your sense of activism, and your unique way of finding creative solutions to complicated problems. So lean on that in your work. Sell your *way of thinking* as much as you would a commodity. Polarization can shorten a sales cycle because it forces customers into a quicker binary choice, to decided yes or no. After all, it's hard to make money from maybes."

The ENERGY leaks to get outside validation for our work, to change someone's mind, or to build just for the moment all come from the same place.

Our urges stem from anxiety.

I don't mean the clinical variety. People I care about have generalized anxiety. It is not a condition to be taken lightly. But what I'm talking about is an anxiety of self. We're not sure if we're showing up *right*. And right often means meeting doing what we do with the guarantee that we will be successful. But, of course, there is no guarantee. We persist in looking for it anyway.

"To stay in the present moment takes concentration. Worries and anxiety about the future are always there, ready to take us away," Thich Nhat Hanh says. "We can see them, acknowledge them, and use our concentration to return to the present moment. When we have concentration, we have a lot of energy. We won't get carried away by visions of past suffering or fears about the future. We dwell stably in the present moment so we can get in touch with the wonders of life, and generate joy and happiness."

According to the National Bureau of Economic Research, the pandemic has cut the length of business meetings 20 percent. In other words, a two-hour in-person meeting is now just over an hour-and-a-half. A full-day meeting can adjourn by mid-afternoon. We've already adjusted to remote calls after several months of off-site, virtual meetings, so it's not a matter of so-called Zoom fatigue. What happened?

"The lockdown introduced a host of new problems requiring unplanned, emergent coordination, much of which could be addressed through impromptu interaction if

527

everyone were in the same office," the report says. "With everyone working at home, however, short meetings could serve to quickly communicate new plans, share work that has been accomplished, increase accountability, calibrate priorities, provide social support, and achieve other purposes that are often handled informally in office settings."

"The unplanned, emergent coordination" is why we go to conferences, meet colleagues at coffee houses, and have happy hours with friends. It is the spontaneous exchange of ENERGY and ideas. The ENERGY-full and the ENERGY-challenged also need to remember that these impromptu opportunities can sap away power from any bigger priority. The ENERGY-full can pile on these random interactions, assuming there will be more strength left over to tackle the most important goals, while the ENERGY-challenged may believe that a quick, unexpected detour will take less strength than it actually will.

Now, with a majority of us working from home, we have to boot up our computer or pick up our phone, schedule these interactions onto a calendar or video conference app, and know that every moment we spend within a meeting could be spent doing the actual thing we care most about. As a long-time WFHer, I always knew to prioritize my physical health and rest, my home environment and, later, my family, as they were constantly right in front of me. Now, once-office-bound people realized that they have a choice, too, on where they put their ENERGY.

Lastly, partnering with ENERGY works best when you know when to let go of an intention. Wisdom is knowing when something cost too much compared to what you will get from it.

It reminds me of Seth Godin talking about the difference between price and cost, which I highlight in *The Ultimate Bite-Sized Entrepreneur*: "Price is a simple number. How much money do I need to hand you to get this thing? Cost is what I had to give up to get this. Cost is how much to feed it, take care of it, maintain it and troubleshoot it. Cost is my lack of focus and my cost of storage. Cost is the externalities, the effluent, the side effects."

For the ENERGY-rich, a misplaced or misguided intention is dangerous because you could just keep going and never truly run out of gas. For the ENERGY-challenged, you don't have the ENERGY to waste going in an unintended direction.

And why do we have revelations when we are laying down immobile in a hospital bed, or looking into the tear-filled eyes of a loved one in emotional pain, or unexpectedly getting the pink slip from our job? Because, as Gandalf says in *The Lord of the Rings* movie adaptation, "Thou shall not pass!" It means ENERGY can no longer pass. Sometimes a roadblock is the only way we actually stop to figure out where exactly our ENERGY is going.

The key to both the ENERGY-rich and the ENERGY-challenged is to honor the season you're in: pursuing, doing, or renewing. Renewing means you are reflecting on what you've done and what you'd like to do next. Pursuing means you're strategizing how you'd like to accomplish what you'd like to do next. Doing is the outward manifestation of both.

"I was, and remain, a mighty daydreamer," business consultant and entrepreneur Natalie Nixon says in *The Creative Leap*. "Daydreams are like a magnetic pull for me. What begins as a glance at a small object blurs into the depths of my mind until I pull myself out of my reverie to go back to the matter at hand. I always feel refreshed when I return back to 'normal.' The reverie serves as a type of marinating time for new ideas."

ENERGY is at its best when it knows where it is going. When put in your best direction, ENERGY put out multiplies and brings back more than what it left as. It creates what economists call a virtuous cycle. It never ends.

"Understanding your creative power, value, and service is your consistent source, your monk's rope, your allies on this journey. It is the ouroboros, the mythological snake eating its own tail. It is nourished forever," I say in *Bring Your Worth*. "Imagine never retiring, not because you need to work to live, but because you live to work. You live to serve. You feed it, and then it feeds you. Forever. Your job, then, isn't to predict the leap to success, nor to wait for success before you begin. Your job is to serve, and in serving, your true worth will always come to you."

It is the belief that circumstances can and will change, and that your actions, in part, will help make that happen. It is understanding the power of your choices and that you actions aren't going into a vacuum.

ENERGY is hope.

Buddhist monk Thich Nhat Hanh gives a sublime definition in his book, *No Mud. No Lotus: The Art of Transforming Suffering*:

"When I lived in Vietnam during the war, it was difficult to see our way through that dark and heavy mud. It seemed like the destruction would just go on and on forever. Every day people would ask me if I thought the war would end soon. It was very difficult to answer, because there was no end in sight. But I knew if I said, 'I don't know,' that would only water their seeds of despair. So when people asked me that question, I replied, 'Everything is impermanent, even war. It will end some day.' Knowing that, we could continue to work for peace. And indeed the war did end."

III.
FUTURE'S PAST

HERE, YOU FORGOT SOMETHING

Direction implies exclusion, and exclusion means that very many psychic elements that could play their part in life are denied the right to exist because they are incompatible with the general attitude. The normal man can follow the general trend without injury to himself; but the man who takes to the back streets and alleys because he cannot endure the broad highway will be the first to discover the psychic elements that are waiting to play their part in the life of the collective.

Carl Jung, The Portable Jung

I write this laying on my back in a wobbly tent somewhere in the Nevada mountains. My partner and I are taking our eldest son, who is in the Cub Scouts, and his little brother camping. It is all our first time, sans me going on a quick trip decades ago with my high school best friend and his highly experienced dad. All I can remember is seeing the tent already made, making corny jokes with my friend all night, and waking up to go to Cedar Point.

Now, my middle age (is forty-something middle age? You tell me.) back is sore from laying on the knotted forest floor, aggressively pressing against the tent bottom. My glamping-oriented partner got a queen-sized inflatable bed; but we naively thought our two sleeping acrobats who, seven and four and no more than 50 pounds each, can hardly stay contained with us in our king bed at home, would miraculously fit nicely with sleeping bags. Daddy is laying on the floor. They are all sleep. I am wide awake. A ridiculously howling mountain wind, at least to my New Jersey ears, has been slapping the hell out of our tent. I was first worried about the tent, us flying off like Toto, and, after an hour or so, I realized we weren't going to fly away, especially with the den leaders helping me mallet the hell out of the spikes, and then I worried about my family, as they – well, we – barely slept the night before because our eldest was restless and scared, and I wanted to make sure the noise and flapping and such didn't wake them, but then I realized an hour or so later that I'm closest to the ground and the wall and the violent sounds were biggest to me and me alone.

So instead, I just lay there. I thought about a castle I thought I made up, then I remembered my partner being there and that they were having a party when we passed by, and then I realized it was a memory, but from what country, and then it was a random castle we walked past in Spain many years ago. I smiled.

I thought about loved ones I missed. One in particular spoke to me through the wind, and I suddenly remembered, after his passing, sitting with my sons at our old home, playing in the front yard and feeling his presence, and then I realized how silly it was for me to not connect the heavy storm winds slapping to that very moment long ago. He would have loved this trip. I began to cry.

And then I thought about what took me to this moment to think about moments. The rocky trail up the mountain. The popcorn sales and Pinewood Derby's. Even the seven years of stay-at-home daddying and potty training. All this conspiring for me to be still enough to excavate these memories long forgotten, to bring them to light, to morn them.

And then, I started writing. Some of the passages you've read started pouring out – "downloading", as one of my mentors says. I jammed them into my iPhone, under dim light and heavy wind.

It is now 6:30 a.m. I've been up since midnight.

But these memories and insights came after worrying about the environment (the storm) and the personal (the family). I spent two hours scared about factors outside of my control. I have neither shame nor guilt about it, and I respect it may have been a necessary series of feelings for me to process. I also know it didn't get me any closer to peace. The deep layers hid behind me accepting my boundaries while simultaneously understanding it wasn't forever. It was just now.

It is crucial we pull up what we've forgotten and let go of what is out of our control. The routines, habits, and strengths we carry are not of the future. You learned hyper-FOCUS because you knew what happened when you didn't pay attention - or perhaps from the fear of losing something if you didn't. You built AGILITY because things in your environment made it seemingly impossible to succeed without adapting to new, often unfair parameters. You leveraged TIME because there were others who had the power to take shortcuts, borrow social capital, and create something based on someone else's perceived legacy. You found ENERGY because any action has an equal and opposite reaction, making it paramount to go longer than others who wouldn't have to work so hard to see outward results. These muscles don't just come out of thin air. They come from your experiences. And without honoring all of your experiences, you'll always have an incomplete view of your power – the power you have for yourself and the power you have to unshackle others. In fact, those powers are one in the same.

"I tell my students, 'When you get these jobs that you have been so brilliantly trained for, just remember that your real job is that if you are free, you need to free somebody else,'" said the late Toni Morrison. "If you have some power, then your job is to empower somebody else."

And starts with you letting go of the tools you do not need anymore. Surviving a toxic relationship when you're young, before you had any true agency, can give you awesome resources and seemingly limitless ingenuity. After all, you're trying to survive, so you need to learn how to FOCUS, be AGILE, leverage TIME or ENERGY quickly. But what happens when you or fateful circumstances change the environment? You still carry that power. You also carry the shadow that comes with it. In my favorite passage from *The Power of Onlyness*, Nilofer Merchant says, "To rebel is to push *against*; to lead is to advocate *for*. To rebel is to say 'we won't;' to lead is to say 'we will.' To rebel is to deny the authority of others; to lead is to invoke your own authority. Rebels attack, while leaders drive toward something."

What happens when what you built your whole army to battle is gone?

When what you created a resistance to crumbles?

When what you are resilient against leaves your life?

Everything becomes a war, often without you realizing it, and the toxic cycle continues. Resistance cannot be the foundation of your power. Resilience cannot be the center of your being. Your perceived enemy cannot be a healthy co-conspirator in your identity. And you cannot grow beyond the fight without recognizing the trauma you still carry from it. How can you fully embrace the sun if you aren't recognizing the shadow?

By morning, everyone was fine. Even I was OK despite getting only an hour or two of sleep.

When we made it home, I unpacked the car alone and noticed a lump beside our house. It was a pretty, seven-inch bird. It was dead.

I gave it a proper burial.

TAKE THE BUILD FROM NOW QUIZ

Curious about your biggest resource at the moment? Take this quick quiz.

Answer each question as instinctively as possible. Match the answers and see your strongest resource. For a deeper discovery, go to www.buildfromnowquiz.com.

Then give the book another read and see how you can maximize your strengths in a new light!

1. I worry most about:
   a. Finishing what I start
   b. Missing opportunities because I'm busy
   c. Losing interest in what I begin
   d. Obsessing over what I'm into at the moment
2. My friends would say I:
   a. Always follow through
   b. Make the most out of uncomfortable situations
   c. Do things in the most efficient manner
   d. Always go the extra mile when it comes to quality
3. I feel most alive when I:
   a. Work from a blank slate
   b. Push myself harder than I ever have before
   c. Know I have room to learn and correct my mistakes
   d. Deep dive into one concept or idea

If I said:
- 1a & 2a
- 1a & 3d or
- 2a & 3d

Then my biggest resource is FOCUS

If I said:
- 1b & 2b
- 1b & 3a or
- 2b & 3a

Then my biggest resource is AGILITY

If I said:
- 1c & 2c
- 1c & 3c or
- 2c & 3c

Then my biggest resource is TIME

If I said:
- 1d & 2d
- 1d & 3b or
- 2d & 3b

Then my biggest resource is ENERGY

If I said none of these matches, then my biggest resources are BALANCED at the moment.

CONNECT WITH DAMON

This book is just the beginning of your growth. Here's how we keep the conversation going.

WATCH THE #BringYourWorth SHOW

http://www.bringyourworth.tv

Join my live TV show as I talk building independent and passive income, strengthening emotional intelligence, and other strategies to improve your side hustle, solopreneurship, and cultural impact.

GET BONUS CONTENT & MORE

http://www.JoinDamon.me

Get your free business worth toolkit to gain even more insight into your next steps. You'll also get exclusive content, early previews of new goodies, and a weekly discussion with fellow creators!

ONE-ON-ONE COACHING AND CONSULTING

http://www.damonbrown.net

I've worked with hundreds of clients and connected with thousands of creatives. I'd love to help you organize your priorities, apply the BUILD FROM NOW method, and make room for your best career. We can set up a time to chat and see if we're a good fit. Reach out at damon@damonbrown.net.

SPEAKING AT YOUR EVENT

http://www.damonbrown.net

I am happy to speak virtually, off-site or in-person worldwide at select events, conferences, and companies. I have spoken at TED, Colombia 4.0 in Bogota, and American University in Washington D.C. Watch my speaker reel at www.damonbrown.net or at www.bringyourworth.tv. Contact me at damon@damonbrown.net.

SIGNIFICANT REFERENCES

- Opening quote: Seth Godin, "13: Let's Get Real or Let's Not Play", from *The Song of Significance* (Penguin, 2023)

BOOK I: THE ULTIMATE BITE-SIZED ENTREPRENEUR

- Opening quote: Scott Dinsmore, "How to find work you love", from TEDxGoldenGatePark (TED Talks, October 2012)

THE BITE-SIZED ENTREPRENEUR

- Opening quote: Steven Pressfield, "The Unlived Life", from *The War of Art* (Black Irish Entertainment, 2012)
- Chapter 1
  - Opening quote: Steven Pressfield, "Resistance is Infallible", from *The War of Art* (Black Irish Entertainment, 2012)
  - Jessica Abel quote: Jessica Abel, "Don't Find Your Passion". Originally published May 26, 2016
  - Adapted from the Inc. column "Forget Inspiration. This Beats Passion Every Single Time". Originally published June 16, 2016
- Chapter 2: Lies We Tell
  - Adapted from the *Inc.* columns "Lies Entrepreneurs Tell Themselves" and "Big Lies Entrepreneurs Tell Themselves".

Originally published August 15, 2015 and October 19, 2015

- Chapter 3: Effective Procrastination
  - ○ Jessica Hirsche quote: Quoted by Animaux Circus, 2016
  - ○ Adapted from the *Inc.* column "How Procrastination Can Supercharge Your Business". Originally published December 21, 2015
- Chapter 4: Idea Debt
  - ○ Kazu Kibuishi quote: Jessica Abel, "Imagine your future projects holding you back". Originally published January 27, 2016
  - ○ Adapted from the *Inc.* column "Why Your Brilliant Ideas Are Holding You Back". Originally published February 28, 2016
- Chapter 5: Busyness
  - ○ Adapted from the *Inc.* column "3 Awful Reasons Why You Are Obsessed with Being Busy". Originally published April 13, 2016
- Chapter 6: A Good Burnout
  - ○ Adapted from the *Inc.* column "How You Can Turn Burnout To Your Advantage". Originally published October 23, 2015
- Chapter 7: Clutter
  - ○ Damon Brown quote: Damon Brown, "Death by Curation: The problem with recording everything", adapted from *Our Virtual Shadow* (TED Books 2013). Originally published September 2, 2013.
  - ○ Adapted from the *Inc.* column "The 2 Types

2016
- Chapter 20: After the Win
  - Ryan Holiday quote: *The Tim Ferriss Show*, "Useful Lessons from Workaholics Anonymous, Corporate Implosions, and More", Originally aired June 25, 2016
  - Adapted from the *Inc.* column "Why Most People Fail Immediately After a Big Success". Originally published July 7, 2016
- Chapter 21
  - Steven Pressfield quote: Steven Pressfield, "The Artist's Life", from *The War of Art* (Black Irish Entertainment, 2012)
  - Adapted from the *Inc.* column "Destroy Average Ideas to Make Brilliant Manure". Originally published March 9, 2016

- Opening quote: Mihaly Csikszentmihalyi, "The Roots of Discontent", from *Flow* (Harper & Row, 1990)
- Chapter 1: Create Limitations
  - Opening quote: Peter Sims, "Failing Quickly to Learn Fast", from *Little Bets* (Simon & Schuster, 2011)
  - Sleeping quote: *Slumberwise*, "Your Ancestors Didn't Sleep Like You". Originally published May 16, 2013
  - Maria Popova reference: *Brain Pickings*, "Why Time Slows Down When We're Afraid, Speeds Up as We Age, and Gets Warped on Vacation". Originally published May 16, 2013
  - Adapted from the *Inc.* columns "Waking Up at 3 Every Morning Made Me Super Productive – Until It Didn't" and "What Having No Time At All Taught Me About Productivity". Originally published July 2, 2015 & July 30, 2015, respectively
- Chapter 2: Know Your Core
  - Martha Stewart quote: "Ask Yourself, What's the Big Idea?", from *The Martha Rules*. (Rodale, 2005)
- Chapter 3: Death By Networking
  - Adapted from the *Inc.* column "Why Too Much Networking Will Make You Less Productive". Originally published August 9, 2016

- Chapter 4: Write It Down
  - Adapted from the *Inc.* columns "The Power of Writing, Not Typing, Your Ideas" and "The Scientific Reason Why You Are Smarter When You Write". Originally published August 7, 2015 & April 28, 2016, respectively
- Chapter 5: Empty Your Schedule
  - Adapted from the *Inc.* column "Why You Need to Add a 'Blank Day' to Your Calendar". Originally published December 18, 2015
- Chapter 7: Walk It Out
  - Adapted from the *Inc.* column "How Walking Can Make You a Better Entrepreneur". Originally published August 31, 2015
- Chapter 8: Stop Measuring Time
  - Pema Chodron quote: "Commitment", *from Comfortable With Uncertainty* (Shambhula, 2003)
- Chapter 9: Do Less With More Impact
  - Opening quote: Steven Pressfield, "The Professional Does Not Wait for Inspiration", from *Turning Pro* (Black Irish Entertainment, 2012)
  - Adapted from the *Inc.* column "Why Being Productive All the Time is a Fool's Errand". Originally published June 16, 2016
- Chapter 11: Alternate Tasks
  - Adapted from the *Inc.* column "How to

Boost Your Productivity by Adding 'Palate Cleansers' to Your Day". Originally published November 18, 2015

- Chapter 12: Overextending Yourself
  - Adapted from the *Inc.* column "4 Surefire Ways to Avoid Overextending Yourself". Originally published June 2, 2016
- Chapter 13: Mastering Time
  - Adapted from the *Inc.* column "3 Ultimate Insider Tips from a Time Management Master". Originally published May 31, 2016
- Chapter 14: Put the Coffee Down
  - Adapted from the *Inc.* column "Why 11 am Coffee Makes You More Productive". Originally published September 23, 2015
- Chapter 15: Know Your Prime Time
  - Adapted from the *Inc.* column "Not Productive Enough? Here's a Smart Way to Fix the Problem". Originally published March 14, 2016
- Chapter 17: Opting Out
  - Opening quote: Mihaly Csikszentmihalyi, "Overview", from *Flow* (Harper & Row, 1990)
  - Rembert Brown quote: *Vulture*, "What Andre 3000 Taught Frank Ocean". Originally published August 25, 2016.
- Chapter 18: Looking for a Crisis
  - Steven Pressfield quotes: "Resistance and self-dramatization" and "Resistance and trouble", both from *The War of Art* (Black

Irish Entertainment 2012)

- o Mark Suster quote: *Both Sides of the Table*, "Do You Suffer from the Urgency Addiction? It's More Common Than You Think". Originally published August 18, 2010.
- o Adapted from the *Inc.* column "An Addiction Most Entrepreneurs Have – and How to Manage It". Originally published June 16, 2016
- Chapter 19: Less, Better Email
  - o Adapted from the *Inc.* column "The 1 Powerful Rule That Will Revolutionize Your Email". Originally published May 10, 2016
- Chapter 20: Creating "Me" Time
  - o Adapted from the *Inc.* column "3 Powerful Ways You Can Make 'Me' Time". Originally published January 12, 2016
- Chapter 22: Silence Is Golden
  - o Duke University quote: *Nautilus*, Daniel A. Gross, "This is Your Brain on Silence". Originally published August 21, 2014.
  - o Adapted from the *Inc.* column "Want to Boost Your Brain Power? Get Silent". Originally published March 29, 2016
- Chapter 23: Bulletproof
  - o Seth Godin quote: *The Tim Ferriss Show*, "Seth Godin on How to Think Small to Go Big". Originally aired August 3, 2016
- Chapter 24: Shadowboxing
  - o Pema Chodron quote: "The Empty Boat",

from Comfortable With Uncertainty (Shambhula, 2003)
- Srinivas Rao quote: *Creative Warriors Podcast*, "Srini Rao – Be Unmistakable". Originally aired August 30, 2016

- Opening quote: Oprah's Super Soul Conversations podcast, "Phil Jackson: The Soul of Success". Originally aired October 9, 2017.
- I: Let Go:
  - Opening quote: Caroline Myss, *Sacred Contracts: Awakening Your Divine Potential* (Harmony 2002)
- Chapter 2: Put Your Mask on First
  - Adapted from the *Inc.* column "How to Stop Burnout with 1 Simple Rule". Originally published September 28, 2016
- Chapter 3: You Need Longer Deadlines
  - Adapted from the *Inc.* column "How Unnecessarily Ambitious Deadlines Can Crush Progress". Originally published October 31, 2016
- Chapter 5: Failure Can Be Success
  - Adapted from the *Inc.* column "How Oprah Conquered Her Biggest Failure (and How You Can, Too". Originally published August 15, 2017
- Chapter 6: Do Good Enough
  - Adapted from the *Inc.* column "Why Good Enough is the Best Path to Serious Success". Originally published February 9, 2017
  - Paulo Coelho quote: Oprah's Super Soul Conversations podcast, "Paulo Coelho, Part 1: What If the Universe Conspired in Your Favor?". Originally aired August 9, 2017.
- Chapter 7: Know Your Sacrifice

Brown on the 1 Question You Need to Ask About People You Truly Dislike". Originally published March 16, 2017

- Chapter 16: It Isn't Your Money
  - o Adapted from the *Inc.* column "A Millionaire Entrepreneur Shares How to Be Happy (and It's Not by Making Lots of Money)". Originally published December 19, 2016
- Chapter 17: Why You Are More Successful Than You Think
  - o Adapted from the *Inc.* column "A Millionaire Entrepreneur Shares How to Be Happy (and It's Not by Making Lots of Money)". Originally published December 5, 2016

MORE FUEL

- Opening quote: Seth Godin, "About to be". Originally published November 29, 2015.
- Chapter 1: Do Less Today to Do More
  - o Adapted from the *Inc.* column "Embrace 'Minimum Viable Days' to Boost Your Productivity". Originally published March 18, 2016
- Chapter 3: Completing is More Important than Starting
  - o Adapted from the *Inc.* column "This Simple, Classic Theory Will Make You Even More Productive". Originally published July 31, 2017
- Chapter 4: Is it Reversible?
  - o Jim Rohn quote: Jim Rohn, *The Art of Exceptional Living* (Nightingale-Conant 2014)
  - o Joseph Campbell quote: Joseph Campbell, *The Hero with a Thousand Faces (The Collected Works of Joseph Campbell)*. (New World Library 2008).
  - o Dr. Michael Bernard Beckwith quote: Oprah's Super Soul Conversations podcast, "Dr. Michael Bernard Beckwith: Manifest the Life of Your Dreams". Originally aired October 25, 2017.
- Chapter 5: Run Parallels
  - o Adapted from the *Inc.* column "How to Not Let Focus Get in the Way of Productivity". Originally published February 28, 2017

Matters Is Your Next One (Portfolio 2017)

- o Louise L. Hay quote: Louise L. Hay, *You Can Heal Your Life* (Hay House 1984)
- Chapter 11: Your Work Will Sometimes Not Be Your Paycheck
  - o Jim Rohn quote: Jim Rohn, *The Art of Exceptional Living* (Nightingale-Conant 2014)
- Chapter 12: Act Like You Meant It to Happen
  - o Chris Young quote: *The Tim Ferris Show*, "#173 Chris Young: Lessons from Geniuses, Billionaires, and Tinkerers". Originally aired July 11, 2016.

  - o *The Daily Stoic* quote: Ryan Holiday and Stephen Hanselman, "June 1st: Always Have a Mental 'Reverse Clause'", from *The Daily Stoic: 366 Meditations on Wisdom, Perseverance, and the Art of Living* (Tim Ferriss 2016)

BOOK II: BRING YOUR WORTH

- Esther & Jerry Hicks. *The Vortex: Where the Law of Attraction Assembles All Cooperative Relationships* (Hay House 2009)
- Steven Pressfield. *The Author's Journey: The Wake of the Hero's Journey and the Lifelong Pursuit of Meaning* (Black Irish Entertainment 2018)
- Brene Brown. *Braving the Wilderness: The Quest for True Belonging and the Courage to Stand Alone* (Random House 2017)
- Elizabeth Gilbert. *Big Magic: Creative Living Beyond Fear* (Riverhead Books 2015).
- Caroline Myss. *Sacred Contracts: Awakening Your Divine Potential* (Harmony 2001)
- Deepak Chopra. *The Spontaneous Fulfillment of Desire: Harnessing the Infinite Power of Coincidence to Create Miracles* (Harmony 2003)
- Mike Michalowicz. *Profit First: Transform Your Business from a Cash-Eating Monster to a Money-Making Machine* (Portfolio 2017)
- Mark Nepo: 7,000 Ways to Listen. *Oprah's Super Soul Conversations.* December 2018
- Jenny Blake: How to Optimize for Revenue and Joy. *The Pivot podcast.* October 2015
- Gay Hendricks. *The Big Leap: Conquer Your Hidden Fear and Take Life to the Next Level* (HarperOne 2009)
- Paulo Coehlo. *The Alchemist* (HarperOne 1989)
- Srinivas Rao. *Unmistakable: Why Only is Better than Best* (Portfolio 2016)

- Laura Vanderkam. *Off the Clock: Feel Less Busy While Getting More Done* (Portfolio 2018)
- Marianne Williamson. *The Law of Divine Compensation: On Work, Money, and Miracles* (HarperOne 2012).

BOOK III: BUILD FROM NOW

I. AN OUTSIDE JOB

THE LOW END OF THE SOUP BOWL

- Toni Morrison quote: Toni Morrison speech, Portland State University. Spoken May 30, 1975. Transcription published in *Array*, "Toni Morrison on Black Artists". July 9, 2014. Currently available online: http://www.arraynow.com/our-blog-archive/2015/8/13/toni-morrison-on-black-artists
- Violet Blue. *ZDNet*, "Silicon Valley's Race Problem." Originally published October 30, 2011. Currently available online: https://www.zdnet.com/article/silicon-valleys-race-problem/
- *Chani Nicholas*, "Horoscopes for the New Moon in Scorpio – November 2020." Currently available online: https://chaninicholas.com/horoscopes-for-the-new-moon-in-scorpio-2020/

- Esther Perel quote: *Steal the Show with Michael Port* podcast, "Unlock Erotic Intelligence in the Bedroom and the Boardroom with Esther Perel." Originally aired December 9, 2015: https://stealtheshow.com/podcast/unlock-erotic-intelligence-esther-perel/

- Chris Rock: *The Daily Show with Trevor Noah.* October 21, 2020. Currently available online: http://www.cc.com/episodes/mdr7q1/the-daily-show-with-trevor-noah-october-21--2020---chris-rock-season-26-ep-26013

- Damon Brown. *Bring Your Worth: Level Up Your Creative Power, Value & Service to the World* (Bring Your Worth 2019).

- Glamour. *Glamour,* "Ava DuVernay's Speech at *Glamour*'s 2019 Women of the Year Awards Must Be Read." Originally published November 12, 2019. Currently available online: https://www.glamour.com/story/ava-duvernay-glamour-women-of-the-year-2019-speech

- Barack Obama: *The Shop: Uninterrupted | President Obama Special.* October 31, 2020. Currently available online: https://www.youtube.com/watch?v=jvy9OWNGPgk

- Thich Nhat Hanh. *No Mud, No Lotus: The Art of Transforming Suffering* (Parallax Press 2014).

- Seth Godin. *The Practice: Shipping Creative Work* (Portfolio 2020).

- Revolt TV, "The Cost of High Fashion" panel with Dapper Dan, Laquan Smith & Jason Bolden. Originally aired November 5th. Currently available online: https://www.youtube.com/watch?v=ZL2tywtSCQg

- John Henry quote: *Earn Your Leisure* podcast, "Hustle & Motivate featuring John Henry." Originally aired October 29, 2019: https://youtu.be/o38ZWUK7w9o
- Next Avenue. *Forbes*, "Cindy Gallop: Disrupting Ageism in Advertising." Originally published October 3, 2019. Currently available online: https://www.forbes.com/sites/nextavenue/2019/10/03/cindy-gallop-disrupting-ageism-in-advertising/
- Seth Godin. *The Practice: Shipping Creative Work* (Portfolio 2020).

- Thich Nhat Hanh quote: *No Mud, No Lotus: The Art of Transforming Suffering* (Parallax Press 2014).
- The Systems Thinker. *The Systems Thinker,* "The Ladder of Inference." Volume 10. Currently available online: https://thesystemsthinker.com/the-ladder-of-inference/
- Don Miguel Ruiz: *The Four Agreements: A Practical Guide to Personal Freedom* (Amber-Allen Publishing 2018).
- Damon Brown. Adapted from the *Inc. Magazine* column, "The Strongest Leaders Use This Simple, Powerful Phrase." Originally published May 31, 2016. Currently available online: https://www.inc.com/damon-brown/the-strongest-leaders-use-this-simple-powerful-phrase-.html
- Damon Brown. *The Ultimate Bite-Sized Entrepreneur Trilogy: 76 Ways to Boost Time, Productivity & Focus On Your Big Idea* (Bring Your Worth 2017).

How to Partner with Focus

- Julian Mitchell quote: *#ChopItUpShow.* "The Business Behind Music and Culture with Julian Mitchell," Episode 10. Originally aired November 11, 2018: https://youtu.be/M8gSvpas6GE
- Damon Brown. *The Bite-Sized Entrepreneur Trilogy: 21 Ways to Ignite Your Passion & Pursue Your Side Hustle* (Bring Your Worth 2016).
- Simon Sinek. *The Infinite Game* (Portfolio 2019).
- Damon Brown. Adapted from the *Inc. Magazine* column, "How Perfectionism is Preventing You from Perfection." Originally published February 28, 2018. Currently available online: https://www.inc.com/damon-brown/how-perfectionism-is-preventing-you-from-perfection.html
- Elizabeth Gilbert, "Success, failure, and the drive to keep creating," from TED. (TED Talks, March 2014). Currently available online: https://www.ted.com/talks/elizabeth_gilbert_success_failure_and_the_drive_to_keep_creating/
- Seth Godin. *The Practice: Shipping Creative Work* (Portfolio 2020).
- Damon Brown, "Why you should strive for good enough," from TEDxToledo. (TED Talks, September 2018). Currently available online:

https://www.ted.com/talks/
damon_brown_why_you_should_strive_for_go
od_enough

- Seth Godin. *The Dip: A Little Book That Teaches You When to Quit (and When to Stick)* (Portfolio 2007).
- Stephen Covey. *First Things First* (Mango Media 2015).
- Elizabeth Alexander, "Creative process: Are you in a period of 'woodshedding'?," from Big Think. (Big Think, April 2020). Currently available online: https://bigthink.com/creative-process-2645857657
- Damon Brown. Adapted from the *Inc. Magazine* column, "A Thanksgiving Story That Will Save You Time and Money." Originally published November 21, 2016. Currently available online: https://www.inc.com/damon-brown/a-thanksgiving-story-that-will-save-you-time-and-money.html
- Jessica Dore. *Jessica Dore,* "October 2020 Tarot Offering." Currently available online: https://www.jessicadore.com/offerings/october-2020-tarot-offering
- Elizabeth Gilbert. *Big Magic: Creative Living Beyond Fear* (Riverhead Books 2015).
- *The Bill Murray Stories: Life Lessons Learned from a Mythical Man* (Double Windsor Films/Old Lime Productions 2018). Directed by Tommy Avallone. Trailer: https://www.youtube.com/watch?v=XC2WIXtWgoc

- Chase Jarvis quote: *The Chase Jarvis Show.* "Creative Therapy with Seth Godin in New York," Episode 172 Originally aired October 16, 2019: https://www.chasejarvis.com/project/chase-jarvis-live-podcast/
- Damon Brown. Adapted from "The Lonely Road". Featured in *The CNF Audio Mag: Issue 1* (Brendan O'Meara 2019).
- *Drink Champs.* "Busta Rhymes on Working With Mariah Carey, Janet Jackson, His New Album & More." Originally aired October 31, 2020: https://www.youtube.com/watch?v=i7nieCNVbE4
- Natalie Nixon. *The Creative Leap: Unleash Curiosity, Improvisation, and Intuition at Work* (Berrett-Koehler Publishers 2020).
- Damon Brown. *The Ultimate Bite-Sized Entrepreneur Trilogy: 76 Ways to Boost Time, Productivity & Focus On Your Big Idea* (Bring Your Worth 2017).
- Damon Brown. Adapted from the *Inc. Magazine* column, "Why You Should Have More Than One Career at the Same Time." Originally published February 28, 2018. Currently available online: https://www.inc.com/damon-brown/why-you-should-have-more-than-one-career-at-same-time.html
- Helena Andrews-Dyer. *The Washington Post*, "Celebrity DJs' live online sets have become

house parties for the homebound: Welcome to Club Quarantine." Originally published March 24, 2020. Currently available online: https://www.washingtonpost.com/arts-entertainment/2020/03/24/dj-dnice-club-quarantine-parties/

- Greg McKeown. *Essentialism: The Disciplined Pursuit of Less* (Currency 2014).
- Damon Brown. Adapted from the *Inc. Magazine* column, "How to Sell Better in 13 Simple Words." Originally published March 3, 2020. Currently available online: https://www.inc.com/damon-brown/how-to-sell-better-in-13-simple-words.html
- Marie Forleo. *Everything is Figureoutable* (Portfolio 2019).
- Seth Godin. *Seth's Blog*, "About Seth's Godin." Currently available online: https://seths.blog/about/
- Damon Brown. *Bring Your Worth: Level Up Your Creative Power, Value & Service to the World* (Bring Your Worth 2019).
- Elizabeth Gilbert. *Big Magic: Creative Living Beyond Fear* (Riverhead Books 2015).

- Adam Grant quote: *The Tim Ferriss Show.* "Adam Grant – The Man Who Does Everything (#399)." Originally aired December 5, 2019: https://tim.blog/2019/12/05/adam-grant/
- Murray Fisher. *Playboy,* "The Playboy Interview: Alex Haley by Murray Fisher." Originally published January 1977. Currently available online: https://alexhaley.com/2019/06/06/alex-haley-interviewed-by-playboy/
- Edwin McDowell. *New York Times,* "Publishing: Dealing with the Delinquent Author." Originally published July 22, 1983. Currently available online: https://www.nytimes.com/1983/07/22/books/publishing-dealing-with-the-delinquent-author.html
- Laura Vanderkam. *Off the Clock: Feel Less Busy While Getting More Done* (Portfolio 2018).
- Shane Parrish. *Farnam Street,* "If you want to perform when the world is watching, you have to do the work when no one is watching." Originally published October 1, 2020. Currently available online: https://www.instagram.com/p/CFzilk0prOH/?igshid=wzukrxmnuijq
- Carol Dweck. *Mindset: The New Psychology of Success* (Ballentine Books 2007).
- Les Brown, "How Bamboo Trees Will Bring Out Your Best Self," from Goalcast. (July 2018). Currently available online: https://

www.goalcast.com/2018/07/10/les-brown-how-bamboo-trees-will-bring-out-your-best-self/

- Nora Salem. *Bitch Media*, "To Well and Back: The Bleak Future of Positive Thinking." Originally published October 28, 2020. Currently available online: https://www.bitchmedia.org/article/goodbye-to-the-wellness-grift

- Damon Brown. Adapted from the *Inc. Magazine* column, "This is Simon Sinek's Guaranteed Secret to Success Most of Us Won't Do." Originally published July 30, 2018. Currently available online: https://www.inc.com/damon-brown/this-is-simon-sineks-guaranteed-secret-to-success-most-of-us-wont-do.html

- Damon Brown. Adapted from the *Inc. Magazine* column, "Forget Five Years. Make the 100-Year Plan." Originally published November 10, 2017. Currently available online: https://www.inc.com/damon-brown/the-five-year-plan-is-old-what-are-you-doing-in-a-century.html

- *The New York Times.* "Jay-Z and Dean Baquet, in Conversation." Originally aired November 30, 2017. Currently available online: https://www.youtube.com/watch?v=XbuQAbG2AZ0

- Josie Rosario quote: "Stop measuring your strength by how much shit you can tolerate." Originally published November 19th. Currently available online: https://www.instagram.com/p/CHxRcX4AsRZ/?igshid=8rtgszo044kl
- Damon Brown. *The Bite-Sized Entrepreneur Trilogy: 21 Ways to Ignite Your Passion & Pursue Your Side Hustle* (Bring Your Worth 2016).
- Greg McKeown. *Essentialism: The Disciplined Pursuit of Less* (Currency 2014).
- Barry Schwartz, "The Paradox of Choice," from TED. (TED Talks, July 2005). Currently available online: https://www.ted.com/talks/barry_schwartz_the_paradox_of_choice/
- Damon Brown. Adapted from the *Inc. Magazine* column, "Why the Most Successful Creatives Love Daily Routines." Originally published December 17, 2019. Currently available online: https://www.inc.com/damon-brown/why-most-successful-creatives-love-daily-routines.html
- Seth Godin. *The Practice: Shipping Creative Work* (Portfolio 2020).
- Paul Jarvis. *Company of One: Why Staying Small is the Next Big Thing for Business* (Mariner Books 2019).
- Tara Haelle. *Elemental,* "Your 'Surge Capacity' Is Depleted – It's Why You Feel Awful." Originally published August 13, 2020. Currently available online: h t t p s : / /

- elemental.medium.com/your-surge-capacity-is-depleted-it-s-why-you-feel-awful-de285d542f4c
- Tricia Hersey. *The Nap Ministry,* "There are so many things that capitalism has stolen, and [one of them is] our dreamspace which is where our power lies..." Originally published October 12, 2020. Currently available online: https://www.instagram.com/p/CGQoexrl6rk/?igshid=1b8eh0nggxqs7
- *Pivot Podcast with Jenny Blake.* "124: Penny & Jenny Show – Embracing Liminal Space (the In-Between)." Originally aired July 7, 2019: http://www.pivotmethod.com/podcast/liminal-space
- Damon Brown. *The Ultimate Bite-Sized Entrepreneur Trilogy: 76 Ways to Boost Time, Productivity & Focus On Your Big Idea* (Bring Your Worth 2017).
- Elizabeth Gilbert, "Success, failure, and the drive to keep creating," from TED. (TED Talks, March 2014). Currently available online: https://www.ted.com/talks/elizabeth_gilbert_success_failure_and_the_drive_to_keep_creating/
- Thich Nhat Hanh. *No Mud, No Lotus: The Art of Transforming Suffering* (Parallax Press 2014).
- Jessica Stillman. *Inc. Magazine,* "The Pandemic Is Making Meetings Less Awful." Originally published August 12, 2020. Currently available online: https://www.inc.com/jessica-stillman/the-pandemic-is-making-meetings-shorter-workdays-longer-new-study-finds.html

- Natalie Nixon. *The Creative Leap: Unleash Curiosity, Improvisation, and Intuition at Work* (Berrett-Koehler Publishers 2020).
- Damon Brown. *Bring Your Worth: Level Up Your Creative Power, Value & Service to the World* (Bring Your Worth 2019).

III. A Future's Past

Here, You Forgot Something

- Carl Jung quote: Carl Jung, edited by Joseph Campbell. *The Portable Jung* (Penguin Classics 1976).
- Pam Houston. *Oprah Magazine*, "The Truest Eye." Originally published November 2003. Currently available online: https://www.oprah.com/omagazine/toni-morrison-talks-love/
- Nilofer Merchant. *The Power of Onlyness: Make Your Wild Ideas Mighty Enough to Dent the World* (Viking 2017).

ACKNOWLEDGEMENTS

Thank you to blood family, chosen family, mentors and supporters. Much love to Parul, Alec, Abhi & Amar, and to Raymond Johnson, Deirdra Bishop, Laura Mintz, and the SF CP crew, as well as to Bernadette Johnson, Tony Howard, David Brown, and folks who raised me. Thanks to Bec Loss, Jeanette Hurt, and *Inc. Magazine* for the uplift.

And to you, for allowing me to join you on your journey.

ABOUT THE AUTHOR

Damon Brown helps side hustlers, solopreneurs, and other non-traditional creatives bloom. As a best-selling author, two-time startup founder, and four-time TED Speaker, Damon co-founded the popular platonic connection app Cuddlr and led it to acquisition within a year, all while being the primary caretaker of his infant son. He now guides others through his private consulting/coaching business, free weekly newsletter at www.JoinDamon.me, and #BringYourWorth show at www.bringyourworth.tv.

THE COMPLETE BRING YOUR WORTH COLLECTION is his 27th book. Notable titles include *Career Remix*, *Our Virtual Shadow*, and the coffeetable book *Playboy's Greatest Covers*.

You can catch Damon in *Playboy*, *Fast Company*, and *Inc. Magazine*, as well as at any locale that serves really spicy food. He lives in Las Vegas, Nevada, with his wife, two young sons, and countless bottles of hot sauce. Connect with him at www.JoinDamon.me or at www.damonbrown.net.